La Comunidad Latina in the United States

*Personal and Political
Strategies for
Transforming Culture*

DAVID T. ABALOS

PRAEGER

Westport, Connecticut
London

Library of Congress Cataloging-in-Publication Data

Abalos, David T.
  La Comunidad Latina in the United States : personal and political
strategies for transforming culture / David T. Abalos.
    p. cm.
  Includes bibliographical references and index.
  ISBN 0–275–95892–2 (alk. paper).—ISBN 0–275–95893–0 (pbk. :
alk. paper)
    1. Hispanic Americans—Cultural assimilation. 2. Hispanic
Americans—Ethnic identity. 3. Hispanic Americans—Conduct of life.
I. Title.
E184.S75A618   1998
305.868073—DC21   97–43953

British Library Cataloguing in Publication Data is available.

Library of Congress Catalog Card Number: 97–43953
ISBN: 0–275–95892–2
        0–275–95893–0 (pbk.)

First published in 1998

Praeger Publishers, 88 Post Road West, Westport, CT 06881
An imprint of Greenwood Publishing Group, Inc.

Printed in the United States of America

The paper used in this book complies with the
Permanent Paper Standard issued by the National
Information Standards Organization (Z39.48–1984).

10 9 8 7 6 5 4 3 2 1

Copyright Acknowledgments

The author and publisher gratefully acknowledge permission to reprint the following material:

Excerpts from Manfred Halpern, "Transformation: Its Theory and Practice in Our Personal, Political, Historical, and Sacred Being," unpublished manuscript; and unpublished papers of Manfred Halpern: "Beyond Present Theory and Practice: Transformation and the Nation State," Paper presented at a national symposium, College of William and Mary, September 24–27, 1993, and "The Archetype of Capitalism: A Critical Analysis in the Light of a Theory of Transformation," Paper presented at the annual meeting of the American Political Association, San Francisco, 1996.

In loving memory of my parents, Luz Gil Avalos and Luis José Avalos and my grandparents, María Hernández Hernández and José Santos Hernández Vivanco, who in the early years of the twentieth century courageously journeyed to this country as pioneers and who together with their fellow countrywomen and countrymen planted and nurtured the roots of la comunidad Latina in the United States. Mom and Dad, Neni and Daddy Joe provided us with the legacy of transformation and love by which to continue the ongoing creation of our community in the twenty-first century. ¡*Muchísimas gracias*! *Que Dios los bendiga y que descansen en paz.*

Contents

Acknowledgments

This book is especially dedicated to the memory of my parents, Luz Gil and Luis José Avalos and my beloved siblings, Marge and Sal. My parents came to this country in the 1920s, leaving behind their families in Michoacán, México. They came here so that we could have a better life. They taught us to be proud of being Mejicanos. But from the very beginning our identity was at stake as the authorities at the border by mistake changed our name from Avalos to Abalos. My father was afraid that if he corrected them it would result in his being denied entry. In Chicago my father was shot and wounded by a police officer who tried to take his money. The officer was convicted and expelled from the force. My mother kept the slug that was removed from my father as a reminder of this close brush with death. I write this book in a spirit of thankfulness and love for my parents, who risked their lives for me so that I might have a new and better life.

Celia, my wife, and my children, David Jerome, Veronica, and Matthew, have been my greatest blessings. My children represent the second generation of my family born in this country. It will be their challenge to create a new and more loving story for their own families and those of others with a life of service.

My students never fail to be an inspiration to me as I invite them to participate with me in the core drama of life, the journey of transformation. I am especially indebted to Ricardo González, Linda Sierra, Myrna Santiago, Robin Cunningham, Kathy Dixon, María Montañez, Nocheline Parent, Sandy Mitchell, Kathy Rosado, Herschel Walker, Carlos López, Phill Szabo, Mary Kirwin Gavin, José Adámes, Gloria Nash, Chavon Smith, Josefa Ruíz, Genis González, Matthew Demian, Jennifer Crist, Levell Sanders, Jennifer Mumby, and Danielle Davis.

My colleagues, especially my Puerto Rican brother, Frank Morales, together with Gisela Webb, Larry Greene, Carlos Rodríguez, George and Paula Tzannetakis, Connie Beale, Diane Bednar, Joyce Strawser, Toni Citarelli, Marty Kropp, Pat Kuchon, Jeff Levy, Toni Malone, Brenda Knight, Sandra Lee, Lloyd McBride, Patrick Sanders, Rosalie Yannazzone, Joe Palenski, Evelyn Plummer, Walt De Bold, Kathleen Rennie, Marge Marren, Phyllis Russo, Janet Easterling, Ana Sierra, Pat Lisanti, William Stoever, Mike McMahon, Dick Adinaro, Cheryl Thompson, Bernadette Wilkowski, Paul Barnas, Paul Holmes, Bob Hallissey, Dennis Garbini, Wilfredo Bonilla, Linda Ulak, and Al Hakim have all been a source of joy and strength for me. Three of my colleagues, Tony Triano, George Reilly, and Bill Mathes, recently died and left a remarkable legacy of love for their students and teaching. I also want to recognize the outstanding staff of the Puerto Rican Institute and of Talent Search, Dra. Lillian Pérez, Johnny Rodríguez, Oscar Marchant, Nitza Aviles, Sonia Ford, Jackie Sánchez, and Salvador "Chava" Rosario, who have been an invaluable source of assistance and affection for me and for our Latina and Latino faculty, staff, and students.

There are many outstanding and deeply caring people who daily fight for the well-being of la comunidad Latina as well as members of all ethnic and racial groups: Celia Dorantes Abalos, Juanita Barbosa, Félix Padilla, Frank Morales, Casto Maldonado, Angel Míllan, Roberto Carmona, Vicente Pérez, Félix López Montálvo, Hilda Hidalgo, María Vizcarróndo de Soto, Ingrid Betancourt, Sylvia Villa, María Elena Campistegüy-Hawkins, José R. Rodríguez, and Susana Casillas.

I have drawn strength from my extended family, often when they were even unaware of how much support they were giving me: Dick and Mary Scaine, Liz, Vinnie, Kate and Luke McMahon, Nick and Marge Martucci, Frank, Vivian, Alex, Tina, and Viviana Morales, Jim Palladino, Joe and Paquita Holland, and Carol, Rick, and Maggie Rose Biunno, Josephine, Joe, Michael, and Elyse Carpenter.

I owe so much of my courage to speak with my own voice to my friend and colleague Manfred Halpern, who taught me the theory of transformation. It was he who encouraged me to be radical—that is, to get to the roots, to the underlying, forming causes of things by asking fundamental questions that would take me to the heart of the matter: testing and living the theory and story of transformation within the experiences of my own life.

Finally, I would like to thank my editors, Dan Eades and Heather Ruland, for their encouragement and genuine friendship throughout the writing of this book. A special thanks also to Marietta Yannetti of Praeger Publishers for the professional and caring manner in which she has assisted me.

Introduction

We know that by the third or fourth decade of the twenty-first century the population of the United States will be 25 percent Spanish speaking. La comunidad Latina in this country will be the third largest population of Latino peoples in the world. Demographic projections are that the Southwest will be 50 to 60 percent Latino. Other states like Illinois, New Jersey, New York, Florida, and Michigan will have substantial increases in the number of women and men from a Latino background. This remarkable growth is now having an effect and will continue to be a tremendous determining factor in the direction of the United States both at home and abroad.

At the same time that the Latino community will be growing, communities of people of color as a whole will be the majority of the population in the nation. This marks the end of an era; the United States as a white, Anglo-Saxon, Protestant nation, never a reality, is now more than ever unreal. Our identity, who we are as a nation, is at stake. Many are alarmed, as we see from the frantic efforts to impose harsh restrictions on immigration. In the schools, the battle is being fought over the curriculum as the dominant seek to continue to socialize the young into the American dream as they have defined it. If current economic trends continue, then the privileged will become more powerful as the income gap between even the traditional middle class and the powerful becomes wider. So many of the issues being debated now in regard to national policy will profoundly affect la comunidad Latina: the minimum wage, aid to education, especially higher education, access to affordable health care, employment in the high-tech area of the economy, housing, social security, and the fight against drugs.

We all know that the Latino community and communities of people of color are in general some of the most vulnerable in the country. Every indicator of poverty, crime, employment, education, and health-related issues identifies us as a people heading toward a difficult future. We also know that we cannot expect the powerful, unless they determine that it is in their own self-interest, to do much about these matters, though they are of dire concern. The dominant are severely hampered by the stories of their own upbringing that they continue to maintain: that they are the powerful because they earned it and continue to deserve what they have. It follows from this that those who are still behind are in this situation because it is their own damn fault. They are either so lazy, so dumb, or so handicapped by nature that they can't make it. For this reason the debate goes on as to whether it is worth it to intervene with social programs. This is an elitism that is permeated with the spirit of capitalism and racism that collude to deform our community.

In the face of such a troubling past and present, what we can and need to do together *now* to create a more human and loving society is our task. Thus we need to ask ourselves as individuals and as a people who we are, what kind of community we want to build, and where the sources of the fundamentally new and more compassionate are to be found. There are many voices advising us that are often at odds with each other. Some say that the answer is in making it in this country, by which they mean getting power and money by playing the system; others think that the solution is in returning to some golden age when Latinas and Latinos knew the meaning of respect and had a sense of shame that kept them faithful to the traditional past; still others believe that this is a war and that we have to concentrate on getting revenge for all the harm that has been done to us even if that means violence; then there are those Latinas and Latinos who realize that our humanity is at stake and who therefore seek to fully express the personal, political, historical, and sacred faces of our being to shape a more just and loving society.

We need a perspective that enables us to discern the deeper, underlying radical meaning of the choices that we have available. I propose in this book, but especially in chapter 1, to offer guidelines by which people like you and me can know the deeper significance of the alternatives available to us. From the perspective of a theory of transformation I will ask the question: In the service of what way of life do I live the stories and relationships of my life? But before I can answer such a question, I have to know something about the realm of deeper, underlying sacred sources known as archetypes. The Sufi philosopher Ibn Arabi (1165–1240) and the Muslim tradition of transformation spoke of the *ta'wil*, that kind of understanding which leads us to the deepest of all sacred sources. To be aware of the archetypal realm is to understand that all of our concrete life has a deeper forming source that determines the ultimate meaning and structure of our lives. Not to be conscious of this reality makes us superficial in the worst sense, for we literally live on the surface and have no depth.

As we create a Latino culture in this country, we need to know which stories in our past have wounded us and which ones have put us in contact with our deepest source. We need to avoid romanticizing the past as well as seeing the official story of American society, capitalism, as the answer. We have to be prepared to critique both cultures by again asking the question: In the service of what way of life do you and I live the stories of our life? in regard to both our Latino heritage and the wider society. This is the task that we shall address in chapter 2.

In chapter 3 I address the stories with which Latina women are struggling to overcome the politics of inequality. Chapter 4 analyzes the situation of students by drawing upon their experiences as they confront the stories and ways of life that held them so that they could not experience transformation.

A perspective that sees our lives as permeated by the living reality of under-lying sacred sources is already intuitively present in a very powerful way in the scholarship and writing of people like Sandra Cisneros, Cherrie Moraga, Gloria Anzaldúa, Leslie Marmon Silko, Oscar Hijuelos, Octavio Paz, Laura Esquivel, René Marqués, and Alberto Pulido, among others. What all of these Latina and Latino writers and scholars have in common is a growing awareness that something is happening to us on the deeper level. They are retelling the story of our search for *el dorado*, gold, in a fundamentally new way, as rediscovering the story of the journey of transformation. They write, create, and teach about people, especially Latina women and Latino men, who are discovering that they are arrested in their lives, who are finding the personal courage to break out of their crumbling containers, politically confronting the stories that gave others the right to possess their lives, and who are embarking on a new story for Latinas and Latinos by creating new turning points in their personal history that can serve as a guide for others who are leaving and breaking away. And, finally, they write and teach about people like you and me, finding the strength to live with great courage to face our problems inspired by the deepest source to de-velop strategies of transformation that will allow us to journey through the core drama of life until we reach its fulfillment in the drama of transformation.

Chapter 5 will be devoted to strategies of transformation. In regard to all of the challenges facing *la comunidad Latina* mentioned above, we cannot begin to develop strategies of transformation to confront our problems unless we trans-form the four faces of our being: the personal, political, historical, and the sacred. There is no place for being permanently victimized or being caught in the deadly game of victimizing others. You and I as Latina women and Latino men can cooperate together with people of goodwill from all backgrounds to intervene in deformational stories and to create the fundamentally new and better in the service of transformation.

In practical terms this means having the courage to confront our own heritage

and freeing ourselves from underlying ways of life and stories that arrest us in
the core drama of life, such as the dramas of capitalism, tribalism, patriarchy,
romantic love, the conquering hero, and a narrow and debilitating nationalism.
It is empowering to be proud to call ourselves a Chicano or Chicana, or Boricua,
Colombian, Cuban, Dominican, Guatemalan, or Peruvian. Many of us have
fought so hard to assert that to be *piel canela*, to be brown, is beautiful. But
we live in a community that needs us to transcend a particular comunidad and
cultura Latina, so that we can also embrace all Latino communities. This kind
of coalition building will serve us in good stead when we interact with an
increasingly multicultural America and world so that we can guide ourselves
and others in shaping an authentic humanity, an open and compassionate inclusion of all human beings.

''In the service of what way of life?'' is the most fundamental question that
we can ask. As we shall see in the context of the book, answering this question
tells us in the service of which of the four underlying archetypal ways of life
and their corresponding sacred sources we are enacting the relationships and
stories of our life, which sacred source either arrests us or frees us as we journey
through the three acts and scenes of the core drama of life, whether we can
respond to new problems, and the capacity of our four faces to be fully present.

For example, when I use the term ''Latino'' or ''Chicana,'' I know nothing
of the quality of a person's life who is so designated unless I can know in the
service of what way of life, in the service of what ultimate sacred source she
or he structures their life. A person who says that she is Latina can be using
this name to indicate her agreement with her past heritage and feel totally in
agreement with that tradition. This use of the term ''Latina'' is in the service
of emanation. This is a way of life in which we are given the truth once and
for all. Our security is assured by the intensity to which we commit ourselves
to the authority that is ultimately based on the will of an all-knowing and all-
powerful lord who punishes all unbelievers. But someone else can use the term
to describe herself in order to get into law school, which will then allow her to
become one of the powerful. Such a person is in the service of incoherence, a
way of life in which the ultimate concern of being is power and the pursuit of
self-interest. In contrast to emanation as a way of life, incoherence inspires us
to question, take risks, and to challenge because these are all forms of rebellion
against the powerful so that we might become one of the privileged. This search
for power takes us over, and so we end by fighting to exclude others, including
other Latinas and Latinos.

To say that I am a Latino can also be used in the service of deformation
because it constitutes a justification for violence legitimized by a declaration of
superiority over other racial and ethnic groups. This way of life is embraced by
those who feel an obsession for revenge, who seek to exercise absolute power
over those who were a cause of pain for them. But now, rather than being the
victim, they become the victimizer. Deformation is a way of life in which we
exit the core drama of life and make life fundamentally worse by turning our-

selves and others into lesser human beings. In contrast to incoherence as a way of life, deformation turns partial human beings into lesser human beings because they are no longer given even the opportunity to compete for power. In fact, the ways of life of incoherence and emanation because of their inherent fragility are often in collusion with deformation. A father, for example, who feels that his container of emanation, which gave him permission to be a patriarchal lord, is in danger of collapsing because of the rebellion of his children, can and often does move to violence. And so to protect his way of life, he exits the core drama and makes life worse. He has no capacity within this traditional way of life to respond to the new problems in life. Since his consciousness is restricted to that of a fixed way of life, all change is heresy worthy of punishment. Those who feel that the ultimate purpose of their life, power, is being threatened, resort to violence in order to sustain their position. This might take the form of beating workers who are trying to form a union or knowingly manufacturing products that will severely injure or kill people. Once this kind of violence is taken, those responsible are no longer on the road to deformation; they are now in the depths of deformation.

In contrast to the three choices in the service of emanation, incoherence, or deformation, those who use the term "Latina" or "Latino" in the service of transformation are proud to be such, but they realize that they are still in the process of growing their own humanity. Overcoming racism and prejudice in regard to our own racial or ethnic group is only part of the process of transformation that allows us, once we know who we are, to take the next step in helping to free all others, including the dominant, by making sure that the structures of racism and inequality will not continue to injure any of us. These four ways of life, the sacred sources that inspires them, and our capacity to choose between them will be further explained, with many examples provided throughout the book.

I have often criticized social scientists who tell us nothing about the deeper, sacred realm of our lives. Like Max Weber, they speak about power and charisma but cannot find a way to determine when the charisma leads us to destruction until *after* it happens. Our own Latina and Latino social scientists have been deeply wounded by following the theoretical emptiness of the dominant schools of the social sciences. So they count people who go to church and rely on labels like santería and popular religiosity. But what they cannot tell us is the quality of the connection to the sacred of that person or community. Neither can they tell us anything about the personal, political, historical, and sacred faces of our being as a consequence of being connected to a particular sacred source. The sacred or religion has become a thing, an abstraction, to be put on a questionnaire so that it will yield some quantifiable numbers that can be spewed out by the SSP program on the computer.

Our theologians are also hampered by their narrow view of the sacred or of religion. We are encouraged to be religious, to listen to the will of God, and to pray for moral guidance. But this is not of much help in the midst of the problems that we face. This is because most, if not all of us were raised to see the world of religion as being above and apart from the world around us. Religion could keep us pure from a world that was only a fleeting reality into which we should not put too much effort. As a result, we did not know that the sacred was being distorted by a denial of its political and historical faces. God also has a political and historical face. To give an example, the lord of sin, shame, and guilt that dominated la comunidad Latina was used to teach us that our personal dreams were selfish, that our task in life was to be uncritically loyal to those in authority, to hand on the tradition as pure and unchanged as we received it, and to see Dios Todopoderoso, God the Almighty, as identifiable with the Church, residing in the minister, living in the tabernacle—but never in our selves.

As long as our relationship to the sacred was structured and given its ultimate meaning by this lord of emanation, we were deeply impoverished as partial beings. Why were we partial beings? Because this lord arrested us and held us in a web of life that denied us the right to participate creatively and critically together with the deepest source of our being. Since our personal face was hidden from us, we could not listen to the inspirations that came from the deepest source. As a consequence of this repression, we had no choice but to practice a politics of loyalty since we had no basis from which to question anything. Since we were cut off from our own deepest voice, unable to challenge the political status quo, we were doomed to repeat the past because history can only be changed by people who hear a new and more loving voice, defy the politics of orthodoxy, and choose to create a new turning point. The transformation of the four faces of our being becomes a reality only if we empty ourselves of the old sacred sources, partial and incomplete lords, so that the deepest sacred can reveal itself in a new way. The central place of the sacred in our lives will be discussed throughout the book.

My hope in writing this book is that it will serve as a guide for people from my community, Latinas and Latinos alike as well as my fellow citizens from all backgrounds, who are looking for a way, for good talk, for a way to articulate, conceptualize, and enact that which can be helpful to us as we face the issues that confront us. The theoretical perspective that I use in the book is an extraordinary blessing because it does not consist of typologies or labels and theorems that have to be memorized; it is a theory that invites us to personally test its validity by participating in the life, death, and resurrection of sacred sources and of ourselves. It helps us to do this by giving us the language to express what many of us have always known in our bones. By means of a theory of transformation, we can name the stories and ways of life that arrest us; we can analyze why and where we got lost on the journey through the core drama of life; and, most importantly, we can learn why it is necessary and how we can in actual fact creatively and critically participate in transformation. Breaking with destructive stories and ways of life that turn us into partial and lesser human beings and creating new and more loving alternatives is the best way to free ourselves of victimhood. To become participants not only in the concreteness of our lives, but in the realm of the deeper sources is to live and act at the heart of life itself.

1

A Theoretical Perspective: In the Service of What Way of Life?

THEORY AS OUR GUIDE

Theory is not an abstraction; it is our participation in a sacred story at the heart of our existence, the core drama of life, which is fulfilled by journeying through all three acts of the drama until we reach transformation.[1] The core drama of life has two aspects that are present to each other: (1) all concrete stories of the journeys of our lives have a deeper meaning; (2) all these stories are grounded and rooted in archetypes, that is, all stories are manifestations of underlying, sacred forming sources that give our stories their ultimate meaning and purpose. Some stories remain connected to sacred sources that are partial, biased, and incomplete, and our anxiety leads us to join with them and we are thus arrested in our journey and fail to reach transformation. Others succeed in regard to achieving transformation and urge us from within to undergo the same passage of transformation: to be born, to die, and to be resurrected. But what is more important is the recognition that we are invited to live and participate in the story of transformation. It is we who inherit archetypal stories and fail to move on by remaining stuck in the journey and never getting beyond the first act of this three-act journey by preserving our stories unconsciously. But through trans-formative action we can enter into rebellion against them in Act II, Scene 1, and in the second scene of Act II uproot the destructive stories and send them into the abyss as we create new and better stories in Act III, Scenes 1 and 2, that allow us to shape a more loving, just, and compassionate society in the service of transformation.

Theory means understanding of and participation in the story and process of transformation. Thus in this book, theory will be reinterpreted, revisioned and, I hope, reexperienced and applied in a personally concrete way in the context of our political, historical, and sacred faces as our participation in the birth, death, and transformation of sacred sources and stories.

It is an extraordinary theory in its ability to tell an old, yet new, story that allows us to see the intimate connection between the personal, political, historical, and the sacred, underlying, deeper meaning of our lives. Furthermore, this theory will give us an opportunity to understand and participate in the most important story of our life, the story of transformation as the core drama, wherein we choose among four ultimate ways of life—one of which ends in destructive death. The reader will be provided with concrete examples, most of which are taken from the experiences of la comunidad Latina in the United States, so that we can understand the four ultimate ways of life. Since the emerging Latino story is about real people like you and me, we will have the opportunity to participate in constructing new and personal manifestations of more just and loving stories and relationships. To understand what is meant by archetypal ways of life, stories, and relationships is to know something crucial about how to shape a new and more compassionate life in U.S. society.

Next, this theory will enable us to understand and analyze the archetypal stories or dramas of our life that affect us as Latina and Latino citizens of a changing nation as we struggle with stories such as capitalism, tribalism, patriarchy, democracy, transforming love, possessive love, and matriarchy. Finally, it will present a means of critiquing and changing the reality of our lives from a clear and compelling normative perspective.

Good theory provides us with an interrelated set of testable generalizations, which fulfill the following requirements: it must allow us to deal with problems that are central to all human relations, formulated in terms and concepts that are not culture bound. Such a theory must allow us to use the same concepts and interrelated hypotheses for intrapersonal, interpersonal, and intergroup relations.

I propose to provide the outlines of the theory of transformation here and to use it in the struggle to analyze and develop strategies of transformation for la comunidad Latina in the United States. This theory will, I hope, help us understand how the relationships and stories connecting our community are being used creatively and/or destructively. The theory can enable us to see that we fail to achieve the meaning of our lives by remaining arrested in Act I of the core drama of life, wherein we unconsciously live the story of uncritical loyalty to the inherited dominant stories of the Latino tradition or to a white, male, Anglo-Saxon culture; moving to Act II, Scene 1, but then becoming caught in rebellion in the story of capitalism as the pursuit of self-interest is to remain a partial self; exiting the journey by turning to the fundamentally worse alternative of violence that results in personal, political, historical, and sacred destruction, is deformation; our only viable alternative and choice is that of transformation in Act III, wherein we make concrete a way of life committed to the persistent creation of fundamentally new and more loving sacred stories.

What is at stake here is our willing and creative participation in the *story* of transformation. This story arises out of our *experiences* of transformation. Once we have experienced transformation, we do not believe in it, that is, turn it into a dogma. But instead we must risk faith, meaning that we risk trust in experiencing this journey in this particular case, in regard to this particular problem. Transformational theory is, above all, *participation* in the drama of the life, death, and resurrection of sacred sources in ourselves and in the stories of our lives. What is so compelling and truthful regarding this theory is that people can live it and test it with their own experiences. It helps us to make sense of our own lives and to see how our experiences hang together as a whole. Let us begin then, in providing our theoretical and conceptual framework, by retelling and revisioning the story of creation and the story of transformation.

RETELLING THE STORY OF THE CREATION OF THE COSMOS: THE CORE DRAMA OF LIFE IS THE STORY OF TRANSFORMATION

According to this creation story, which contradicts the account of creation as told in the Book of Genesis, the deepest source of all sources, what Meister Eckhardt called the god beyond god, created first of all the most important story: the archetypal story of transformation, as the core drama of life. This is a three-act drama that must be enacted again and again. Why? Because the source of all sacred sources is still creating the universe.[2] From its inception, creation was intended to bring forth the fundamentally new and better. The core drama of life, fulfilled in the story of transformation, requires participation in all of its three acts between the deepest source and us, the concretely created. Our deepest source is not perfect, that is, complete: the source of all continues to create. Neither our sacred source nor we are perfect. So together with the deepest sacred we break and relink again and again in order to reemerge in a new and better unity. This is another way of saying that we and the source of all sources need to live and journey continually through the core drama of transformation. But this participation demands freedom to say yes or no. Who are the participants? We are, since we are the only creation able to persist in transformation without a preprogrammed specific outcome.

Other key participants in the core drama of life are archetypal, sacred forces. Why do I speak of sacred forces in the plural? Because we could not feel deeply attracted to Act I, in the service of the way of life of emanation and be seduced to remain in it and to arrest and consolidate our lives here unless an archetypal, sacred force or the lord of emanation was also free to say no and to separate itself from the story of transformation and hold us there. Similarly, we could not break away from the seductive security of Act I and then get caught in Act II, unless an archetypal source, the lord of incoherence, could separate itself from the core drama of transformation and hold us there. We could not be sucked into the abyss of deformation unless an archetypal force, symbolized by Satan, the lord of nothing, had the power to pull us down as we give into fantasies of superiority based on gender, nation, race, or religion to cover our insecurity.

Why do we need these archetypal forces or lords that can frustrate the story of transformation created by the deepest source of transformation? This is not a puppet show. The story of transformation has to offer us and the archetypal forces, the lords of emanation, incoherence and deformation, the capacity and freedom to say no and yes to this story, which constitutes the heart of creation. Therefore, the lord of emanation arrests the story in Act I, and we can be overwhelmed and continue to repress our feelings and doubts in order to allow Act I to remain a viable container. We cannot act at all without archetypal sources to pattern our actions; but neither are archetypal forces complete without us. For this reason we have to ask always the question In the service of which lord, or archetypal source, am I inspired to act?

All sacred sources in the core drama of life are free to act once they have been created by the deepest source of our being. Some of these sacred, archetypal sources repress their knowledge of the deepest ground of our being so that it is difficult for us to hear and understand when the voice of the god beyond god reaches out to us in order to further transformation. For example, according to the Mayan book of creation, The Popol Vuh, some gods became jealous of human beings because "they could see all things," and they could know the deepest of all sources and also give the sacred a concrete presence in the world by making conscious decisions.[3] Evil came into the world when we and the archetypal sacred source symbolized as Satan betrayed the drama of transformation and moved to consciously create destructive death or deformation by exiting from the story.

The source of transformation, the deepest source of our being, began creation by creating the story of transformation as the core drama of life because only that story fulfills the need for persistent transformation. But the deepest source gave us and archetypal sources the freedom to prevent transformation by participating in fragmentation and destruction. Nevertheless evil is not a necessary by-product of freedom. We can choose to move through the story together with the deepest ground of our being again and again without exiting from the drama and descending into the abyss of deformation, which makes life fundamentally new, but worse. To practice transformation is to continuously say no to the archetypal lords who enchant us in emanation, enchain us in fragments of power in incoherence, or suck us into the abyss of deformation. We need to free ourselves from these sacred sources, to be filled anew by our deepest sacred source. The deepest sacred does not stand by passively but enters the core drama of life again and again. But the god beyond god cannot command transformation; therefore the deepest ground of our being needs our participation to renew and widen transformation.

In this drama all of us of the very nature of being human can participate in the structure of the story of transformation. Increasingly in the modern age the most important choice is between deformation and transformation. To choose to make life fundamentally more loving and compassionate is to participate with one another and with the god of transformation as the deepest ground of our being.[4]

There is a marvelously redemptive aspect to the story of transformation; it consists in our ability to realize in what story we were caught and in what way of life we enacted a decision. We are now free to reject the destructive stories and ways of life and to choose more just and loving relationships in the service of transformation. This participatory nature of the story of transformation prevents the loss of our precious time; we do not need to punish ourselves because of hurt pride, guilt, or anger. We are now empowered to put an end to our guilt by creating alternatives in such a way that we simultaneously accept responsibility for what was done and decide to do something to heal the injury caused by living destructive stories.

This great blessing of the story of transformation is due to the inherent mercy of the deepest source of transformation, the source of the fundamentally more loving and compassionate. It is a witness to the inherent dynamic of the structure of the universe, one based on love. It is never too late, either for ourselves or for others. But we must not freeze ourselves, or others, in cultural stereotypes. To do so violates the very nature of the universe, which is a constant invitation from the ground of our being to dry our tears and resume the task of co-creating the universe.

To conclude, we know that different partial, and lesser lords were present from the beginning of the creation. But only in the story of transformation as the fulfillment of the core drama of life could human beings have a necessary role in creation—necessary because the source of all sources, that has no concreteness, required human beings to give creation a concrete face. This co-creation between the source of sources and human beings made us the object of jealousy to the lord of a final and fixed truth since this source of emanation could only dominate in the realm of a once-and-for-all creation. Through us the sacred has real feet on the ground and can continue to create. But the fullness of this co-creation can take place only if we realize our inner sacredness by embarking on the journey of transformation.[5]

THE THREE ACTS OF THE CORE DRAMA OF LIFE

The underlying patterning force of the story of transformation is the only way of life in the service of which we are capacitated with the imagination to participate in creating the fundamentally more just and compassionate in all aspects of our life.

Telling the story of this drama tells us something we are rarely told: How in actual practice can we transform ourselves? How can we actually find a fundamentally better way and test it by translating it into practice together with our neighbors?[6]

The three-act drama of transformation is the deepest act of life.[7] When we arrest life, and therefore our journey, in one of these acts before we reach the third act, we stunt and contain our life in a fragment of the story of transformation. And because it is only a fragment of life, it leaves us partial selves, fragile, wounded, and angry, no matter how much power we may accumulate within it.[8]

We always begin in emanation in Act I, Scene 1. In the first scene of Act I, we are caught in the enchantment of overwhelming sources. Because we are uncritically loyal to established stories we have learned, we can arrest our lives here and turn this scene into an entire way of life in the service of emanation. This is an overarching way of life in which we consistently experience feelings of sin, shame, and guilt whenever we begin to ask fundamental questions. The result is that those wielding power are legitimized by the lord of emanation. In this way the few, as the will of this lord, control the many; they serve not the deepest source of our being, but a lord that has split off from the deepest sacred source. This lord of jealousy possesses its people, and the people, on their part, obey because of fear and the security given to them. This is the sacred origin of repression, which means that people unconsciously control themselves and abandon all resistance because they come to love their masters and this lord of the way of emanation, leading them to participate in their own subjugation. The symbolic drawing in Figure 1.1 and the interpretation provided in this chapter, together with the intuitive understanding of the reader, are intended to point toward a deeper and fuller understanding of the core drama of life.

We therefore live the inherited stories of our lives as final and ultimate because they are the outer flow of the revelation of a mysterious, overwhelming source of power, the lord of emanation. The lord of emanation impoverishes us all, even the deepest of all sources, because of the emphasis on continuity and cooperation with the status quo. We are forbidden to create conflict or change; our justice is enforcement of a revealed law, and the cost is the repression of all four faces of our being, the personal, political, historical, and sacred. When we arrest our entire lives here and turn Act I, Scene 1, into an entire way of life of emanation, we live all of our inherited stories as the final will of an all-powerful lord.

In addition, cut off from our deepest source, caught in the embrace of this lord, we cannot develop a new consciousness, creativity, new linkages to others, or new shared goals, and we find it difficult to understand what we continue to hear from our deepest source. In contrast, it is the lesser and partial lords of the

Figure 1.1
The Core Drama of Life

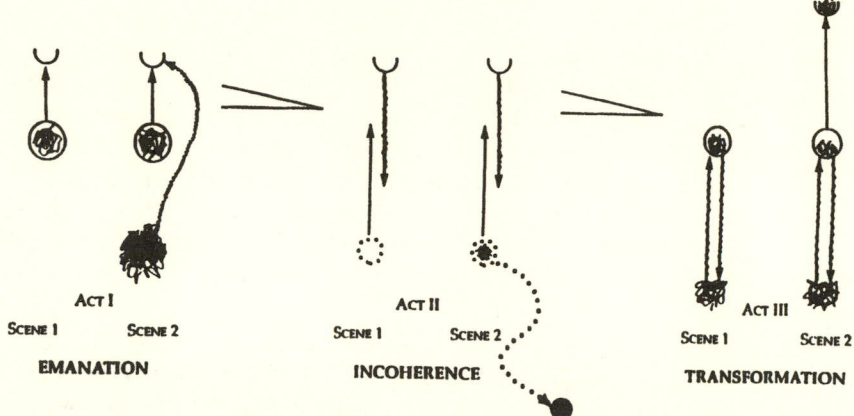

established order upon which the sociologists of religion focus their attention. The sociology of religion studies institutionalized religion, unaware of the realm of the deepest, underlying sacred, forming sources and the difference between these sacred forces. The story of transformation will allow us to reject these lesser lords who seek to be "the" lord and to point to the deepest transforming sacred source.[9]

And yet the way of life of emanation, arrested in Act I, Scene 1, is fragile precisely because of the structure of the story of transformation. This is a cosmos of continuous creation; we need to enact the story of transformation again and again in order to turn the fundamentally new toward the fundamentally better. We can only realize transformation in regard to one aspect of our life at a time; it is never total. The men and women of the countertradition, which is at least 2,500 years old, knew that they were unfinished, that the world was incomplete, and that the sacred was still creating itself in the cosmos.

For this reason there are two scenes in Act I. Scene 2 is filled with desires, new ideas, doubts, intuitions, and experiences that have their origin in sacred sources, beyond the official voice of conscience. It is our inner voice, rooted in underlying sacred sources, that undermines the repression. Increasingly we know that there is something more, an unrealized aspect of our lives that must be explored. But we cannot assume that these new voices are to the good. We need to test them to discern whether they are fundamentally new and better or destructive. Once we consciously determine that the new inspiration comes from the deepest source of transformation, we leave Act I, Scene 1, and break with those who have held us there. The threat, challenge, and opportunity of the inner voice are what people as famous as Albert Einstein and Isaac Newton, as well as people like you and me, respond to when we answer to a new, feeling. Change in the service of transformation always begins as a threat, as a heresy, as a radical departure from the norm. There is always something threatening in a real act of freedom.[10]

The way of life of emanation is everywhere dying. People are no longer willing to deny their own fundamentally new experiences, ideas, and hopes. Some, however, will chose to repress the new. We owe much to those who are seen as deviants, heretics, and outsiders. I vividly remember my mother referring to me as a child with no shame because I dared to question her, the Catholic Church, or God. Initially, though, I repressed my inner voice in Act I, Scene 2. I was afraid to question my mother's religious beliefs and the authority of the Church. Manfred Halpern says that

when this arrested fragment of life breaks, people who have lost or feel that they are losing the seeming security of acting as the outward embodiment of a mysterious source may also be tempted towards deformation—promising to lead us to a great restoration but it leads to destructive death.[11]

This promise to restore or maintain the glory of the past and to bolster a deteriorating story that possessed us and held us in the first act of the core drama of life helps us to understand the deep fear that many parents have felt when their children rebelled. Many resorted to violence when the children dared to raise questions regarding their inherited values. My mother could not accept such challenges because the story of patriarchy in which she was arrested in Act I, Scene 1, would not allow her to see other possibilities.

When we take Act I, Scene 2—that is, our new doubts and intuitions— seriously, we enter into Act II, Scene 1, wherein we break with our parents and other authority figures and embark upon a path of open rebellion. But in the first scene of Act II, we are also free to arrest the journey and institutionalize rebellion against the way of life of incoherence in which we enact stories and a culture that organizes the competition for power. This is where we are as a culture enacting the story of the market society or capitalism.[12] This story gives us a false sense of freedom, which comes from not yet knowing who we are. But since we live in a hostile world, rather than continue the journey, many begin to create fortresses in a world that they do not understand.

It is important to emphasize that this is not only a rational, personal choice; people have not become "secularized" merely by rejecting the lord of emanation of institutionalized religion. Other sacred forces are present. The lord of incoherence, the lord of power, attracts us and inspires us to remain rooted in the first scene of Act II. This lord replaces the lord of emanational truth. But the lord of incoherence is also a partial and lesser lord who hinders our ability to reach the deepest sacred, the source of the fundamentally new and better. The lord of incoherence inspires us to believe that power and self-interest are the only things that give meaning to life. Whenever we fail to understand our emanational relationship to this overarching drama, this way of life takes us over. The lord of incoherence is the sacred source present in the depths who inspires the story of capitalism but because the modern age considers the sacred as superstitions, we can no longer name what drives and obsesses us. Therefore, we get trapped in stories that possess us and turn us against each other in a perpetual competition that turns our relationships into contests of mutual suspicion and fear.

At best in the story of capitalism in the service of incoherence arrested in Act II, Scene 1 as a fragment of the core drama of life, we can agree on procedures that keep us from killing each other as we struggle with each other in the name of self-interest. The language and the deeds of love and compassion are not welcome in the public realm.[13] To overcome our vulnerability, we seek power, thus of course increasing our anxiety. There is no security. We turn this attempt to organize insecurity, without being able to name it, into a whole way of life of incoherence.

Since we have only broken with our actual antagonists in Act II, Scene 1, we remain vulnerable to the lord, to the archetypal story and the way of life in the depths that hold on to us. Thus it is not enough to break on the concrete level with our fathers or lovers; we have to experience a deeper breaking, but this time critically and consciously, by emptying our soul in Act II, Scene 2, of the archetypal story in which we are caught and the deeper, overarching way of life that inspired and gave mysterious power to others. We need now to empty ourselves of the archetypal story and the way of life in the service of which we live the stories of our life. If we merely reject our concrete expressions, we will repeat what we had rejected. It is because we do not understand the power of these sacred stories, which are concrete manifestations of underlying patterning forces, and the necessity of emptying ourselves of them that we repeat history, that is, the same stories of our lives in the service of ways of life that constitute mere fragments of the core drama of life.

Most of us remain unaware of the world of archetypal, sacred forces that constitute the grounding of stories that possess us when we remain unconscious of them. We mistakenly believe that we are changing, even transforming, our lives when we only break with the actual concrete actors of our stories in Act II, Scene 1. But because we fail to empty ourselves on the deeper level in Act II, Scene 2, of the story enacted in the service of partial ways of life that gave them their power, we wake up one day and realize that only the outer appearances have changed; the story remains just as powerful, or more so, than before.

Deformation constitutes the road into the exit from the core drama. At the second scene of Act II we make a decisive choice to empty ourselves of the stories that have possessed us, or we turn to violence and send ourselves and others into the abyss. From being the victims, we become the victimizers. Increasingly in the modern age, deformation is becoming prevalent. Because of the inherent fragility of emanation as a dying way of life and of incoherence as a way of life, people whose emanational container is threatened or whose power is at stake will turn toward violence to preserve their way of life and thus exit the core drama of life and make life fundamentally worse in the service of deformation. A good example of this is the Taliban in Afghanistan, who seek to create a story of uncritical loyalty to their version of traditional Islam. But since emanation as a way of life has lost its meaning for many Muslims, who have been seduced by the freedom to pursue power and self-interest in incoherence as a way of life, they are no longer willing to return and submit to what is in fact a fantasy of orthodox views. Therefore they are tortured and killed; what is alleged to be a return to the past thus ends in deformation.

The tobacco industry is now naked before the public because of the revelation of studies that it commissioned that proved thirty years ago that smoking was addictive and that there was a clear linkage between smoking and cancer. The industry suppressed these studies, which would undermine tobacco profits and power. So for the sake of power it was willing to let people die. What may have begun as an attempt to reform a particular set of practices in the story of capitalism in the service of incoherence as a way of life now becomes capitalism in the service of deformation, destructive death at the exit from the core drama. This exposes the lie that the pursuit of profits is a cool and rational business pursued by honorable people. The story and ways of life take us over. Our obligation is to become conscious of these underlying sources and to refuse to become their vessels. This is the real, and deeper, meaning of just saying no.

Without this deeper rejection of the archetypal story and way of life in which service we enacted the drama, we have not really freed ourselves to create a new and better story. There can be no revenge in the story of transformation, only the courage to engage but then go beyond the oppressor to deal with the deeper causes, the stories and partial ways of life.

Once we have emptied ourselves in Act II, Scene 2, we free ourselves from unbearable archetypal dramas and the ways of life of emanation, incoherence, and deformation since they are arrested fragments, and in the case of deformation, the exit from the drama of transformation, and send them, not ourselves or others, into the abyss at the exit from the core drama. As Halpern has put it, "We now free ourselves in Act III, Scene 1 to hear anew from the deepest source of our being and in the second scene of Act III we try out in practice with our neighbors to see if our new vision is in fact fundamentally better."[14] The story of transformation is radically different; this sacred story needs and demands our participation. To empty ourselves three times over in Act II, Scene 2, that is, of our actual concrete antagonist, of the underlying story that oppressed us and of the way of life in which both the powerful and the powerless were caught, is to prepare ourselves to be filled anew by the deepest source in Act III. The way of life of transformation provides the only context within which we can express the capacity, freedom, and wholeness of being human both in our concrete creation and in our sacred depths and thus fully realize love and justice. The deepest source is free to continuously recreate the world only when we are prepared to participate in its transformation. In this way we incarnate the sacred source that inspires us, that actually breathes within us. Participation in persistent transformation belongs to each of us of the very nature of our humanity. Each of us has the awesome responsibility and joy of living the story and journey of transformation in all aspects of our lives.

Now that we have been introduced to the core drama of life and to the four ways of life in which we enact the four faces of our being and the stories that we live daily, let us go on to consider how we structure our daily lives by enacting nine archetypal relationships in the service of different ways of life.

Our analysis is grounded firmly on a theory of transformation that asserts that a structure to the universe is provided by the core drama of our lives, the story of transformation. The core drama of life, as we have seen, consists of three acts; within the matrix of these three acts we enact archetypal ways of life, the stories of our lives and archetypal relationships. The theory of transformation sees the encounter between self, other, and the sacred with respect to concrete problems as the most fundamental dialectic in human life. According to this view, the quality of the connections between individuals, groups, families, ideas, and our personal and sacred sources is what gives us the capacity to simultaneously be free to change, yet continue our connections to others, to be able to conflict, yet cooperate, and to work toward a more compassionate justice for all.

What constitutes our first worldwide revolution consists precisely in the breaking of the concrete, inherited manifestations of archetypal relationships and the dying way of life of emanation. (Increasingly in our own time, incoherence as a way of life is also proving to be fragile as we confront many kinds of problems that cannot be resolved by the pursuit of power and calculated self-interest.) Everywhere in the world societies and cultures founded on an ultimate truth and ways of doing things as the will of an all-powerful lord are being undermined and subverted. This collapse of meaning and purpose gives rise to a profound terror that opens up both destructive and creative possibilities.

The concrete manifestations of inherited archetypal relationships and stories enacted within the way of life of emanation are breaking because they can no longer give us the capacity to respond to the flow of life, to the changes that demand a new kind of self, a renewed relationship to those around us, and a mutual creation with our underlying depths. This way of life cannot allow any new consciousness or creativity since the final revelation has been provided for the people.

The nine archetypal relationships—emanation, subjection, isolation, buffering, direct bargaining, autonomy, incoherence, deformation, and transformation—are always enacted in the service of four ultimate ways of life, the ways of life of emanation, incoherence, deformation, and transformation. These are the patterns in the service of fundamentally different ways of life by which we shape daily life and live the stories of our lives. We and those around us encounter difficulties when the concrete, inherited manifestations of these underlying patterns no longer give us the ability to deal with the five issues of daily, human performance: continuity and change, collaboration and conflict, and the achieving of justice. Each concrete form of an archetypal relationship gives us a different ability to cope with these five issues of performance.

Usually the repertory of archetypal relationships available to people has been limited by the societies in which they were raised to one dominant and two or three subdominant relationships in dealing with most problems of life. For example, most Latina women were living until recently in the way of life of emanation in Act I, Scene 1, of the core drama. They were limited to the use of five relationships: the relationships of emanation, subjection, isolation, buffering, and direct bargaining. As I will explain below, these five relationships are the officially sanctioned relationships that sustained and maintained the realm of emanation.

In the container of emanation most Latina women in Latin America and in the Latino barrios of this country were socialized to relate to their elders in only these five ways. These five patterns of relating provide people with a maximum of continuity and cooperation and shield them from conflict and change; the benefit, or justice, rendered by these relationships is that they provide security, but at the cost of not being able to speak about one's own desires and needs if these contradict the society's norms. Latinas entered into rebellion when they found it unbearable to continue to see their lives as mere extensions of their fathers, lovers and husbands, with their lives arrested in Act I, Scene 1, of the core drama of life. The price of this security was too high because it meant to continue to repress the four faces of their being and their own desires. Therefore they sought a change of relationships so that they could experience a new kind of justice: accepting and living their own desires and needs.

These relationships enacted within four ways of life will be fully explained through examples taken from the lives of Latina women and Latino men throughout the book. Our goal is to understand how to take the concrete, inherited manifestations of these nine archetypal patterns into our own hands so that as they break, we can create new concrete combinations of them and restore to all of us the capacity to change our lives and society. We can identify those patterns which have to be struggled against by naming them clearly as patterns that, in their present concrete form and in the service of our present way of life, cripple the human capacity to reexperience self, other, and our deepest creative source.

Now that this introduction is given, let us proceed to consider in depth the nine relationships available to us by which we pattern daily life. Within our discussion of the nine encounters we shall also return to the story of transformation and of choosing among archetypal stories enacted within the four ways of life.

What are the archetypal patterns of relationships that link the lives of all of us? From one moment to the next, our theory sensitizes us to the realization that our task is to deal with constant change. Our lives are always in the process of creation, nourishment, death and re-creation. This perpetual process of change is given shape by the nine archetypal relationships, and they in turn are given their deeper meaning by the archetypal stories and the four archetypal ways of life within which we enact relationships. Practiced within a particular story and way of life, each of our nine archetypal relationships has its own capacity to relate ourselves to self, to the other members of our society, to problems, and to the sacred.

NINE ARCHETYPAL RELATIONSHIPS

For all encounters between self and other in all recorded human history and in all societies, there exist only nine forms of relationship that give people the capacity to deal simultaneously with continuity and change, collaboration and conflict, and the achieving of justice. The hypothesis that there are nine and only nine archetypal forms applies to all intrapersonal, interpersonal, and intergroup relations. It applies to all groups, from family or affinity groups to political parties or nations and to the human species as a whole. This hypothesis applies to relations between individuals and groups, whether formal or informal, stable or fluctuating. It applies to our relations to concepts, symbols, ideas, values, feelings, norms, and problems. This hypothesis also applies to our connection to those sources of energizing and forming which we may call transpersonal, which others have called the unconscious, the sacred or god. This hypothesis applies to all encounters in all of recorded history and in all human societies. Because this hypothesis applies to all such human experiences, all readers already possess sufficient factual information to test this hypothesis.[15]

Let us now proceed to an explanation of the nine forms of encounter enacted in the service of four different ways of life. To be able to tell which relationships are allowed by a particular society tells us what any person or group is free to express and also what it is that they are forced to repress. Presently in the world there are very few persons who feel free to create all nine relationships, with the exception of deformation, which is always destructive. No current society encourages or even allows the free use of all eight relationships in the service of transformation, and so they discourage our full human capacity.

EMANATION

This is an encounter in which you or I treat a person, such as our son or wife, solely as an extension of ourselves. If our son accepts the denial of his own separate identity it is because of the mysterious and overwhelming power of the source of this emanation— the underlying archetypal sacred source of this relationship that gives fathers their mysterious power over their sons. If our sons dutifully obey, we and the archetypal source in the depths, the relationship of emanation, reward them with total security. All of us began life as children without power adequate to meet the powerful others in our home. We therefore necessarily yielded our identity to the mysterious and overwhelming power of our mothers until we freed ourselves to risk losing total security. However, some fathers or mothers seek to retain all members of their household as emanations of themselves. Others treat their property or their employees in this way. Many individuals remain eager to submerge themselves as loyal extensions of a political movement, a dogma or a lover.[16]

The relationship of emanation is the most prevalent relationship, even in the time in which we live. It points out an unexamined, unconscious, uncritical, relationship to a mysterious and overwhelming source that contains us and within which we live our inherited stories. Indeed we are not even conscious of archetypal stories. We may see emanation manifested in the lives of many Latina women, who see themselves as mere extensions of husbands and families; they see themselves as the expression of their husband's personality, without any independent views of their own. Most Latino men and Latina women were raised in inherited stories, especially patriarchy, in which we were trained to believe that the limits of our lives were determined by our fathers or matriarchal mothers.

It is a relationship in which many of us as Latinos agree to be passive as we cooperate with others at the cost of repressing conflict. Both parties agree to achieve continuity by implicitly accepting or rejecting change, taking our cue from our fathers, mothers, or bosses. In this way we grant mysterious and over-whelming power to them in exchange for total security.[17] Emanation keeps us firmly embedded in Act I, Scene 1, of the core drama of transformation. But later in this chapter we will see that emanation is not in itself destructive. The relationship of emanation can be enacted in profoundly different ways that are determined by which of four different ways of life it serves. For example, in the service of transformation, emanation can be used temporarily to nurture the young; the flow of emanation can then be broken to allow for emergence rather than containment.

SUBJECTION

In the relationship of subjection both myself and my mother are fully present, but in reality both of us are denied a full presence and an identity of our own. The relationship is still asymmetrical; it still rests upon the experience of overwhelming power. But this power, which was mysterious in emanation, becomes naked in subjection—I now clearly see who is blocking my freedom, how the denial of access to money controls me and I see my own resistance.[18]

We see subjection in the European American determining the curriculum in the schools and the teacher demanding that children speak English at all times, the father or husband solely controlling the spending of the family's money. Subjection exists whenever I control others as a means to my own end, whether I base this control on the naked power of standards of efficiency, or simply on the power of the gun.

In subjection, conflict is no longer repressed, but suppressed. Too often in their own education Latino children know that they cannot be themselves by speaking their own mother tongue and telling the stories of their heritage. Explicit rules defined solely by the dominant culture tell us how to behave. Everywhere the powerful often combine emanation and subjection when relating to the less powerful. Thus most newly arrived Latinos are still prepared to relate to authority figures in this country with the same deference and respect given in the previous homeland. The dominant group, therefore, assures continuity and change in accordance with its power. Justice means that if you want to survive, then you better go along with those who have the power to hurt you. Almost always, especially in regard to matters of educational policy, members of la comunidad Latina who were not considered to be part of the elite survived by giving up their right to create conflict or change on their own in regard to matters of the curriculum so that their children would not be hurt.

BUFFERING

This is a relationship in which conflict and change are managed by intermediaries. Buffering is carried out by a mediator, broker, or by a concept.[19]

Comadres (godmothers) were very important mediators for Latina young women as they sought to break away from the oppressive hold of their parents. As in all patriarchal societies, Latinas used buffering to create conflict and change in a socially acceptable manner by having others who are seen as the peers of their parents intervene on their behalf. They also avoided ever contradicting their parents, because to do so is a sin. Justice in buffering is obtaining some better situation through the intervention of a third party. Thus godparents, a teacher, or a member of the clergy, because of their influence with parents, were able to achieve considerable exceptions from the strict rules of the family to participate in different kinds of activities. The problem here is that our freedom relies on the ability and skill of the mediator; our self-determination is therefore limited and we can become too dependent on others.

ISOLATION

People who live in emanational relationships to others cannot bear isolation.

In this relationship two people or groups agree to leave each other alone. Both sides agree to avoid any conflict that would lead to change between them. In this case justice, that is, the result of this kind of relating means a degree of freedom—but at the price of not attempting to affect change in the others. Isolation cannot be achieved alone. The other must agree to cooperate. If one or the other party attempts to isolate without an agreement to avoid conflict, change or new forms of justice by the other party produces incoherence, not isolation.[20]

Patriarchal males such as César in Oscar Hijuelos's *The Mambo Kings Play Songs of Love*[21] and Tomás in Humberto Solas's *Lucía*,[22] who possessed their wives in relationships of emanation, assumed that their spouses would always want to be near them since they were the source of emanation who gave the women their reason for living and therefore refused to allow them to exercise physical isolation. Latina women could and do practice emotional isolation in which they are allowed to withdraw into themselves and are left alone as a substitute for being unable to physically withdraw.

DIRECT BARGAINING

In this relationship, individuals and groups collaborate in allowing conflict in order to bring about change with each other directly. Justice consists in the better bargain that one side or the other may achieve. But real advance in self determination is the right to struggle with another to seek a better and more advantageous bargain as the balance of power changes.[23]

By means of gifts or favors, the less powerful seek to gain some bargaining leverage by creating a sense of indebtedness between themselves and the powerful. In fact, the one who provides the favor is often heard to say "You owe me one." As is clearly shown in Laura Esquivel's novel *Like Water for Chocolate*, women knew for many years that the way to get a better bargain from men was through the bargaining power of sex and food. In exchange for these services, their husbands often relented and allowed them certain favors. But the use of direct bargaining in the service of emanation and incoherence is one of the most effective ways to head off real transformation. When a man senses that his wife is becoming dangerously close to rebellion, he could resort to offering her a better deal within the story of patriarchy. By giving her a new car, he could lead a woman to feel guilty that she could ever question his love. Thus too often women go back to normal, that is, to the relationship of emanation enacted in the story of patriarchy in the service of emanation that kept them arrested in Act I, Scene 1, of the core drama of life that caused the problem in the first place. In this way the story of male dominance was reformed, that is, made easier but not done away with. Thus the anger of women is reduced to catharsis, emotional outbreaks that end by sending them back to their enchained container so that real change is avoided, since the husband remains in sole command.

AUTONOMY

This is a relationship in which both parties are entitled to claim power based on custom, law, status, value, education or competence that both share. Justice in the encounter of autonomy is the reciprocal right of each to sustain or enlarge their area of power. In the wider society, autonomy is the form of encounter which allows us to separate yet keep in constant tension the three branches of government, to charter the limited liability corporation, to create autonomy yet collaboration among professions, scholarly disciplines, and bureaucracies.[24]

The relationship of autonomy, together with direct bargaining, are the most powerful patterns in official U.S. society. They are necessary to survive in this country. Autonomy in the service of incoherence on the personal level demands aggressive, calculating individuals who know how to protect their interests by enlarging their area of power or who know when to defend their boundary against another bureaucrat who seeks to redraw the area under his jurisdiction to include one's own. It is essentially a relationship that justifies the attainment of power after power. The relationship of autonomy on the societal level is the relationship enacted when the rights of Latino parents to participate in the education of their children is involved. The struggle between the community and teachers is often a question of autonomous jurisdictions, those of the certified experts and of the parents. On the personal level, it is a young student going to university and becoming a teacher so that she can achieve economic autonomy and other rights based on explicit contractual principles. Latina women, for much of our history, were not allowed to exercise this relationship. Women's dependency, even when they worked outside the home, was ensured whenever a woman often handed over her check. Once again this relationship can be subverted and used in the service of transformation such that a competent doctor uses her skills and the autonomy granted to her as a physician to protect the rights of patients rather than to enhance her own personal power.

INCOHERENCE

Incoherence in our theory is that relationship in which two people face each other in the same place and at the same time but are unwilling or unable to agree on how to relate. Incoherence is a painful experience of the broken connections that had previously connected them. It is the experience of discontinuity rather than continuity; of change that is unintended and uncontrolled; it is conflict because they cannot agree on any form of collaboration, leading to injustice for both self and others. It is two people or two parties standing in the presence of each other and not knowing how to agree.[25]

Recently, a Latina woman related to me that she was so angry with her husband when she discovered that he had an affair that she rebelled against him. All of the inherited relationships by which she and her husband related to each other were shattered: she no longer saw her husband as the source of her mystery in emanation; she refused to accept his commands in subjection; she rejected the rationalizations as buffering (All men are like me) that her husband used to disarm her anger; she did not want to bargain with him since she refused to consider this betrayal as the basis for getting concessions because of any guilt that he might feel; consequently she and her husband stood in the presence of each other and could not agree on how to relate, hence the relationship of incoherence. What exacerbated the incoherence was that she now exercised the relationship of autonomy by going back to school and getting a part-time job without her husband's consent: wife and husband stood in the presence of each other unable to agree on which relationship to use. This Latina woman listened to her inner voice in Act I, Scene 2, and entered into rebellion in Act II, Scene 1: she broke with the person with whom she was previously linked in emanation in Act I, Scene 1. She is now moving toward transformation as she intends to free herself not only from this marriage, but from the underlying story of patriarchy that gave men permission to be unfaithful. Her family is opposed to what she is doing because the members still remain caught in the core drama in Act I. They want her to return to her husband in order to remain in Act I, Scene 1, in the relationship of emanation as a mere extension of their father/husband's life.

When she asked her husband to leave, it was truly an act of incoherence; from the perspective of the way of life of emanation it was a sin. Her husband and family used all of the psychic artillery of sin, shame, and guilt to attempt to restore her to her senses. She missed her husband and loved him, but she would no longer accept him at the expense of her own life. Her mother argued that if she loved him, she would swallow her pride and let him come back, go back to "normal," the way things used to be in Act I, Scene 1, the dying way of life of emanation.

The result is that this woman and her family are no longer able to relate; they are now relating in different worlds and mean fundamentally different realities in their use of the word "love." What accounts for this is that they are now living in different ultimate ways of life and in different acts of the core drama. The relationships of emanation, subjection, buffering, and direct bargaining enacted in the service of emanation are broke, and to the repertory were added the relationships of isolation, autonomy, incoherence, and transformation.

DEFORMATION

Deformation is a relationship in which we make connection with a particular person, object, idea, or feeling which from that first moment moves us into the road to destructive death. We have been feeling depressed for so long that we take cocaine to get a high; we join with a gang to defend the purity of our neighborhood so that we feel for the first time that we really do belong here. This is not a relationship of emanation but in fact a sacred source that is demonic.[26]

It is easy to confuse this relationship with emanation and transformation because it carries such a mysteriously overwhelming power. In truth, it is pseudoemanational, a fake emanation, because it is in the guise of emanation. The presence of this relationship means that we are on the road to destructive death in key aspects of our life. For example, when a male slaps a woman in order to hold her in the container of emanation, he goes beyond the relationship of subjection. Threatened males see their life and everything they stand for disintegrating; they not only want to punish women, but to cripple them. They are unable to respond to new demands on the part of their daughters, lovers, or wives. They respond to two fundamentally opposed inspirations: create a truly open relationship and risk themselves for the sake of the women and themselves or crush them as the persons who meant the end of their privileged yet repressed self. This latter choice brings men to the brink because they think that without the world as they know it they will not know what to do. What they refuse to see or accept is that this world is already being dismantled.

Happily, we can be inspired anew at any time to stop and to break with any archetypal relationship, empty ourselves of any archetypal story, any way of life. But that requires our connecting to a more powerful sacred source than those that lead us to destructive death, the deepest source of transformation. Only this god is powerful enough to help us to empty ourselves of both the concrete and the archetypal bonds that now enchant, but enchain us.

TRANSFORMATION

The relationship of transformation is a relationship in which our consciousness is no longer the mere embodiment of an external source of emanation. People like you and me have become conscious of those sources in the depths which constitute the archetypal dramas and stories of our lives. To enact this relationship is to know that we can participate in fundamentally new and better dramas and relationships. We can create, nourish, allow to die and re-create new forms of the relationships to deal with new problems and thus woo new combinations into being.[27]

People who create a new sense of self, break inherited relationships, and reject in Act II, Scene 2, the archetypal stories in the service of emanation, incoherence, and deformation that possessed their souls and create new linkages to others previously forbidden to them and who create alternative stories of their lives based on mutuality have enacted the drama of transformation. In Act III, Scene 1, people are inspired by a new vision of how to shape life anew. In the second scene of Act III, this new intuition is actually put into practice. One of the results of this newfound wholeness is that it enables people to enact not only all eight relationships (excluding the ninth relationship of deformation, which cannot be enacted in the service of transformation), but an infinite number of concrete manifestations of each relationship. This is what is meant to participate in the process of creating, uprooting, nourishing, and destroying in order to create and transform time and again.

What looks like transformation, however, can be distorted if it is in reality reformation. Transformation in the service of emanation is not possible; the very logic of emanation as a way of life precludes the emergence of the fundamentally new as a form of the worst heresy. Change that may be called transfor-

Figure 1.2
Four Archetypal Ways of Life

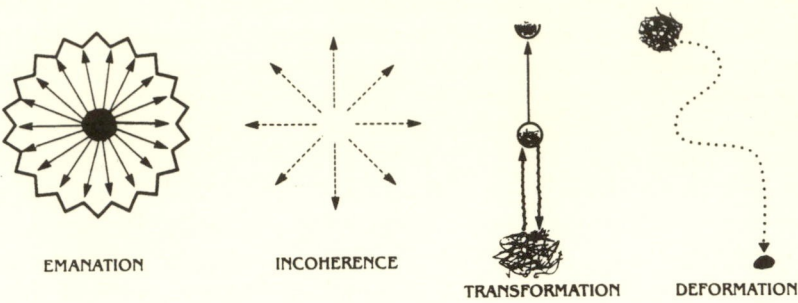

EMANATION   INCOHERENCE

TRANSFORMATION   DEFORMATION

mation is reformation when a person alters his or her personality, but in order to be more loyal to a lover, church, hero, or mother. Transformation is frustrated as reformation in the way of life of emanation when a woman becomes the first doctor in her family's history, but she herself did not choose to practice medicine and became a doctor only to remain loyal to her parents' wishes. This is not a transformation, but one which was performed in response to the question How can I ultimately show uncritical loyalty to mysterious others? Such a person is really arrested in Act I, Scene 2, since she was inspired to become someone new but then responded in this scene of the core drama by becoming a better extension of someone else and thus returns to Act I, Scene 1, with even more intensity. Transformation always means the creation of the fundamentally more loving and just alternatives in all aspects of our life. Transformation will be further discussed as a whole way of life later in this chapter.

All societies shape our ego. Through socialization the community introduces us to the acceptable repertory of concrete forms of the nine archetypal relationships. That is to say that not all nine forms of our archetypal relationships are seen as positive options. Consequently, people are forbidden to choose and to enact certain relationships; often we are not even aware of the existence of alternatives. The same is true for the archetypal dramas and archetypal ways of life that are available to us. In U.S. society the archetypal story and way of life, which we are all led to believe and accept as natural, is that of capitalism in the service of the way of life of incoherence, the legitimation of the pursuit of self-interest.

The nine archetypal relationships however, do not stand alone. Each of the nine archetypal relationships in its concrete manifestations derives its deeper meaning and value from a wider context, a whole way of life, either that of emanation, incoherence, transformation, or deformation (see Figure 1.2). The four ways of life determine the quality of our stories and relationships; consequently, the eight archetypal relationships are neither negative nor creative in themselves; only deformation is always destructive. Their quality or ultimate meaning is given to them within the way of life in which we choose to enact them. Emanation, incoherence, deformation, and transformation as archetypal relationships differ from emanation, incoherence, deformation, and transformation as whole ways of life. We will always specify which we mean, the relationship or the entire way of life.[28]

THE WAY OF LIFE OF EMANATION

The deeper and larger context within which traditional societies lived the stories of their lives and enacted their repertory of relationships was the way of life of emanation, arrested in Act I, Scene 1, of the core drama of transformation.

Politics in the service of emanation (for example, in the service of a fixed faith or tradition) holds us within containers in which all we can and need to do together is already codified and ritualized, and declared to be no longer a problem except for the skill and intensity with which we affirm, elaborate, deepen or refine what we are already performing together.[29]

In this way of life, we are told that all the truth has been given once and for all. Because we cannot ask fundamentally new kinds of questions to respond to new problems, this way of life is everywhere in the world being questioned and undermined.[30]

Any attempt to leave the way of life of emanation arrested in Act I, Scene I, means breaking with the inherited concrete manifestations and underlying archetypal relationships in such a way that it will lead to a change of relationships for self and others. This is clearly heresy and dangerous to a cosmos blessed once and for all by the lord of emanation. In the past people were killed for such thoughts and behavior, which appeared to the orthodox to be the demonic come to life. It has always been dangerous for people living in closed societies to practice the heresy of personally contacting the sacred so as to participate in continuous creation. Betonie, the medicine man who analyzes the new forms of death in Leslie Marmon Silko's *Ceremony*, is disliked by his people because he insists on listening to new voices that allow him to respond to destructive death with new and better ceremonies of transformation. Life for too many of the people is arrested in Act I of the core drama as the will of an all-powerful lord.

A society arrested in the way of life of emanation has never been dull or boring. Each person always differed in the specific ways in which they expressed these archetypal relations. From one moment to the next a person was bargaining for a better deal, seeking a friend to mediate with a mutual acquaintance, hoping to find security through attaching themselves to a more powerful source of mystery, a saint or patron, or simply surviving by standing in line for hours to get employment or better benefits or to buy the necessities of life.

In the following pages, we will be looking more closely at this limited repertory and some of the archetypal dramas that will allow us to see actual daily behavior in the Latino community. We will go beyond mere descriptions of the breaking of the concrete and inherited manifestations of archetypal relationships practiced in the service of the dying way of life of emanation and the rejection of other sacred stories to consider how we might transform such incoherence. However, as long as the inherited relationships and stories in the service of emanation in Act I remain in effect, we do not have the ability to cope with new forms of change and conflict since we are all socialized to favor continuity and collaboration with the status quo; change means the terror of insecurity and injustice. Because of this too often we remain limited and partial selves who cannot respond to new problems.

THE WAY OF LIFE OF INCOHERENCE

The relationship of incoherence breaks open the way of life of emanation arrested in Act I, Scenes 1 and 2. But if the relationship of incoherence, which was necessary to polarize the members of a group frozen in inherited patterns, becomes permanently arrested in Act II, Scene 1, it then becomes another way of shaping life, the way of life of incoherence. In this way of life we feel increasingly vulnerable in a world of fragmented individuals who feel no commitment to one another. This is a drama, a way of life that holds together as a story of institutionalized rebellion.

Politics in the service of incoherence takes account of the fact that in the modern age, most of our concrete inherited forms of relationships are breaking, but therefore builds fortresses in a desert it cannot overcome. The guardians who would contain us within these fragments insist upon removing much of what we can and need to do together from what they define as politics. They treat politics solely as an arena for contests of power. They seek to give their histories the appearance of final legitimacy (as if they were the true heirs of faith and tradition) in order to justify the exclusion from this arena of all fundamentally new issues and encounters which do not serve their already established power. Hence they compel most people to accept politics as the acknowledgment of dependency upon the powerful and to deny the value and importance of their own miseries and joys.[31]

In the relationship of incoherence, a Latina stands in the presence of her way of life, her culture, her relatives, and her self and can no longer relate in the expected manner, according to inherited patterns. Her connections to self and others are breaking. But rather than allow the relationship of incoherence to lead to a fundamentally new and more loving way by entering Scene 2 of Act II, in order to empty herself of destructive, inherited archetypal stories, she now settles for less, learns to live with incoherence, arrests the core drama in Act II, Scene 1, and incoherence thereby becomes the way of life of incoherence.

The relationship of incoherence in the way of life of emanation was always a sin because it constituted a rejection of the final revelation of the truth. In the way of life of incoherence we have entered into a whole new drama or story of our life. This is a story that holds together around the reality of constant rebellion, insecurity, and the power of the powerful while it lasts. We cannot count on any absolute meaning or the loyalty of anyone. The past is regarded as superstitious, powerless, old-fashioned, or foolish. To realize the American dream, one must become like the dominant and accept its values, especially the pursuit of power that arrests everyone in Act II, Scene 1, of the core drama.

To lose contact with one's deepest self and to reject others and one's own sacred sources is to live with incoherence, arrested in Act II of the core drama. The only certainty now is the insecurity of knowing that nothing is secure or lasting. Since in this way of life we cannot know or acknowledge any ultimate meaning or value or love, we must get what we can while the going is good. This anxiety feeds a constant need to compete. Success is always limited to organizing the incoherence so that the powerful can protect themselves from the powerless and assert their right to become more powerful fragments.

Because we come to believe that only power can alleviate the terror that we experience, we are taken over by the story, so that it has an emanational hold over us. This is because as an archetypal way of life incoherence is part of the deeper realm of underlying sacred forces. But since it is only a fragment of the story of transformation, we cannot discover our wholeness while held in the service of incoherence's embrace.

EXITING THE CORE DRAMA: THE WAY OF LIFE OF DEFORMATION

In discussing the way of life of deformation as the exit from the core drama of transformation, I will draw upon examples from the story of Cleófilas in Sandra Cisneros's story "Woman Hollering Creek."[32]

The way of life of deformation is that context within which life is made fundamentally both new and worse. It is the exit from the core drama into the abyss. This way of life diminishes our humanity and cripples our capacity.[33]

The ways of life of emanation and incoherence are fragile and ever vulnerable to leading us to destructive death in deformation. The whole of life from the perspective of the core drama is a persistent process of creation. Incoherence that is, an experience of broken connections that previously bound us together, is therefore bound to increase. In the arrested way of life of emanation, some parents and spouses decide that there is only one way: the use of physical, psychic, or financial violence to force the rebellious wife or children to return to the old ways. But a wife or children cannot go back to a container that is now demystified; the subjection previously exercised and blessed by a lord, because it was part of the legitimacy of the way of life of emanation, is now considered illegitimate. In Act I, in the service of emanation, what gave subjection its legitimacy is that an individual believed that he or she deserved the punishment, given the rules of the game that were broken and accepted by all. The appropriate amount of submission restored this person to good standing in the family and the proper order of things.

Now, however, this cosmic view has collapsed, so that what was once considered acceptable is now seen as unbearable and untenable. But it should also be said here that violence was always an acceptable part of the strategy to preserve the way of life of emanation. Therefore deformation both as a relationship and as a way of life was available as an ally to maintain the container of emanation. Wives were beaten as a matter of right for men. It was not necessary for a woman to be in open rebellion to be assaulted. The greatest and ever-growing danger in these circumstances is that the hidden resentment of the husband would erupt in an irrational manner in the form of violence. Juan Pedro, in ''Woman Hollering Creek,'' believed that it was his right as a man to beat his wife, Cleófilas, just to let her know who was boss. It was her duty to accept this violence. In this way both men and women for generations in the Latino community have colluded in practicing the relationship of deformation as victim and victimizer. By practicing the relationship of deformation, Juan Pedro and Latino men like him were already exiting the core drama and living in the service of deformation in regard to this aspect of their lives, the story of patriarchy. Soon the way of life of deformation threatened to totally destroy them, both physically and psychically. After every beating Juan Pedro would apologize like a child who had done something wrong; Cleófilas felt that she must have done something to have caused such an eruption of anger, so she readily forgave him. They thus entered into a conspiracy that guaranteed that the violence would go on in a morbid sadistic/masochistic drama in the service of deformation.

This is deformation because it makes life fundamentally worse. Juan Pedro is frustrated in his inability to hold onto his male ego which is inextricably related to life in Act I in the service of emanation. He has promised Cleófilas a better life. But he has little education and a low-paying job. They live in poverty, and he constantly berates Cleófilas for spending too much. His male ego is badly bruised by his inability to make it in this society. His self-image is distorted by the exalted role that the culture gives him. To maintain his fragmented self, Juan Pedro increasingly turns toward the abyss of violence and thereby exits the core drama. He is unhappy, but he does not know what to do except to try to compensate for his sense of powerlessness by exercising total power over his wife. He finally fails to intimidate Cleófilas, who gets up the courage to leave him. Juan Pedro's refusal to go forward through the core drama exposes the wounded nature of his partial self. Partial selves are essentially people who have arrested their lives in the truncated ways of life of emanation and incoherence. People living within these ways of life are constantly living on the edge of the abyss. Why is this so? Because when Act I is arrested as the way of life of emanation, people must guard against any new inspirations from the depths because this way of life tells them that it is not possible for there to be anything new under the sun.

Since we cannot escape our unconscious, the underlying realm of sacred sources, this attempt to prevent the emergence of the fundamentally new has failed and will continue to fail. Thus Cleófilas is inspired to follow her feelings and leave.

A person dedicated to an arrested way of living cannot allow any new feelings within themselves or in those around her or him. People must continue to repress, deny, and destroy new ideas, feelings, intuitions, and stories that question their way of life. The logic of this means that people are prepared to constantly violate themselves and others in order to keep their family and world intact. This inability to acknowledge crucial aspects of their lives is what constitutes the danger of being a partial self. In order to preserve a stunted identity in a truncated world, the road to violence opens up again and again. For this reason, to question is seen as an act of disloyalty that demands a swift retaliation.

In regard to the core drama, those who remain arrested in Acts I or II because of loyalty to others and repression of self or the desire for power are profoundly threatened by those others who do not accept or who are excluded from participating in the life of the society. In Act II, arrested in the service of incoherence, the greatest fear is the loss of power or inability to gain power. Anybody who gets in the way is expendable. This way of life possesses our soul so that we are not free to be compassionate or loving.

The fragility of repression in the way of life of emanation and the obsessive pursuit of power in the service of incoherence tempts the true believers and the powerful toward increased violence. This makes life fundamentally worse and turns history downward into the abyss. The poor and excluded also face the reality of deformation in the public realm. In 1992 the Latino jobless rate was 12 percent, double that of non-Latino whites; only 50 percent of Latinos had a high school education in comparison to 84 percent for the non-Latino white population. Ten percent of Latinas and Latinos held bachelor's degrees while non-Latino whites were at 24 percent; the median income of Latino families is about 24,000, as opposed to 40,500 for non-Latino whites. About 28 percent of all Latinas and Latinos were living in poverty as of 1990. Young Latina women are especially at risk to be caught in a cycle of poverty since they represent fully 25 percent of dropouts nationwide. This high dropout rate is related to another concern. In 1991, 24 percent of all Latino families were headed by women. In 1988, 53 percent of all single-parent Latino households headed by women lived at or near the poverty level. In 1990, 30 percent of all Latino men and Latina women have no health care at all, which means that close to seven million lack access to health care. As of June 1993, according to the Centers for Disease Control, in regard to AIDS, 20 percent of women reported to have AIDS/HIV were Latinas, and in the Puerto Rican community it is an epidemic with the rate of AIDS seven times higher than that among the non-Latino population.[34] These statistics are alarming because la comunidad Latina in the

United States is already the largest ethnic group in the nation. The future well-being of the country is inextricably tied to the growth and development of the Latino community. And yet the number of teenage addicts, children born with AIDS, school dropouts, the unemployed, and poverty levels continue to grow. Fully 39 percent of all Latino children, 45 percent of African-American children, and 20 percent of all children in the United States live in poverty. Poor children from all backgrounds are becoming an endangered species.

This points to the impact of the wider society's structures and attitudes that cause serious violence to the Latino community. Much of the destructive behavior in the Latino community is a suicidal rebellion against the violence of the drama of tribalism: being excluded from proper housing, education, employment, and access to health care. It is very difficult to measure to what extent the community is wounding itself from within because of the dying way of life of emanation and to what extent the harm is being done by the powerful in the service of incoherence and the deformative violence of the external society. What is clear is that it is due both to the internal wounding and the external assault. A society permeated by the ways of life of incoherence and deformation creates an environment in which people are turned into faceless persons who often respond with violence to assert their presence.

THE WAY OF LIFE OF TRANSFORMATION

The way of life of transformation is the most crucial story in the universe of human relations. The other three ways of life are truncated fragments of the core drama of life that cannot provide us with the necessary vision, imagination, or creativity to respond to our problems. To live in the service of transformation is to persist in continuous creation of the fundamentally new and more loving by journeying through the core drama again and again. The structure of the universe only makes sense if there is a source of the fundamentally more just and compassionate.[35]

Acting in the service of transformation in Act III, Scenes 1 and 2, of the core drama, means rejecting the inherited and assimilated stories of uncritical loyalty, power, and deformation in our lives so that we may choose the story of life: creating and nourishing fundamentally new and better relationships. To journey through the story of transformation as the core drama of life is the vocation to which all of us are called. Anybody who prevents this journey for himself or for others violates a sacred process. A decisive breakthrough has been accomplished when we realize that our greatest freedom is that we can become conscious of the different stories and relationships in which archetypal forces manifest themselves and prepare ourselves to choose some and reject others and even participate in creating new archetypal stories. This kind of participation takes place in Act III, Scenes 1 and 2. We complete what inspired us in Act I, Scene 2, when we first heard from the deepest source of our being but were not yet ready to understand. In this act of the core drama of life we are empowered as individuals to cooperate with the source of all sources in order to share in the continuous work of creation.[36]

THE FOUR FACES OF OUR BEING: THE PERSONAL, POLITICAL, HISTORICAL, AND SACRED IN THE SERVICE OF TRANSFORMATION

The process of transformation takes place first of all in the individual's depths, in our personal face; the archetypal source that crippled us and used our egos as its incarnation is now understood and consciously rejected in Act II, Scene 2, so that we are prepared to be renewed by the sources. But each of us as a person has four faces: the personal, political, historical, and sacred. Thus when we reject a particular father or lover or ruler, there is a political dimension. Our personal face was shaped and misshaped by the body politic, that is, the larger society with its stories, relationships, and archetypal ways of life that formed the meaning and purpose of both our personal and political history. Therefore when we say no, we are not only responding to particular persons who represent the society; on the deeper level we are breaking with the official politics, lords, stories, and ways of life enacted in that society. Only a person can choose to be political; our personal face is necessary to choose a new turning point in the creation of a new history; the deepest source of our being knows us as a unique and individual person.[37]

We cannot settle only for the transformation of our personal face; the four faces of our being are always present, and we ignore any one of them at our peril. We have to reach beyond our personal lives to the political and historical networks that severely limit our capacity. To resist the racism in one's personal life requires also a struggle against structural deformation in the society that continues to cripple others and also to threaten the tenuous personal liberation achieved. We must be political, that is, performing together with our neighbors what we can and need to do in order to liberate ourselves from the dramas of control and power that are justified in the wider society in the concrete and in the depths, by sacred forces. To cast out demons in our personal lives and in society means that we have freed our sacred face from the lesser lords of emanation, incoherence, and deformation and connected it to the deepest sacred and historical means to create a new turning point by struggling with both the immediate, concrete tyranny and its underlying forming source and ultimate ways of life.[38]

STRATEGIES OF TRANSFORMATION

By rejecting the inherited ways of life and the stories of our lives as Latinas and Latinos, we enter into the relationship of incoherence in Act II, Scene 1, wherein we break with the official personal, political, historical, and sacred faces of our being. And then, in the second scene of Act II, we break on the deeper level from archetypal stories and ways of life so that we can be filled anew in order to create the fundamentally more loving and just in Act III. But we cannot create a new history or politics once and for all. That is the failure of utopian politics. Although we have experienced transformation in regard to a particular problem, we will have to make this choice again and again as new problems emerge. This prevents us from stereotyping, from establishing a new orthodoxy, or from declaring that the revolution has been won for all time. We cannot stereotype because at every moment we must test each relationship, each drama, and ask finally: In the service of what way of life am I helping to give concrete form to these archetypal forces? It follows from this that no previous incarnation will be authentic once and for all; we must persistently choose, nourish, break, and create again and again so that we can shape life anew.

Enacting new relationships and stories in our lives as more loving and just faces of our deepest underlying source is the meaning of justice relevant for our times. It means to enact ways of relating and living and being that were not there before. This is to truly relate theory to practice: our participation in the life, death, and resurrection of sacred sources. The old stories and ways of life needed our involvement to remain alive and active, and by withdrawing from them we deny them life. Now by politically allying ourselves to the deepest source of transformation, we can participate in making transformation concretely alive and present in our society. This is our new won freedom in Act III, Scenes 1 and 2, not only to choose among existing archetypal dramas but to create new ones that will do justice to ourselves, to others, and to the source of sources.

This kind of participation is utterly democratic because it is available to each person. This theory is committed to awakening in each of us the capacity we have to tell a new story with personal, political, historical, and sacred implications. For this reason we need guides who witness to the process and awaken it in each of us. When any one of us enacts a transformation, we have made a personal breakthrough and created a new kind of politics by changing our environment for the better. For example, by creating neighborhood centers that serve the young, the sick, the unemployed, and the elderly, thus changing the parameters of what we can and need to do together, we have also shaped a new historical path, inspired by a new and loving sacred source. Breaking inherited patterns that condemned people to docility and silence and replaced them with new and better ways of relating to each other enabled members of the community to participate in the decisions that affect their lives.[39]

Only in the service of transformation is our capacity—our unconscious, consciousness, creativity, linking with others, and our use of just means—kept in lively tension with the changing realities of life, for in the way of life of transformation, the concrete realization of transformation is never experienced as a final solution. To enter into the relationship of transformation becomes the final moment of a particular turn in the process of transformation. Nourishing this new experience of transformation will inevitably reveal new suffering and threats and new joys and opportunities. To live in the service of transformation is therefore persistently to experience an archetypal process of breaking relationships, moving into incoherence, and entering into the relationship of transformation anew. Through this same process, chains of emanations are turned into links of transformation.[40]

Unlike the arrested ways of life of emanation, incoherence, and the destructive way of deformation, the way of life of transformation frees us from fear and empowers us to step forward militantly, yet nonviolently, with urgency and energy, to protect and enhance our humanity and that of others. Since each of us is sacred as a face of the transforming god, our politics allows us to care and love others as we love and care for ourselves.

"Strategies of transformation" means enacting new forms of the eight archetypal relationships in the service of transformation, to participate in uprooting the inherited and destructive archetypal dramas/stories of our lives. This emptying of ourselves of destructive social and political dramas allows us to initiate a new history wherein, for the first time, people are capacitated together to create new forms of the relationship of autonomy, no longer in the service of incoherence, wherein we seek to enlarge the domain of our personal power, but now in the service of transformation. Our guide throughout this way of transforming life is not a master or lord that commands us. It is the deepest sacred source, the god of transformation who invites us to participate on a common journey that will result in transforming the personal, political, historical, and sacred faces of our lives. To be aggressive, to step forward urgently in this way of life allows us to end the repression, suppression, and murder of self and others, both psychically and physically. The transforming of self and other, the world and the sacred means taking decisive and courageous steps in the service of love and compassion.

It is a great blessing that we can discern between the ways of life and stories that are to the good and those that are destructive. We are not predetermined to remain locked into a strategy of power or death. To choose strategies of aggressive response in the service of transformation will require a constant choice and willingness to enact a transforming solution to each particular problem. The three ways of life of emanation, incoherence, and deformation, because of their wounding of the self, turn us into impotent and partial selves. In contrast, the persistent call to take the journey of transformation in regard to new problems is a witness to the indispensability of our loving and personal participation as whole persons. Without our involvement as practitioners of transformation, the source of all sources will not be able to have a more just, loving, concrete, and sensual face.[41]

Throughout the pages that follow, we will give numerous examples of the strategies needed by Latinas and Latinos to practice transformation. Any good theory must help us to see and understand what we have been living but have not fully understood. To revision our lives through a theory of transformation based on reflection and action exposes the threat of our present situation as well as the promise if we choose to live what most of us have intuitively known in our deepest depths.

APPLYING THEORY TO PRACTICE

Now that the reader has been introduced to the theory of transformation, I now wish to apply theory to practice by telling my own story as a Chicano/ Mexican/Latino male and my struggle for transformation. It is in this personal vein that I now wish to continue to develop the theory of transformation. As I use the concepts of the theory, I hope to make them more accessible by giving concrete examples to put the theory, so to speak, on solid ground. After all, what is crucial for any theory is for you and me to be able to apply it to practice to realize whether it in fact helps us to understand our reality more clearly and practice it in a fundamentally new and better way. Thus a good theory is like a good teacher. The finest teachers never put anything in us; they guide us by providing us with the concepts, the words, that will help us to name and bring to fruition through practice what has always been in us. Above all, what the theory of transformation will enable each of us to do is to tell our own story, for the story of transformation is our unique, individual story as well as the story of humanity. Thus, in reality, to seek and find our own self is also to search and find the humanity of the other.

The theory of transformation that helped me so much to understand my own life as well as the wider world around me will serve as our guide as I reenvision, reinterpret and re-create my own Latino experience in the United States. As we have seen above, ours is a theory that allows us to participate in the most important story of our lives, the core drama of transformation. This participation allows us to choose between partial and biased ways of life or transformation as a way of life that gives us the opportunity to bring together the fullness of the personal, political, historical, and sacred faces of our lives. By applying theory to practice in this personal way, my hope is that it will help readers to see not only my journey and their own but also that of la comunidad Latina as its members struggle to recreate a new culture and identity in the service of transformation by choosing among stories and ways of life.

What we are coming to understand is that the challenge of creating a new and more loving Latino culture in the United States is grounded in deeper sacred, forming forces. People like you and me give a new expression to what it means to be human by coming to know, critiquing, and transforming our stories. As Latina women and Latino men and individuals from all backgrounds, we are manifesting the four faces of our being by making a personal decision to tell a new story that had been rendered invisible. Through our political face we can together give shape to an environment in which we become aware of and are free to critique our stories. And we need to do this. Together we can create a new turning point for la comunidad Latina and for our nation, a new aspect of the story of democracy that is an affirmation that each of us has a sacred face as a manifestation of the deepest of all sacred sources. Most of us were never told that each of us, by the very nature of our humanity, has these four faces, by which we shape daily life. Furthermore, in the Latino culture we were seldom if ever taught about the human propensity to enshrine cultures once and for all and the challenge to keep them alive and open so that they can be constantly renewed and transformed through our conscious participation. We too often simply become a part of the culture and unconsciously accept the prohibition against critiquing the stories by allowing ourselves to be made into uncritical participants. In this way our Latino heritage takes on a life of its own, and we become the mere recipients rather than the persistent creators of our cultures.

MY JOURNEY OF TRANSFORMATION

In the winter of 1942 my secure container was decisively broken when my father died. My mother was to become my sole source of emotional and economic support. Luz Gil Avalos was left with six children, no education, no knowledge of English, no source of income, and $1,500 that she had managed to put aside. My mother had followed my father, Luís José, to the United States, where he had come to find a job. My mother never questioned her duty to be with my father and the tradition that never allowed her to challenge him when he decided what was best for the family. My parents brought with them to this country the stories and relationships enacted in the service of the way of life of emanation that they had inherited from their parents and their parents before them. To the best of my knowledge my parents did not question these givens of their life. My mother felt especially vulnerable in this country and so insisted that we learn the traditional way of life of rural Mexico. This is what she had to hang on to in a hostile environment. Above all, my mother wanted to be left alone by the wider society and to create a wall around us inside which Mexico still reigned. The one great institution that gave my mother and father comfort and allowed them to remember Mexico was the Catholic Church. My mother was very suspicious of Anglos, Americanos, or European Americans. But priests she trusted because they were emissaries of the Church that was universal.

LIVING BETWEEN TWO WORLDS

From my birth I lived in two worlds, the Mexican universe of my parents and the world of "white people," of whom we were taught to be wary. My mother had the greatest influence on me since my father was gone when I was not yet three years old.

In the language of the theory of transformation, I was raised in the story of patriarchy in the service of emanation. I began my life in the merciful container in Act I, Scene 1, as an extension of my parents. They raised me with a repertory of four relationships: emanation, subjection, buffering, and direct bargaining. In the context of the family I was not allowed to enact the relationships of autonomy, isolation, incoherence, deformation, or transformation. Those four relationships which we did practice encouraged dependence. In the performance of the nitty-gritty of everyday life I was raised to emphasize continuity and cooperation with those in authority and to avoid conflict and change in exchange for the justice of security. I was not to listen to my own consciousness, and my creativity was limited to being obedient. Seeking linkages to those outside of the family was discouraged. There was little attempt to establish shared goals except those that my father determined, and I was cut off from my deeper self. Nobody sat me down and explained it like this, but I knew from my experience in my home which relationships were allowed and which were forbidden. In regard to the four faces of my being, my personal dreams were not taken seriously, since the survival of the family is what mattered; politically I was expected to be uncritically loyal to my parents; my historical face was to be determined by the past so that I was expected to be like my father; the sacred was not in me but in my parents, the priests, the Church.

But the other world was also calling. I knew as a very young boy that we, that I, could not shut out the larger world of the so-called Anglos. Playing outside meant that I met people from that other world. Shopping, school, doctors all meant that we could not avoid the white world. But my mother was adamant that once we crossed the threshold the outside world was to be excluded. "In my house you only speak Spanish, not your damn English." My mother already knew that the larger world was beginning to assault the world of her emanational past. Since the death of my father, my mother had taken over the story of patriarchy by becoming a matriarch, a feminine patriarch. The shock to our container had to be repaired by asserting what my mother knew best: taking control. "I am now your father and your mother. I give the orders in this house." My father could not have said it better.

I watched my mother raise us the way my father had, giving preference to the boys and expecting the girls to do the usual domestic chores. In the language of the theory, my mother moved forcefully to renew the container of emanation in Act I, Scene 1, by enforcing the story of patriarchy in the service of emanation. The sacred lord that inspires this way of life was the ultimate appeal of my mother as she raised us with large doses of repression: sin, shame, and guilt. She insisted that we give her the same emanational respect that my father had received; if not, she could and did resort to subjecting us to obey her; we had few buffers who could speak on our behalf to get us some relief from the crushing weight of living in two worlds, neither of which was very helpful. My personal face was not only ignored in the rush of circumstances, but as I moved to rebel against my mother's authority and her view of American society, my face was slapped. My mother had to hold us in check. She could not accept any further threat to our endangered existence. Therefore my political face strained to remain loyal even as I found my mother's view of the world increasingly more unreal. My mother's insistence that I simply repeat the past since it was superior to the American alternative made it difficult for me even to think of doing anything else. The sacred was on my mother's side, and so I often felt that what I wanted must be from the evil one that tempted me to rebel.

For me the greatest conflict was feeling that my mother was wrong but feeling guilty as I disagreed with her. As a child of eight and nine I remember telling my mother that I did not accept her ideas about many things. If I had listened to my mother, I would not have been able to survive in the wider society. My mother was angry, lost and afraid as she faced her future alone without the emanational force of my father or her family, all of whom were in Mexico. This demonstrated for me the fragility of the way of life of emanation. This is a way of life in which all of the truth has been given to us. It cannot respond to fundamentally new kinds of problems. My mother spent years hoping that some-one would come along that would be able to give her the kind of security, not happiness, that my father had provided. As time went on, my mother became contemptuous of men and felt that she did not need a man to survive. She would become the man of the house. My mother wanted to repeat the past, and we, I, had to help her to accomplish that.

I couldn't explain it at the time, but I knew what my mother was doing. She wanted us to collude with her continuation of the story of patriarchy and ma-triarchy arrested in Act I, Scene 1, in the service of emanation. The relationships of dependence—emanation, subjection, buffering and direct bargaining—were insisted upon, and when we resisted too much, my mother did use the relation-ship of deformation, that is, a relationship in which she used violence to return us to a crumbling container, thus once again demonstrating the fragility of em-anation as a way of life. Since emanation as a way of life could not respond to new problems, my mother resorted to punishment, which opens the road to deformation. In this way deformation as a way of life colludes with emanation to prevent transformation. I could not enact the relationship of autonomy by speaking or having ideas of my own; nor could I exercise isolation; I had no right to create incoherence by doubting; so there could be no transformation. Because of the lord of sin, shame, and guilt, I was to repress my personal face, accede uncritically to all demands, relive the past as my own history, and live in fear and trembling of the lord of emanation.

But the center could not hold. My mother was not able to be the kind of physical force necessary to uphold this world. Frequent illness and her inability to cope with the other world caused the container to further disintegrate. My mother was not able to physically control six children who were daily growing and demanding more and more from their mother. It is very difficult to maintain the mystique of invulnerability when your mother stands helplessly in front of school officials because of her lack of English. When my mother "failed" to protect me at school and I had to speak for her in other situations, it filled me with rage. I wanted her to be my source of emanation, but she couldn't do it. She was outside her world. When we returned home, my mother would be uncontrollably angry because she was put in a situation by *esos güeros*, those white people, who humiliated her and made her feel powerless.

THE WORLD OF LOS ANGLOS, LOS AMERICANOS:
BEATING THEM AT THEIR OWN GAME

I could sense my mother's sense of powerlessness. She had been disappointed in the ability of men to take the place of "the only one who had the right to tell her what to do," my father. My mother was not naive. She saw the family falling apart in spite of her efforts. One sister was so hurt by the loss of my father that she became rebellious. She refused to go to school, which brought the feared and hated official America to the door. My oldest brother joined a gang. I went along at times and was both afraid of and excited by the exploits of fighting, stealing watermelons from freight cars, and jumping on the back of trolley cars. The emanational world of the past was helpless in the streets of America.

My mother moved quickly to secure the economic well-being of the family. For a woman with no formal education who could not read or write, she found within herself an extraordinary courage, love, and ability. She rented a flat with three bedrooms, moved all of us into two rooms, and rented out the "spare" bedroom so that she could pay the rent. After accumulating enough money, my mother bought our first home. She followed the same pattern of cramming us into a portion of the house and renting to as many as three to six people in the remaining space. As a result my mother was soon able to buy a new and better home in a nicer part of town. This time my mother rented a back apartment and the whole of the upstairs. We became more economically secure, but we seldom saw the benefits when it came to anything beyond bare essentials.

My mother was so afraid that she would not be able to make it in the wider society that she was determined to beat white America at its own game. My mother became obsessed with money. Over the years, through pinching pennies and denying herself and us any joy from the money, she put away a substantial sum of money. What my mother never realized was that white America had won. Money for my mother became the concrete expression of the story of capitalism. *"El dinero,"* money became an end in itself. In this way my mother crossed into the other world and assimilated into the archetypal story of capitalism, the official story of U.S. society. This aspect of my mother's life became arrested in the first scene of Act II in the service of incoherence. She rebelled against white America but got caught in the game as she continued to rebel against the powerful. My mother learned the previously forbidden relationship of autonomy that made it possible for her to close herself off from the wider society and to carry on a running battle with city inspectors, real estate agents, renters, lawyers, and other officials. She sought to obtain more and more security. Since life was so brutal, we couldn't afford to spend. Higher taxes would send my mother into a rage. Now she had to continue to rebel against the powerful by making more money to assure her newly won power.

But now my mother lived between two worlds. She felt guilty about making money and often spoke of returning to a purer life, the life that she knew in

Mexico. To safeguard this world, she continued to insist on keeping Mexico in our home by relating to us in the old repertory of emanation, subjection, direct bargaining, and buffering. She slowly conceded some space to the outside world and the place that we were beginning to make for ourselves in it. After all, there were benefits to be had when your sons all worked and brought in money to augment the family resources. Money also became a weapon with which to maintain the inherited past. My mother often scolded us that we would see none of her money if we failed to be loyal to her. Money had become everything when there was none, and now money was still everything when there was more of it.

From our theoretical perspective, my mother had now dramatically changed the four faces of her being. My mother no longer repressed her personal face but used it to reveal only those fragments that she felt would help her to protect her new-won power. My mother became very good at hiding her face. In her bargaining with others she learned that you did not reveal your true hand to anyone. Her political face became one of attaching herself to those in the community who had connections, those who had power, who could help her. History for my mother was no longer simply repeating a past, but time became interest on savings of the hard-earned money that was in the bank. It seems harsh to say but my mother now served two lords, the lord of emanation that she brought from Mexico and the lord of incoherence and self-interest who took her over in this country.

THE FRAGILITY OF EMANATION AND INCOHERENCE AS WAYS OF LIFE: COLLUDING WITH DEFORMATION

When my mother felt threatened by me or one of my siblings, she often resorted to physical force. She felt justified in this because it was not only her authority but also that of the lord of emanation that gave her the right. I often resisted my mother, not because I didn't love and respect her, but because I badly needed attention. I wanted very much for my mother to love me, to nurture me, and to acknowledge my presence. But given the story of patriarchy in the service of the way of life of emanation and how it had wounded my mother, she wanted me, as a little man of the house, to nurture her. Whenever I gave my mother money or performed some service for her, she would say that *Dios te pagará*, God would repay me. I went to work seven days a week as a paperboy when I was twelve years old. From that time on, I paid for all of my personal expenses, including dental work, tuition, clothes, entertainment, the phone bill, the milk bill, and other expenses. I wanted to help my mother and also to become independent. I was deeply affected by the emphasis on money in our home, even after it was no longer a question of survival. I began to hate money and the references that my mother made to it. I wanted to be pure and above it all, so I gave money away quite freely. As a result, money became overly important as I rebelled against it and my mother. But unless we empty ourselves on the deeper level of the story of money, capitalism, we will only succeed in repressing it for the time being. So in this way I also became arrested in Act II, Scene 1, in constant rebellion against money and therefore still controlled by it.

I saw my mother do things for the sake of money that profoundly shook me. I wanted to be accepted in the society of priests and nuns, who were my teachers and parish ministers. They held out a world for me that promised acceptance and above all deliverance from the permanent exile that my mother wanted to live. To save money, my mother ignored a slash that I had in my head as the result of being hit by a car. My sister went without a coat because of my mother's fear of not having enough money. My teeth were badly decayed by the time I had the ability to take care of them. What all of this points out is that the stories of patriarchy/matriarchy in the service of emanation and capitalism in the service of incoherence take us over and control our lives. Because we come to see life as not being livable without these stories and ways of life, we are prone to violence in their defense, thus entering into deformation. My mother fought to hang onto emanation as a way of life, even if it meant not being able to respond to the needs of her children in a new world. So taken was my mother with powerlessness that she found herself in situations where in order to keep her power she hurt others. This is the logic of partial ways of life that keep us arrested in fragments of the core drama of life. Precisely because we are arrested as partial selves, we cannot respond to fundamentally new kinds of problems. Total unquestioning obedience and power above all precludes any response that will endanger loyalty and power.

Now that I know of the realm of underlying sacred sources, and of how we participate with them, there is no doubt in my mind that my family was the victim of wounding stories and partial ways of life that made it almost impossible for us to transform our lives. And yet there were other choices. As we will see later in the book, my mother had choices; we had choices. My mother could have fought my father from the beginning of their marriage. When given the opportunity, she refused. When my father died, my Aunt Margarita offered her a home in Mexico City; my mother declined. My mother could have learned English, encouraged us to make the best of this country, spent her resources on our needs, and so on. She could have raised us with a deep respect for our Mexican heritage without using it as a fortress. And yet my mother had a very realistic understanding of the dominant in this country and warned me to keep a safe distance from it. In my dash to be accepted here, it was good advice. I only wish that my mother had been able to become financially secure without allowing the money to have taken her and us over. It was possible for my mother to have raised us to preserve the best in the Mexican tradition and to take the opportunity that this country had to offer to build a more human life. The sadness is that she could have emptied herself of the stories enacted in the ways of life of emanation and incoherence in order to live her life fully in the way of life of transformation. But she did not.

Because of these choices, my mother was both a victim and a participant together with sacred sources that possessed her and caused her to lose her way. Thus her partial rebellion against the world of emanation, especially in regard to men, never became a step toward transformation, but a permanent rebellion that kept her caught between the two ways of life of emanation and incoherence that colluded with deformation.

After living in the United States for forty-five years, my mother returned to Mexico to live. But she was immediately disillusioned. Things were not the way they used to be. Mexico had changed. The world of the ranch on which she had been raised was fast disappearing. Again my mother felt caught between a romanticized past in the world of emanation and the new Mexico, caught up in the market economy of capitalism, with all of the emphasis on power and money that had affected my mother in the United States. After five years of trying to make the old world come back, my mother returned to live in Detroit.

MY JOURNEY THROUGH THE CORE DRAMA OF LIFE

All of the above was painfully necessary for me to reveal, so that the reader could know me and the sacred sources that shaped my life. As a child I was a victim of the underlying sources that provided the structure of life for my culture and my parents. By the time I was eight and nine, I began to make choices. I intuitively understood that my life was in danger. The earliest memory that I have of my mother is a scene in which she is sitting down crying as she prayed for help. I was later told that this was just after my father had died. I recall the desperation in my mother's voice and the terror that it caused in me as my anchor slipped away. I now know that my mother was wounded by the story of patriarchy and uncritical loyalty in the service of emanation. She felt that she had no right to question those in authority like her parents or my father. It took my mother forty years before she was able without guilt to speak about how my father had not allowed her any voice in the finances of the family. As a result, she was not prepared to face life without him. But long before his death, my mother learned to be silent and not to create any conflict or change and to accept her place. Soon after they were married, out of jealousy, my grandmother demanded that her son, my father, choose between his wife and his mother. My father, to the great disappointment of my mother, chose his mother over his wife. From that time on, my mother revealed that she felt less affection for my father. When she told me this story, I felt so bad and wanted only to love my mother for all that she had faced in her life.

I vividly remember the poverty that followed my father's death. I had such mixed feelings about my mother. I felt guilty because I wanted to love her, and yet I was disappointed in her because she couldn't protect me in our Mexican home or in the outer, larger world. I saw things as a child that have stayed with me through the years. I was awakened by fighting between a Mexican male and female who were boarders in our home; the woman wanted to stab her husband to protect herself. On another occasion, my brother and I were present as a man, a boarder in our house, hit our mother and we screamed. As children we saw women assaulted and abused by men. Men who rented rooms became abusive and caused great fear in us. For this reason, for years I found it very difficult to be proud to be a Mexican/Chicano male. Men were the enemy, and so I turned against my own masculinity and Mexican heritage, since I identified it with the abusive males of my youth.

Since my secure container was taken away from me before I was ready or able to leave, I searched for another container of emanation. In our early years the container of emanation in Act I, Scene 1, is a necessary and merciful vessel that all children need. The problem is that too many traditions do not see the period of the merciful container as the beginning of transformation, but as the culmination of a previous transformation that will last for all time. I knew that I had to have acceptance, love, and security. I was very vulnerable to anyone who could offer me even the semblance of acceptance. I searched for a father, a family, a group that would give me a place in their lives. When I was eight years old, I learned that my sister's fiancé was getting ready to leave town. I jumped up from my lunch and ran without stopping for eighteen long blocks, only to learn that he had already left. I was very disappointed but glad that I had made the effort. Two things were happening here: on the one hand I badly needed him emotionally, as a father, but I also wanted to do something, to intervene in some way to change my life, and to show to what lengths I was willing to go to prove my loyalty so that I would be accepted.

I wanted to make the crumbling world of emanation work for me. I was willing to be completely loyal to somebody whom I trusted. I longed for the story of patriarchy without knowing what to call my need. What good was a personal face of my being when I had no idea as to who I was? I wanted to give my personal face away to somebody worthy of it. If somebody would only love me, I was prepared to dedicate my political face to their desires. I did not want history to change only to bless me with the recurrence of strong relationships and stories that would give me a place. I prayed not to the deepest sacred as the source of my sacred face but to that lord of emanation begging that I not be condemned for being bad. I remember as a boy of six asking my brother Louie to reassure me that I would not be condemned for eternity in the fires of hell for skipping Mass that Sunday. I was afraid to go to bed for fear that I would not wake up and would find myself paying the penalty for sinning against the lord of emanation.

I looked for heroes so that I could be in an emanational relationship to them. The Marines, especially those who landed on Guadalcanal, Tarawa, and Iwo Jima were to me the epitome of courage, manhood, dedication, and dangerous adventure. The lives of the saints inspired me as a boy, especially saints like Sebastian who was killed by arrows because he refused to renounce the faith. Finally, I found a family, a competing emanational source, that would fill the void left by the fragmenting of my Mexican family and heritage: the Catholic Church.

Just as I was moving in my own life toward deformation, I discovered another kind of Marines, Irish-Catholic priests. Why was I moving toward deformation at the early age of eight and nine? This was occurring in two ways. First as a victim of deformation, I experienced the racism to be found in the story of tribalism that turns people of color into invisible and inferior people. When I was six years old, I was with my brother and a group of other Mexican boys. We went to Tiger Stadium (then Briggs Stadium) to see if we could get into the park to see the Detroit Tigers play ball. We had no money, so we begged the guard at the turnstile to let us in. He said he would if we went to the drinking fountain and washed our faces. We were surprised. Is that all? No problem. We ran to the fountain that was only a few feet away and began to scoop up water into our hands, so that we could wash our faces. For a split second I happened to look up and to catch the look on the guard's face: it was a look of supreme contempt. He was mocking us and enjoyed our humiliation. I knew as a boy of six that he was a racist who in his own way was calling us dirty Mexicans. I felt terrible, but frozen by the experience of such hatred. I may be wrong about this, but I have thought about this experience many times over the years and I know, I just know, based on the unsophisticated immediacy of a child's knowing, that he disliked us. At school I had to fight because I was a Mexican. I was called a dirty Mexican and told to go back to where I belonged. I witnessed my mother being thrown to the ground by a taxi driver, who took off while she was leaning on the cab to catch her balance. I yelled at him and cried with anger against him and my mother for putting me in a situation that I couldn't handle. My mother had also told me the story of how my father had been shot by a policeman in Chicago because my father refused to give him money. Whatever the cause of the confrontation, I knew that my father was shot, and my mother was terrified that he would die.

But above all, I was moving toward a deep hatred and fear of white people, who caused me to be ashamed of my own mother and Mexican heritage. In the presence of white women such as teachers or nurses in official positions of authority, my mother felt inferior. These white women almost always spoke condescendingly to my mother and used me or my siblings as the interpreter.

The violence that I had seen and felt in our home, together with the violence of racism, filled me with anger. I already felt as a boy of six and seven that I could not count on my Mexican heritage to sustain me. I identified my culture with poverty, male violence, with being an outsider, with outdated traditions that didn't work, and with a mother who spoke Spanish and refused to learn English as a protest against the way we were treated. So I was angry with a mother wedded to a culture that did not help me to focus my young life. The cumulative effect of these negative experiences surrounding Mexican culture made it impossible for me to romanticize the culture and to remain in Act I in the service of emanation. I was seeking for a competing emanation without knowing it. One such emanational source arose in the Mexican gang to which my brother already belonged. At such an early age I discovered a way to express all the anger that I felt.

One way of escaping from the rejection of the dominant culture was assimilation. But you needed money and power and a group that was looking for you to assimilate. The powerful in the other world did not care about us; we were no threat and of no interest to them. Besides they were seen as the enemy, the *Anglos, los americanos*, whites, who called us wetbacks. Because of the lack of money at home, I felt very insecure. I felt powerless to do anything about the most basic issues, such as good food and clothing. But I was not interested in money and power; hell, I wanted to be loved and accepted. I never thought about power and money, but I now realize that the sense of powerlessness made me vulnerable to the fantasy of total power. As my connections to my mother and my culture became more tenuous, I was dangerously trying to restore the container of emanation without knowing it.

Why was this a danger? Because in order to restore a lost security, people are vulnerable to those who say, ''I have the answer, just follow me.'' For me and for many Latina and Latino youth the gang becomes a very seductive emanational substitute that can fill the void created by the collapse of one's culture, one's stories, that is, one's sacred sources, and the very way of life in this country. The Mexican gang to which my brother belonged offered me the following: a family that could care for me and protect me in a dangerous world; a place where I could begin to define my manhood; participation in a group that could defiantly declare that we were Mexicans and proud of it; an emotional setting that helped us to break away from our increasingly female, single-parent homes by allowing male bonding; a testing ground for developing our courage and loyalty in difficult circumstances; a territorial imperative that was to be defended as one's home turf, one's homeboy neighborhood; and a vehicle for getting revenge on the society that had rejected us. This was all about loyalty to a group invested with emanational power that was more important than the individuals.

For our total obedience and loyalty, we received the intoxication of immersion in a group; this had nothing to do with finding out who you were. My personal face was never further from me as I sought to see my face only in the faces of the most powerful in the gang, those who were the most daring. As we looked to establish ourselves in an emanational container, it became increasingly deformational. We erased our own faces as we smashed the face of the outsider. It was a politics of violence and revenge against those who dared to make us invisible and inferior. History was now made worse by fragmented individuals who repeated the story of racism and tribalism that victimized us. The sacred source that inspired our sacred faces was the lord of nothing, which reveled in our violence and self-destruction as we exited the core drama of life.

Thus this was no return to the world of emanation; this was a pseudoemanation, a fake. We could not return to the seamless container of emanation. We lived in a world of broken connections, where people even from our own heritage no longer shared the same ideas, emotions, and hopes. We found ourselves in a world of fragmented individuals who pursued self-interest and power and who cared very little for community or shared values. In such a broken world, we sought security and even absolute power over our lives and those of others. We had no money or prestige or power as defined by the dominant. But what we did have was power to end our lives and those of others through violence. There was something very nihilistic about us organized in gangs. Nothing was important but us and our loyalty to each other. This uncritical loyalty to the gang, and especially to the leader, led us to fight, steal, drop out of school, turn to drugs, and escalate the violence as a sign that we were loyal above all. We were not making it in the world of capitalism in the way of life of incoherence arrested in Act II, Scene 1, of the core drama of life; and the connections to the way of life of emanation inherited from our parents were dissolving. This made us very vulnerable to the way of life of deformation that ends by exiting a person from the core drama of life to someplace where life is fundamentally worse.

On one occasion as we went looking for trouble, I was determined to cement my position in the gang by proving that I could be just as courageous in my violence as the toughest in the gang. We cornered a group of white boys in Clark Park (a recreation center in Detroit not far from Tiger Stadium) and began to goad them into a fight. They refused to be provoked. This was my opportunity. I grabbed the boy who was my size and punched him in the face. He fell to his knees, crying and holding his face. I was immediately overcome with a sense of utter despair at what I had done. I didn't feel good or tough, I felt sick. But the members of the gang were all praise and congratulated my brother on what a fighter I was.

Ironically, I decided then and there that I would never hit someone that way again. But we lived in a violent neighborhood, where I was never sure who would come after me. I could under these circumstances have learned how to become mean and to kill my feelings of compassion. Between the danger in the hood and my need to purge myself of anger, it would have been only a matter of time before I entered into deformation as a victimizer.

EMANATION IN THE SERVICE OF EMANATION AS REFORMATION

The second scene of Act I is a blessing. From this point of the core drama of life, even though we have passed this way before, just prior to our first rebellion, we hear once again from other deeper sources and from the deepest source of transformation. We often repress these voices, but they will not go away. We experience doubts, new insights, feelings, or intuitive understandings that lead us to question the life that we have. But these voices from the depths are not always to the good. As competing emanational impulses they challenge the emanational hold of our current stories. As an inspiration from the deeper realm we have to determine what sacred source is manifesting itself by asking the questions: In the service of what way of life does this new idea come forth? What sacred source is speaking to me?

As a young boy I did not know how to ask such a question, but I did begin to intuitively deal with one thing: when a person or feeling erupted in my life, did it affirm me as a person? Ultimately, the gang did not care about me for myself but to the extent that I strengthened the group. I was only important if I gave myself away to the rest. I remember defying people in power if I sensed that they didn't care about me, but about their own authority. I recall thinking that if someone honestly loved me and cared about me, I would respond.

An Irish Catholic priest was for me a guide of reformation, not transformation. He walked into my life as an emanational force representing Act I, Scene 2, as a concrete manifestation of the lord of emanation. As a competing emanational force, he did me a great service by drawing me away from the possessive cycle of gang violence in the service of deformation at the exit from the core drama of life and into the first Scene of Act I. He offered me a deep friendship based on love and caring. He demonstrated this by providing concrete alternatives: sports, education, and belonging to the altar boy association. As a priest, he also introduced me to the community of the Catholic Church in a kinder and more powerful way than I had known before. One of the links that provided my family with continuity had been its Catholic faith. But the Church was a community that still belonged to the Irish and other white people. As a Mexican I never felt that I really belonged. Indeed, the Mexican community had a special Mass in Spanish in the chapel, which was separated from the main church. I went to Saint Anne's Church and attended the parish school; I observed firsthand the class difference between our family and those of other ethnic groups. There were times when I skipped school because I had no clothes to wear. I was embarrassed by my last name and my Mexican heritage. When the nuns asked for parents to volunteer to drive the students on an outing, I felt excluded, since we had no car and my mother would never consent to such participation.

But now I had discovered a good opportunity. As an altar boy, I was at the right hand of acceptance. All I had to do was to reach out and grab the ring. For the next seven years, from the time I was ten until I was seventeen, I found a new container of emanation that could replace the fragile web of my home life, provide me with an alternative identity than that of the gang which I had left by the time I was nine years old, and give me the necessary security to build a foundation for life. The relationship of emanation with this charismatic priest was in the service of emanation. He accepted me *as a Mexican* and relied on me to teach him certain aspects of the Mexican heritage. He got me involved in team sports, baseball and basketball, which introduced me to my classmates in a new way. He took me to hockey games and introduced me to his family. But above all he got me into the altar boys, which was a privileged group with its own hierarchy dominated by the older Irish-Catholic boys. The nuns gave special preference to this group of boys.

Father got me in through the back door. He taught me and one of my Mexican friends from Texas how to serve Mass in the Mexican chapel. He drilled us in our learning of Latin, the language then used in the celebration of the Mass. During Mass he told us what to do next. He was so free with the rubrics from which the other priests never deviated. But we were not allowed into the big church or into the regular altar boy organization which was controlled by the nuns. They resented a priest's intrusion into the realm of their patronage. I was determined that I was going to crack the circle of privilege. I did this by being available literally day and night, whether it was for evening rosary, early Mass, weddings on Saturdays, summer novenas. Before long, all of the priests knew me and asked for me, so that in the hierarchy of power the nuns could no longer keep me out. Members of the Ladies Altar Society adopted me and became my Irish mothers. Soon I was the top altar boy. As time went on, the older boys graduated, and I was able to outdo my peers. This was no small matter. I was now accepted as a Mexican youth who had succeeded in the wider world of the parish.

My priest as father figure had left for a parish assignment in Texas long ago, but he had left behind a determined young man. I have no doubt that he wished me well, not for himself but for myself. He guided me to inner resources and the courage to express those energies as nobody else had been able to do. For the first time, I thought that maybe I could be both a Mexican *and* a member of the wider world around me. I was beginning to feel good about who I was.

But there was a problem. I was uneasy, for I realized that I was accepted as one of the "good" Mexicans. I had proven myself by meeting somebody else's standards, Anglo standards. I wanted so much to be accepted that I tested the limits of their willingness to allow me to belong. I had as girlfriends only white young girls, from the time that I was twelve. I was surprised that they were responsive to me. In a strange way, even though it was confusing, I felt that several of these young women had given me a gift. They had helped me to accept myself and my sexuality. As a Mexican young man, this was crucial because for me sex had been identified with abusive males. I had witnessed male/female relationships as unequal, based on male domination. I began to believe that I was now beyond that or at least that it didn't have to be this way.

But there is no doubt that I was assimilating into the Irish-Catholic world. Belonging, security, acceptance, good standing in a group, being loved by everyone is what I craved. But acceptance by whom? The world of the powerful for me was the Irish-Catholic. I knew that the epitome of success, privilege, and power was the priesthood. This was my final initiation into the world of the others. It was not long before the priests and nuns began to groom me for the priesthood. They observed me as I went to Mass and communion every day, was always present at evening services, that I filled my Sunday envelope with money far beyond that expected of a young boy. The nuns tutored me so that

I could get the grades that would allow me to transfer in my junior year of high school to an all-boy prep school where I could begin to prepare myself in earnest for the priesthood.

EMANATION IN THE SERVICE OF PARTIAL
WAYS OF LIFE

The emanational pull of my parish priest in the service of emanation was in the service of a partial way of life that caused me to lose my way. I now got stuck in the journey, in the core drama, in the first scene of Act I. He had clearly helped me to get off the road to deformation by attracting me to himself and to the Catholic Church. But he stopped and helped me to arrest my journey so that I could not understand and practice my story. He offered me a more powerful fragment of emanation to substitute for the breaking of the emanational world of my Mexican heritage. Thus the story of uncritical loyalty that my mother had demanded was now firmly dedicated to the Church. Furthermore, the story was enacted in the service of emanation. This was therefore not a transformation but a reformation, since the changes made this story and way of life more seductive, by giving me security. In addition, I was deeply attracted to the privilege and status of the Catholic Church in the dangerous world of power. This means that I was joining the powerful in the service of incoherence, which arrested me in this aspect of my life in the first scene of Act II. I was rebelling against and rejecting my own community, which was identified with powerlessness. All of the good feelings I had developed about myself and others were dominated by the desire to be acceptable to the more powerful. I was taken over by a false consciousness. I felt good about my personal desires as long as they corresponded to what others wanted of me; my political face had become more compassionate toward others, but in a condescending way. I saw myself creating a new story as an educated Mexican young man who could be a good lawyer, but it was really an old story of the poor joining the game of the powerful; and for the first time I acknowledged the deeper currents within me of the sacred, but a sacred that commanded me to deny myself.

Above all, I recall thinking when I was fifteen and sixteen that I wanted to do something meaningful with my life. At this time, I began to develop a powerful sense of destiny. I fought actively against a pessimism, a fate that there was nothing that I could do to change my life nor environment. "La vida no vale nada. Siempre comienza llorando y llorando siempre se acaba. La vida no vale nada" (Life isn't worth a damn. It begins in pain and always ends in pain. Life isn't worth a damn.) I heard this Mexican folk song (*música ranchera*) many times as a young boy. It made me angry and depressed; there seemed to be no way to become someone.

By the age of fifteen I had clearly ruled out as choices trying to restore the broken web of emanation of my Mexican heritage. I could not and did not accept my heritage in an uncritical way. But ironically, I did give to the official Catholic

Church an uncritical loyalty that I intensified as time went on. I was afraid of money and power and thought that I could avoid these aspects of the story of capitalism by denying their power in my life. I had learned how to enact the previously forbidden relationships of autonomy, isolation, and incoherence, as well as how to practice the relationship of direct bargaining in a new way. I became competent and independent as a paperboy. I learned how to organize a large route of 200 customers on the west side of Detroit. By the time I was fourteen, I had to collect, deliver papers daily in all sorts of weather, make weekly collections, keep accurate records, sell insurance sponsored by the paper, canvas for new customers, and learn how to get along with people from diverse backgrounds and economic status. I got so good at all of this that I won six trips and numerous other awards and prizes, as well as the independence that came with earning thirty dollars a week. This competence earned for me a great deal of autonomy and bargaining power, and not only with my mother. I also had respect from my peers and their families, who saw me as a hardworking young man. I was responsible, dependable, and efficient, and therefore acceptable.

I had enacted the story of capitalism in the service of incoherence, which arrested me as a partial self in the first scene of Act II. All of this helped me to develop a powerful sense of myself. I was beginning to see the source of emanation and mystery in myself rather than seeing it only in the strong people around me whom I admired. I thought that I had gone a long way toward healing my self, wounded by racism and the rage that it engendered, only to have it erupt in more powerful and irrational ways later in my life. As a young boy of 14, there can be no doubt that I had changed for the better. I did not want to pursue revenge on others, especially European Americans or whites, not only because I wanted to be accepted by them but also because I sensed in myself a growing awareness of my own self-worth. But at this point in my life my sense of mystery was blocked by the ways of life of emanation and incoherence that made me vulnerable to deformation. I was still searching for myself in the first two acts of the core drama of life.

Why did I come to see the first scene of Act I as transformation, when in fact it was a reformation that led me in the wrong direction for many years? There came into my life very powerful emanational characters, especially another priest, who wanted to use my Mexican heritage as a way to expand and maintain the influence of the Catholic Church in the Mexican community. I was considered a good candidate once I was ordained to work in the Mexican Missions in south Texas among the Mexican people. There was great concern, since Protestant evangelical groups were beginning to make inroads in converting the people to their sectarian beliefs. In addition, the priest who wanted to sponsor me was in competition with other priests to see how many young men they could recruit for the seminary. This priest did everything he could to win my confidence, and he succeeded. I wanted to be just like him. He was handsome, charismatic, a very good speaker, a respected teacher, and someone you felt good being with. This priest wanted me to be an extension of him, by thinking like him and to act as he wanted me to be. I was so caught up with him that I lost myself again in a relationship of emanation in the service of emanation arrested in Act I, Scene 1, of the core drama. I fell back into the relationships of dependence in relationship to him: emanation, subjection, buffering, and direct bargaining. I was not allowed to practice isolation from him, nor to be autonomous. I could certainly not break the connections resulting in the relationship of incoherence, and so there could be no transformation. And yet in other aspects of my life, I did become independent; I exercised independence with members of my family, broke connections with friends who I felt were going in the wrong direction. But there was no transformation, only reformation. That is, I became better at the stories that I was living. I became more intensely loyal to the Catholic Church, lived the story of the hero with the priests, stayed away from patriarchal males, but failed to deal with the story of patriarchy in the depths by turning to a more acceptable kind of benign patriarchy, the world of priests. I denied problems by repressing sexuality under the guise of purity and denied my simmering anger.

The reason for the failure to transform was that I was under the impression that if I rejected actual individuals who represented what I most feared, then I would be free. But in rebelling against individuals and entering into Act II, Scene 1, I failed to go beyond this disconnecting to a deeper breaking with the underlying sacred sources that gave those rejected their mysterious hold over me. I did not enter into the second scene of Act II wherein I needed to empty myself of the story that possessed me and the way of life within whose service I enacted that drama. As a result I experienced a false consciousness, believing that I had changed my life in the sense of transformation and conversion when I had really only changed the players in the same stories and ways of life; and therefore I practiced reformation. Now, rather than being in emanation to my mother or to the gang, I was in emanation to the Catholic Church, everything European-American or white, priests and concepts of purity. Some might argue that this kind of emanation was at least a betterment of my life. It was certainly better than life in the service of deformation. But I was still left incapable of criticizing, not able to create conflict and change, but seeing collaborative loyalty and continuous obedience as the most important virtues. I spoke about love, but it was to be a stingy, empty love, laced with a suspicion of sex, passion, and emotion. I did not realize at the time that this was another way of escaping my Mexican past. Once again my personal face was obscured for the sake of others. Politically, I was uncritically loyal to the Catholic Church. I only wanted to repeat the history of the great saints of the past, not to let my own story become the beginning, a new turning point. I reverted to repressing the messages that came from the deepest source, and when they did come, I interpreted them from the perspective of the lord of emanation. If feelings threatened my beliefs, I dismissed them as temptations. If I found myself resisting guilt, I felt sorry that I couldn't be sorry. I was deeply in repression and in denial of my own self.

The year before I left my home in Detroit to study for the priesthood was especially significant. I had made a decision to repress my sexuality and to concentrate all of my efforts on academics. I channeled my passion into my intellectual development. I had to prove myself in the all-Catholic boys' prep school that I had attended since my junior year in high school. It taught me discipline and hard work, exactly the formula that I needed so that I could make it in the Irish-Catholic world of priests and nuns. But unexpectedly I began to experience very powerful feelings that if left unchecked threatened to upset my plans to study for the priesthood. The year before I left home for the seminary I grew close to two women: my mother and a young woman whom I had dated for the past four years. It is almost as if I knew on a deeper level that I was leaving the world of women for that of men and the story of patriarchy. I had long talks with my mother and often went out with her. When I graduated from high school, she was there and showed a lot of pride in me. As the time grew closer for my departure, I began to miss her. The day that I was to leave I got up early and my mother was upset. She cried as I left for the train station, and it hurt me very much when she showed such a depth of love and emotion for me. But I had begun some time prior to prepare myself to choke off my feelings.

The other person with whom I had developed an emotional bond was a young woman with whom I felt completely at ease. I could be myself with her; I was so happy to be with her that I sang to her. Since she was a good Catholic and knew something of my desire to become a priest, we silently colluded in repressing each other's sexuality for the sake of my vocation. We shunned any open affection, and I was threatened by her sexuality. I did not tell her that I was leaving for the seminary in Rochester, New York until the night before. It was one of the most difficult things that I have ever done. It was very painful. But given my life in the service of emanation, I believed that the harder it was, then all the greater was the love of God. I identified suffering with love. Love had become for me denial of affection, denial of pleasure, denial of feelings, denial of sex, repression of my personal, political, historical, and sacred face. And yet when I was asked why I wanted to be a priest, I would reply: "For the love of God and His people." I didn't have the foggiest notion as to what love really meant.

This split between my intellectual, academic side and my sexual, feeling, passionate side was to be a serious problem for many years to come. I was a partial and fragmented self who willingly participated in denying my own desires; in order to be loyal to others, I was disloyal to myself; and therefore I could not create a new story for myself and others but only repeat the stories of those who were more sacred and valuable than me. This kind of denial of myself shows the inherent limits of the way of life of emanation. I could not be faithful to myself and listen to my own needs. In denying myself, I colluded with deformation: I was telling myself that I was not valuable. I came close to canceling my own personal face as a result of being loyal to others who wanted me to live their history in the name of the lord of emanation.

REENTERING THE CORE DRAMA OF LIFE: LISTENING
TO THE DEEPEST SOURCE

Following my graduation from high school, I began my studies for the priesthood. I felt that now I could center my life around this goal. This would resolve my quest for self, my sexual identity, my career for life, allow me to be the "good" Mexican, and provide me with the challenge that my own heroic sense urged me to conquer. I was finally, I thought, pursuing my destiny. But I was deeply troubled by the nagging reality that I was not happy. Yet in the realm of emanation, your personal face and desires must be sacrificed to the quest itself. I prayed and said to the lord of emanation whom I addressed as "the" god at the time: "I have finally come to do your will. If I am not happy, it does not matter, since doing your will is what counts."

The whole of our training during our first year in the seminary was intended to repress and suppress our will and desires. No food between meals, no secular music, no television, no uncensored mail, no talking for most of the day, no newspapers, and no unauthorized contact with outsiders, even our own family. We were to cut ties with the world so that the priests as our teachers and spiritual advisors could mold us in their image and likeness. This was emanation and subjection with a vengeance. But if you could take it, you proved that you had a vocation. As a result of this training, I was able to cut myself off from the realm of the deepest source for at least two years.

One of the great blessings of the core drama of life is that the deepest source intervenes again and again, even against our will. Of course, since we have been convinced that the lord of emanation is "the" lord, the first reaction is to see the new inspirations, literally the new breathing within us, as heresy and sin. The temptations came in Act I, Scene 2, in the form of sexual desires that were overpowering and could neither be ignored nor tamed by prayer and fasting, both of which I tried. Other temptations arose from older seminarians, some of whom questioned the manner in which we were being prepared for the priesthood. I considered them to be complainers and avoided them.

The relationship of emanation in the service of emanation was so pervasive that it reached into all aspects of my life. Politically, I could see no wrong in the United States. So intense was my desire to belong that once I began to make it in the Catholic world of the Irish, I took on their politics of American nationalism. As part of my preparation for the priesthood, I was sent to Canada, to the University of Toronto. I felt secure as a candidate for the priesthood and as an American who was proud that we had just elected John Kennedy the first Roman Catholic as president. My life was of a whole cloth of emanation. All I had to do was stay focused, and my future was safe.

It all came crashing down at the same time. I could no longer deny my sexuality, even though I still didn't know how to express it, since I had taken a vow of celibacy that I looked upon as a matter of life and death, grace and mortal sin. My relationship of emanation to the United States was undermined by professors who challenged, probed, and questioned U.S. foreign policy. I was angry and confused, for I respected them for their scholarship. But then I began to do research and realized that I could no longer uncritically defend my country. My whole ego had been shaped around unquestioning loyalty to others. I felt as if I was betraying not only the sacred source of emanation in church and state but also myself. All of the anger that I thought I had resolved came back in a rush. I now responded to the doubts by entering into open rebellion against my superiors as representatives of the Church and American nationalism. I was angry because I felt that I had been tricked and lied to. I came to do the will of the lord of emanation, and that lord had refused, indeed was unable, to give me the necessary help to stay the course. When reading U.S. State Department documents, I now saw clearly that American history, especially diplomatic history, was replete with official versions, that is, lies. This revelation was devastating for me. In the world of emanation there can only be the moral certitude of right or wrong; there is no room for paradox, contradiction, or moral subtleties.

I learned from my personal anguish that the lord of emanation and those who are inspired by this source cannot respond to fundamentally new kinds of questions. My superiors could not answer my questions. They began to wonder whether I was material for the ministry. Most of them, but not all, knew how to deal with problems only by denying their validity. The more I pressed, the more they had to enforce the world of emanation. If I was onto something, they would have to doubt their world, and this most refused to do.

There was actually a warning that was sent from Rome to all spiritual directors of seminarians, instructing them to counsel their charges who were having serious difficulties with sex to leave the seminary. I was still too naive to recognize to what extent this directive was out of touch with the reality of our lives. If this order had been carried out, it would have meant a virtual emptying of all seminaries.

So the Catholic Church resorted to a policy that it used long before the current controversy over gays in the military: "Don't ask. Don't tell." This official approach breeds an environment of pain and guilt. The hierarchy knows that there are many good men and women under vows who are in trouble. But the official Church, in order to preserve its sense of superiority over other Christians and to continue to possess the loyalty of its nuns and priests in the relationship of emanation, refuses to change Church policy regarding married priests, celibacy, and women priests. In this way the lives of men and women are wounded for the sake of maintaining a mystique of emanation that has nothing to do with creating a more loving and just world.

MOVING TOWARD TRANSFORMATION

Since I could not resolve my sexual identity and discover my own story, I left the seminary after seven years. It was an extraordinary experience that has marked my life in ways that I am still discovering. I met some deeply caring and loving human beings, who guided me toward transformation. When I was depressed following the breakdown of the world of emanation, there were friends who spent hours reassuring me and helping me to heal.

There was a transformation that took place in one aspect of my life. I wanted an education even before I had decided to study for the priesthood. I hoped to make a contribution with and for others. While at the University of Toronto, I discovered a creativity and intelligence of which I was unaware. Those in charge of our education were worried that I would not be able to handle the course of studies at the University of Toronto. I accepted this as another challenge: the little Mexican youth in me had to prove himself again. And although this may have started out as another example of emanation, living up to the expectations of my heroes, it didn't end this way. The first thing that I learned was a new kind of discipline: a creative discipline that led me to my own inner resources. I studied for hours at a time. By the time I had graduated I could sit and study for seven to eight hours a day. But it was pure drudgery until I began to feel and intuit the issues being raised in class. Then I knew that it was mine, no longer the words of a teacher, but something that had come from some unknown depths within me. I no longer memorized but *stood under* the material as in under-stand. I could feel ideas as my hands began to sweat. I had succeeded in making all knowledge personal, a part of me that helped me to become more fully myself and more human. For my exam in metaphysics, I wrote only what I could intuit. I wrote the exam in a stream of consciousness. I received the highest grade in the class. I wrote all of my English literature papers in this way. Above all, what I had discovered was my own creative imagination, the source of my inspiration for the rest of my ongoing education. To enact transformation in this area of my life, it was necessary for me to break with the official teachings encased in emanation, to rebel against teachers who demanded rote learning of any kind. On the deeper level, I broke with the story of the teacher and the priest as the all-knowing hero in the second scene of Act II. This story, which had been such a powerful and seductive drama in my life was, together with the way of life of emanation, sent into the exit from the core drama.

Once I had freed myself on the deeper level of these partial sacred sources, my personal and sacred faces were filled with the inspiration to be a different kind of teacher. And in the second scene of Act III, I enacted the political and historical face of my being by practicing the story of teaching in the service of transformation. In this kind of teaching, the goal is to guide students to their own creative imagination so that they can create their own story. I have been blessed with an ability to assist students to tell their own story, with the theory of transformation as our guide. To tell their story is to discover the four faces of their being, where they are in the core drama of life, what stories they are living, and in the service of what way of life. Once they are aware of what sacred sources they are in contact with, they can make choices to intervene against their fate and create a destiny that is fundamentally more loving and just.

TRANSFORMATION AS A PERMANENT PROCESS

As a teacher I experienced the joy of transformation in Act III, Scenes 1 and 2, as a fulfillment of the core drama of life. It was a profoundly healing experience. As a young Mexican boy growing up in poverty in Detroit, I had been hurt by what I call the story of the wounded self. I was traumatized by physical and emotional abuse, the loss of a parent, and alcohol abuse. I never knew when I left the house if I would be physically assaulted by members of a neighborhood gang. I spent one entire summer running from a group that wanted to beat me. I felt abandoned because my father had died when I was only two years old. He was not there to protect me when people abused alcohol and threatened me and my family. These traumas severely undercut my sense of self-worth and led me to blame my mother and my Mexican culture. My desire to assimilate and to reject my Mexican background was a cry for help. In relationship to the wider society, I also felt the pain of racism and classism. The feelings of powerlessness and helplessness that I felt as a child were the cause of an anger that was so intense that I had problems repressing it.

But against the expectation of failure on the part of many, I had succeeded. The beauty of transformation is that once we have known it in one part of our life, we want to apply it to all of our problems. To be able to participate in transformation in such a remarkable way as a teacher centered and grounded my life. I now had a perspective from which to re-vision everything that had happened to me and to know it in a new way. To be whole in one part of our life is a witness to the hope that we can accomplish this time after time. To be whole is to heal. The hurts that I suffered were now the basis for strength and compassion. To be whole is not to be perfect or finished, but to experience yourself as a valuable person with a sacred face. These understandings and the feelings that came with them swept away a great deal of the brokenness and anger that came from being a wounded self. To tell your story heals and restores. My face, which had been despised because I was a Mexican, because I was rebelling, because I was poor, now came forth with my insights and hopes because it was connected to my sacred face, which was linked to the deepest source of transformation. This discovery of my capacity to bring forth the depths in my own unique way gave me the courage to be political, that is, to bring about changes in the world around me, so that a new and more loving history replaced the inherited past.

I also learned that for me and la comunidad Latina the pursuit of self-interest and power could not be an alternative for the dying world of emanation. The way of life of incoherence that arrests us as partial selves has no capacity to heal our fragmented self; it can only compensate for the fear and anger that accompanied the loss of emanation as a way of life. The search for the compensatory part of life opens up an abyss of unfulfilled desires. Money, drugs, addictions of all kinds, and the search for security become a relentless escape from not knowing who we are. We cannot make ourselves vulnerable because we live in the midst of the story of capitalism in the service of incoherence. To be vulnerable or wounded is to place ourselves in danger because we live in a world of competition for power. Any weakness is exploited. In this story we have to hide our personal face since it is wounded. We cannot tell our story and discover the wholeness of our sacred face since the lord of incoherence blocks our access to the deepest source of transformation and continues to whisper in our inner souls that power is the answer. Our political and historical faces are driven by the pursuit of power.

Nor is the story of revenge in the service of deformation an option for us as members of the Latino community. Why is this? Because revenge, of its very nature, means that we want to hurt others as we were hurt. We have not emptied ourselves in Act II, Scene 2, of the story and the way of life that victimized us. For example, the Spaniards practiced racism against the indigenous peoples of Latin America. But rather than letting the story go into the abyss, mestizos looked down upon the full-blooded Indians. In this country, as in Latin America, light-skinned children are preferred. There is intragroup as well as intergroup racism. Latinos speak about whites as prejudiced, but then some Mexican parents refuse to allow their children to date Puerto Ricans because they have "*sangre negra*," black blood. Many Cubans will not identify with poor Cubans, who are usually black. So upon whom will we avenge ourselves? This is the madness of revenge. It sends the victims and the victimizers into the abyss at the exit from the core drama. It is the story of racism and the deeper way of life of deformation inspired by the lord of nothing that are the enemies. These powerful sacred sources can only be overcome by our participating together with the deepest sacred source, the god of transformation.

FROM MEXICAN AMERICAN TO CHICANO

I was deeply affected by the Chicano movement of the late 1960s. This awakening of the Mexican people, together with the rebellion of women, students, African Americans, Asian Americans, American Indians, and gays, marked a decisive turning point in the history of this country. The key here was self-definition, the creation of one's own identity and the refusal to be named by others according to the criteria determined by the standard of white, European American, and male.

I became so enchanted by the Chicano movement in an emanational sense that once again I was tempted to see white people as the problem. I called myself a Chicano, a militant Mexican, who refused the politics of accommodation for the politics of confrontation. Intellectually and academically, I was caught up in deconstructionism. It was necessary to tear down and sweep away the paradigms of oppression. This was an important step to prepare us to create alternatives. But the sadness is that many of us went through the tearing down and then became cynical. You couldn't trust anyone over thirty, white males were forever the oppressors, straights could not understand gays and lesbians, if you weren't Chicano you couldn't teach me anything.

I vividly remember reading Erik Erikson's *Gandhi's Truth* at this time and feeling my anger slowly recede. Ghandi and Erikson helped me to understand that to confront the enemy is to face the story in yourself. For this reason both the antagonist and your own self had to be approached nonviolently. Only this method would allow the person to accept their personal collusion with violence and to move to put a stop to it.[42] In addition, to follow the logic of extreme nationalism that uncritically celebrated everything that was Chicano would mean that I would deny what I had experienced in transformation and regress to being arrested in an emanational linkage to deformation as a way of life. This was contrary to who I was as a person and as a teacher.

But I was tempted, which demonstrates that even though we send a story and way of life into the abyss, very powerful fragments remain that threaten to possess us once more. I had also been blessed by some crucial guides on my journey who accepted me as a Chicano and wanted me to explore my heritage as a source of creativity in my scholarship and teaching. The irony is that neither of these men was Chicano or Latino. Frank Sullivan was a brilliant teacher who hired me for a special program working with inner-city youth. He gave me the freedom as a young teacher to create my own style of teaching. He encouraged me to experiment. Manfred Halpern was for me the kind of teacher and scholar I wanted to be. It was he who led me gently but firmly through the theory of transformation into the realm of deeper underlying forming sources. For a time I was in emanation to him, until he helped me to understand that the theory of transformation does not belong to anyone but needs each of us to participate, requires each of us to be fully present with our four faces. As we worked together on the theory of transformation, I rediscovered him as a friend and colleague. Practicing the tribalism inherent in blind nationalism in the service of deformation meant that I would have to deny Frank Sullivan and Manfred Halpern because they were not Chicanos. This I could not do and would not do. There had to be a way for me to be both Chicano and open to people from all ethnic and racial backgrounds.

It was a blessing to remember and reexperience my Mexican/Latino heritage in the service of transformation. I reached back and restored in a new way what it meant to be a Mejicano/Chicano. I realized that I had the opportunity to help create a new culture with my community in this country. It was up to us to nurture those aspects of the culture which were transformative and to critique and break with destructive stories and the three ways of life of emanation, incoherence, and deformation because they are only fragments of the core drama that arrest and deny our humanity. Not everything Mexican and Latino was good; there was no sense in being a chauvinist with a brown face. If I rejected the way of life of emanation in which my mother had raised me, I also refused to see assimilation into the story of capitalism as the answer for la comunidad Latina. Of its very nature, this story means that only some of us will make it, that only some are *intended* to make it and some are intended to fail. The story is rigged. The greatest fear of the powerful, and that includes those Latinas and Latinos who are in the service of incoherence, is real competition. Everything is done to make sure that the competition will be uneven and unequal. Once you are taken over by this story and way of life, you no longer care about those who are left behind, except as charitable deductions. The ultimate concern of this way of life is self-interest, not compassion and justice. In the story of capitalism in the service of incoherence that arrests us in Act II, Scene 1, of the core drama of life, it is not possible for us to respond to problems that demand a different kind of consciousness.

LA COMUNIDAD LATINA AT RISK: THE COLLUSION BETWEEN INCOHERENCE AND DEFORMATION

Some Latinos get caught up in their efforts to survive in this country in what begins as the story of capitalism in the service of incoherence and ends in the destructive death of deformation. I am speaking here of underground capitalism, crime, and especially of drugs and dealing in drugs. There are those in la comunidad Latina who see drugs as a business enterprise. They invest in drugs and sell them for a profit. The fact that it is illegal is ignored and justified as being like numbers. "Everybody does it, so what is the harm? If they don't get it from me, they will get from someone else." With such a drug as marijuana, the danger was not immediately apparent, but many have taken the step toward the most dangerous substances, like heroin and crack cocaine, which, quite simply, possesses and takes over the user's life. Drug dealing is so seductive because of the incredible amount of money that can be made in a matter of days or hours. The drug pimp becomes a quasi hero in the community because he may support child-care centers or build a new swimming pool for the children. But those same children are in danger from the violence and death that always travel with drugs.

Many Latinas and Latinos cannot get jobs or good-paying jobs and find it increasingly difficult to make it in this country. As a result, they are prone to see drug dealers as successful. Many of our youth enter into relationships of pseudoemanation with the drug lords and see them as their heroes. Once the money and power seduce them, they are gone. The hustle takes them over. If it is necessary to sell drugs to children to keep the profits coming, then it will have to be done. Anybody who threatens the trade by going to the police or a competing gang can be killed. Young and old alike are battered daily by the inequities of the story of capitalism and the racism that surrounds us and are vulnerable to all kinds of escape. By taking drugs, they mortgage their paychecks and lives to dealers who look to be paid off. As a result, families are driven deeper into poverty and despair. This situation forces others into crime to survive. There is no end to the destruction caused by drugs. They destroy the fabric of the community and take away our humanity. Shattered communities and families mean crime, increased drug use, and infected needles that spread the AIDS virus, dropping out of school, early pregnancy, gang violence, and the perpetuation of the cycle of poverty, despair, crime, and more poverty. Drugs and involvement in other forms of organized crime place our communities in the hell of deformation. It is a path of self-destructiveness that diminishes our humanity as we exit the core drama into the abyss. This is one of the greatest challenges for the Latino community. All efforts need to be taken to prevent the way of life of deformation from becoming the dominant way of life for our community.[43]

WHAT IS TO BE DONE? THE UNFINISHED AGENDA

Transformation needs to become a reality in all aspects of our life. It is never complete once and for all. In my struggle to transform my life, I faced the following stories: patriarchy, matriarchy, uncritical loyalty, romantic love, capitalism, racism, and the wounded self.

THE ARCHETYPAL DRAMA OF PATRIARCHY/ MATRIARCHY

I now know that I had not succeeded in ridding myself of the story of patriarchy. This deadly story has done so much to debilitate la comunidad Latina. Our families, which means our ability to prepare the next generation, are at stake. At the heart of the matter in regard to our families are male/female relationships and how, as a result of the story of patriarchy in the service of emanation as a dying way of life and deformation, we wound our women and therefore our men. Returning to my own story, which I believe transcends my own experience and provides the words for many others, my marriage was permeated by the story of patriarchy. Because I had left the community and my family to go to school and to study for the priesthood, I thought that male domination was behind me. I had broken on the concrete level with patriarchal males, but I did not empty myself on the deeper underlying realm of the archetypal story. As a result I hurt our marriage, in ways of which I was not even conscious.[44]

My mother, following the death of my father, became a matriarchal/patriarchal mother. That is, she now practiced the story of patriarchy with a feminine face. She raised us as if my father were still present, not realizing that it was the story that still held her in a tight grip. As a boy, I fought my mother and resisted her control. I felt overwhelmed and yet abandoned by my mother, who didn't have the time or the energy to devote to me. I craved attention but seldom received it, except from my sisters, especially Marge, who was like a mother to me.

As I grew older, my sisters married and moved away. I became closer to my mother but continued to resist her. I saw my mother as someone who lived in the past and spoke highly only of Mexico and the life that she had had there. Her life expressed a hidden resentment against my father, who had asked her to follow him to this country. She spoke with harshness about the United States. She was here against her will. I wanted to belong, as I have said, and I saw my mother's resistance as another aspect of her being stuck in the past. I was also afraid of my mother because as I got closer to finishing high school, I was concerned that I was becoming too attached to her and that I would be obligated to remain at home to take care of her. In addition, as a good Catholic I was concerned about the state of my mother's soul. She had not gone to confession or received Holy Communion in years. According to Catholic teaching, she was in danger of eternal damnation. There was no way that I could let that happen. So I worked on my mother for months until she finally consented to receive the sacraments. I was greatly relieved because this now freed me to leave home with an easier conscience. I wanted to get away. But this also developed in me a fear and suspicion of affection, because it might be used to trap me.

I carried these ambivalent feelings toward my mother into my relationships with women, without understanding their implications. Because of my desire to be acceptable to white, European-American people, I dated primarily white young women. Since I had decided to become a priest, I was very leery of sex and affection by the time that I was in my junior year in high school. So the fear of my mother and my Mexican culture became connected to wanting to assimilate, get away from my fear of suffocating affection and settling for relatively safe relationships to young women whom I must not allow to become threats to my destiny. My mother, my heritage, sex, and possessive obligations with women caused me deep fear.

I had no awareness of these issues when I met and later married my wife, Celia. After leaving the seminary, I wanted to develop a lasting and good sexual relationship with a woman. I had willingly given up sexual relationships with women but felt that I was now ready. I spoke to Celia about what our marriage and family would be like with anticipation. I was caught completely by surprise when I froze up on Celia. I behaved badly. I became everything that I had renounced and denounced in the Mejicano/Latino males who were part of my life and community. I was a bossy, controlling, mean, aloof, and emotionally cold patriarchal male. Underneath, I was totally confused and depressed. How and why did this happen to me? After many years of marriage, I still had no answer to this question.

For six years I sought the answer in Jungian analysis. I discovered that once I married Celia, she ceased in my feelings to be my lover. What brought about the change was her pregnancy and the birth of our first child. I now experienced Celia as a mother, my mother, with all the fears surrounding that relationship. I responded to the return of the story of patriarchy/matriarchy by dominating and controlling Celia. I reasserted the other face, the masculine face, of the archetypal story of patriarchy/matriarchy because I was afraid I would be smothered. This was the only way that I knew how to deal with the power of under-lying archetypal forces that I did not understand.

This inability to relate to Celia as a lover meant that we could not guide each other toward the realization of the four faces of our being. Celia and I have had long discussions of what our marriage did to us while we were trapped by the story of patriarchy in the service of fragments of the way of life of emanation. We could not sustain the heavy cost of this relationship, because neither of us could be a self fully present. I moved toward deformation by taking out my anger on Celia. She colluded with me by seeing me as her father, who once again was punishing her for wanting to be a strong and independent woman with her own desires and dreams. The price of this was a heavy one. Celia denied her own personal face by negating her self-worth and turning her life into a constant desire to please me, and I took advantage of this kind of self-cancellation. I thereby participated in erasing my own face by seeing myself through the eyes of Celia, who refused for the most part to challenge me. With her political face, she gave me power over her life as she sought to find meaning in being loyal to me. With our historical faces, both Celia and I repeated the dramas of our parents, who were also caught in the same stories and ways of life. Our sacred faces were obscured and crippled by the lords of emanation and deformation that said that there was nothing else that we could do. We were both victims of this story and of the deeper ways of life in which we enacted this drama of patriarchy. This to me is a classic example of a battered family. There was no physical assault. But we cannot take much solace when we see how we hurt each other and our children by not being fully present to and for each other.

I believe that in the Latino community and in the wider society our marriage and family are all too common. Our marriage gave me an insight into what was happening to other couples and families. Now I know better than ever before why Latina women and Latino men practice either a politics of loyalty or dis-appointed rage, why they fail to create a new history and do not see themselves as participants with the sacred faces of their being together with the deep-est source of transformation. The politics of so many of our families has dis-abled us.

I do not want to blame anybody, but to get to the roots of our problem. We have it within our ability to refuse to continue to be victims. Celia and I sought help from each other and from others. Together we experienced an awakening in which some deeper voices were speaking to us, which is what Act I, Scene 2, is all about. But for a time we heard the wrong sacred sources, as we tried to reform our marriage first through being better at living the inherited relation-ships and stories from our past, especially emanation and subjection, practiced in the story of patriarchy; then we tried bargaining from positions of power, as we both became competent professionals; then we tried ignoring the presence of the other, as we denied each other's pain. In all of these earlier attempts to deal with our marriage by incremental change, we sought to change the existing story from within, but without realizing that the story of patriarchy enacted in the service of emanation, incoherence, or deformation could never be fulfilling.

What it was that we needed to do together was to make a personal, political, historical, and sacred decision to vomit out the story of matriarchy/patriarchy into the abyss and to take back our own lives. Sandra Cisneros in her short story, "Woman Hollering Creek," writes about this radical move from being a victim, a *llorón/llorona*, to being a *gritón/gritona*, people who shout out their resistance *and change their life* on the deeper level by emptying themselves of the stories and ways of life that denied their full participation in the core drama of life.[45]

Because Latina women were so undermined by the stories of our emanational past, Latino males and the community as a whole lost a great deal of their creative participation. Too often I have heard how Latinas kept the family together. But as a community we did not allow Latinas to express the personal and sacred faces of their being and denied them participation that would express their political and historical faces both within and outside the home. We have a habit as a community of referring to our mothers as saints, because of all the suffering that they endured from our fathers and Anglo society, often without complaining. They always kept the home fires burning. But because their endeavors were restricted to the home, it impoverished the community in its political and historical fight against the stories of racism and capitalism that we faced in the wider society. Latinas were selfless, which means that their personal faces and sacredness were denied. Latino men veiled and silenced Latina women because of a deep fear that if they got involved in the public realm with their personal abilities—which would empower the political and historical faces of their being—male authority would be eclipsed. This might be due to the fact that in traditional Latino societies, as well as in this society, Latino men could only be powerful at home, by dominating the women. Thus, to prevent the collapse of their patriarchal authority in the crumbling way of life of emanation, Latino men turned to deformation to force Latina women back to a container that no longer worked for anyone. Once a woman gained some autonomy in the public arena, it exposed the weakness of men, who were excluded for reasons of race and class from their rightful involvement. In this situation Latino males were rebels: they responded to the deformation of racism and classism in the wider society by practicing the deformation of patriarchal violence against themselves and their own families. But there is no excuse for such fear and behavior. Together Latina women can say with Herbert Biberman's Esperanza, as she spoke back to her husband in *The Salt of the Earth*: "If you do not want the Anglos to control you, then neither do we want our men to control us."[46]

Let us look a little more closely at the ways in which Latina women have been for the past thirty years freeing themselves and therefore helping to liberate Latino men and la comunidad Latina from destructive stories and ways of life that arrest us in the core drama of life. Latinas moving toward transformation recognized that they were living stories that arrested them in the core drama of life. They knew on at least an intuitive level that they were living dramas that held great power over their lives. So when they fought to go away to college and to live in dorms, they helped all of us to free ourselves from the stories of patriarchy and possessive love and from a way of life that held women and all of us in the deadly embrace of a partial way of life. When they got to college or to the workplace, they realized that they were not yet free. Once again, they had to fight for their selves against their fathers and the guilt instilled in them by parents by resisting jealous lovers and professors who doubted their ability to do well. On campuses they faced issues of race, class, and gender that threatened to undo their fragile self-confidence. Then once they began to become successful, they fought to include the community in their victory and to resist the temptation to join the powerful in the story of capitalism in the service of incoherence. Then there came the struggle to avoid feelings and acts of deformational revenge for all of the hurt they had encountered in their relationships to men.

Latinas who were married when they heard from their deepest self fought to go to work or to return to school to redeem the dreams that they had repressed. Many Latino males were deeply threatened by this rejection of the story of patriarchy and the way of life of emanation. Their legitimation of control based on their manhood had been eroded. They found themselves with broken emanational relationships in the midst of the story of capitalism, in which, because of racism and ethnocentrism, they were not allowed to compete. Thus they saw their tradition dying and their failure to make it here as an assault on their identity. The only place where they felt they could counterattack was in the home. Thus to hang onto stories, relationships, and ways of life that were fragmenting, they turned to violence in the service of deformation.

But there is another way. Men and women in the Latino community are not prisoners of the past. Once we become conscious of the stories and the ways of life that have arrested us in the core drama, we can choose to free ourselves on the deeper level of these obstacles to transformation. But we need to confront these stories and ways of life that live in and move through us as they control our creativity. No transformation is complete for all time, nor all embracing. We can only experience transformation in regard to one problem, one story, one aspect of our life at a time.[47]

In my own marriage I now realized that I could use all of the eight relationships in the way of life of transformation that would allow us to continue yet change, cooperate yet disagree, so that together we could experience the justice of expressing in their wholeness our own personal, political, historical, and sacred faces. In the relationship of emanation, I can temporarily hug Celia when she is depressed and tell her that everything will be all right and so prepare her to return to the fullness of her own life. In subjection, Celia can refuse to give me the keys to the car because I am foolishly trying to go to work with a serious infection. In buffering, we can both cover for each other as mediators with others who seek an unwarranted demand on our time. In isolation, we can be happy when we are apart, knowing that when we see each other again, we will have more to share about what happened to us since last we talked. In direct bargaining, we agree to divide and share the work that has to be done in the daily stuff of life. In autonomy, we each respect the realm of competence of the other and support each other in the development of our talents while at the same time learning something of one another's area of expertise, so that both of us can grow in new ways. In the relationship of incoherence, we admit when we do not know how to relate to each other and agree to continue communicating until we can discover in the relationship of transformation what it is that caused the break between us, so that we can move quickly to create new and more fruitful manifestations of the other relationships. The only relationship of the nine archetypal relationships that cannot be used in the way of life of transformation and the one that must be consciously and vigorously rejected is deformation, which only serves to put us on the road to destructive death.[48]

Celia and I have not solved all the difficulties of our marriage, but we face our lives every day with the realization that our marriage belongs to us and that we are no longer unconsciously victimized by the stories of patriarchy/matriarchy and possessive love in the service of partial ways of life that wounded us and arrested us as partial selves.

NOTES

1. Manfred Halpern first taught me the theory of transformation, which he had rediscovered when I was his graduate student at Princeton University. He is presently writing his own manuscript, "Transformation: Its Theory and Practice in Our Personal, Political, Historical and Sacred Being." I have gained greatly from having read the chapters of his manuscript in the writing of this book. For earlier versions of the theory of transformation and applications of the theory of transformation see David T. Abalos, *The Latino Family and the Politics of Transformation* (Westport, CT, London: Praeger, 1993) and *Latinos in the United States: The Sacred and the Political* (Notre Dame, IN: University of Notre Dame Press, 1986) and *Strategies of Transformation Toward a Multicultural Society Fulfilling the Story of Democracy* (Westport, CT, London: Praeger, 1996).

2. Halpern, "Transformation," chapter 1.

3. Miguel León Portilla, ed., *Native Mesoamerican Spirituality* (New York, Ramsey, Toronto: Paulist Press, 1980). For an explanation of The Popol Vuh from the perspective of transformation, see also David T. Abalos, "Rediscovering the Sacred Among Latinos: A Critique from the Perspective of a Theory of Transformation." *Latino Studies Journal* 3, no. 2 (May 1992), pp. 10–11.

4. Manfred Halpern, "Why Are Most of Us Partial Selves? Why Do Partial Selves Enter the Road into Deformation?" (paper presented at the annual meeting of the American Political Science Association, Washington, DC, 1991).

5. Ibid.

6. Manfred Halpern, "Beyond Present Theory and Practice: Transformation and the Nation State" (paper presented at a national symposium, "Beyond the Nation-State: Transforming Visions of Human Society," College of William and Mary, Williamsburg,

VA, September 24–27, 1993). To be published in *Transformational Politics: Theory, Study and Practice* (SUNY, 1998), edited by Ed Schwerin, Christa Slaton, and Stephen Woolpert.

   7. Halpern, "Transformation," chapter 1.

   8. Ibid.

   9. Ibid., chapter 13.

   10. Ralph Ellison, *Invisible Man* (New York: Vintage Books, 1972).

   11. Halpern, "Toward an Ecology."

   12. David T. Abalos, *Strategies*, p. 18.

   13. Cornell West, *Race Matters* (Boston: Beacon Press, 1993).

   14. Halpern, "Transformation," chapter 1.

   15. Ibid., chapter 7.

   16. Much of the summary above and the quotes from Halpern's theory are taken from "Transformation," chapter 7, "Archetypal Relationships," and from "Four Contrasting Repertories of Human Relations in Islam: Two Pre-Modern and Two Modern Ways of Dealing with Continuity and Change, Collaboration and Conflict and Achieving Justice," in *Psychological Dimensions of Near Eastern Studies*, ed. L. Carl Brown and Norman Itzkowitz (Princeton, NJ: Darwin Press, 1977), p. 62.

   17. Ibid., p. 64.

   18. Halpern, "Transformation," chapter 1, pp. 9–10.

   19. Ibid., p. 12.

   20. Halpern, "Four Contrasting Repertories," pp. 77–78.

   21. Oscar Hijuelos, *The Mambo Kings Play Songs of Love* (New York, Toronto, and London: Harper and Row, Perennial Library, 1990).

   22. Humberto Solas, *Lucía*, produced in Havana, Cuba, 1968.

   23. Halpern, "Transformation," pp. 13–14.

   24. Halpern, "Four Contrasting Repertories," pp. 78–79.

   25. Halpern, "Transformation," chapter 1.

   26. Ibid., p. 18.

   27. Ibid., chapter 7.

   28. Ibid., chapter 3.

   29. Ibid.

   30. Ibid., chapter 4.

   31. Ibid.

   32. Sandra Cisneros, *Woman Hollering Creek and Other Stories* (New York: Vintage Books, 1991).

   33. Halpern, "Transformation," chapter 5.

   34. This statistical profile of some of the dangers facing la comunidad Latina was largely drawn from two papers: Curt Idrogo, "Hispanic Americans," in *A Guide to Multicultural Resources, 1997–1998* (Fort Atkinson, WI: 1997); and Rev. Ferdinand Fuentes, "An Overview of the Hispanic Context in the United States" (paper presented at the United Church of Christ Latino and Latina Leadership Summit, Cleveland: OH, 1994).

   35. Halpern, "Transformation," p. 48.

   36. Abalos, *Strategies*, p. 25.

   37. Ibid., p. 39.

   38. Ibid.

   39. Ibid., p. 40.

   40. Halpern, "Transformation," chapter 7.

41. Abalos, *Strategies*, pp. 41–42.

42. Erik Erikson, *Gandhi's Truth: On the Origins of Militant Non-Violence* (New York: W. W. Norton, 1968).

43. Abalos, *The Latino Family*, chapter 4.

44. Ibid., chapters 4 and 5.

45. Sandra Cisneros, *Woman Hollering Creek*.

46. Herbert J. Biberman, *The Salt of the Earth*, produced by Independent Productions Corporation and the International Union of Mine, Mill and Smelter Workers, 1953.

47. Abalos, *The Latino Family*, chapter 5.

48. Ibid.

2

The Personal, Political, Historical, and Sacred Faces of la Cultura Latina

To know yourself is to know your lord.

—*Ibn Arabi*

Culturally . . . returning to the source means not a recreating of the past but the building of the future: not to restore the past or to worship it as a false idol, but to build an authentic future, one which subsumes our past, not denies it.

—*Juan Gómez Quiñones*

INTRODUCTION

In *I Heard the Owl Call My Name*, a novel about American Indians in the Northwest, Margaret Craven has one of her characters state, "no village, no culture, can remain static."[1] This is because a culture that does not prepare people to deal with fundamentally new problems disables them so that they are rendered wounded, partial selves.[2]

If we are to confront radically new issues, we cannot use tradition as a container to protect us because people do not simply inherit and hand on a cultural past by telling the old stories. Of the very nature of our humanity, we have a historical face that needs us to actually make history by responding to the personal and political voices inspired in us by the deepest source. Indeed, whenever a culture or a community stops taking responsibility for the stories it lives, because it unconsciously repeats and reenacts them, such a society becomes ahistorical. Thus the past and history are not synonymous. The past is what shaped us to be who we are; thus history is more than just living and repeating a story or a common cultural inheritance. We need to be participants in the uprooting, creation, and nurturance of our cultural stories in order to earn our historical calling.

THE FOUR FACES OF CULTURE AND THE STORIES OF OUR LIVES

Culture, for purposes of our discussion here, will be defined as "a network of stories that hang together in order to create a cosmos of meaning for the members of a society." The reason that I adopt this unorthodox definition is that it corresponds more closely than technical terms to the lived experience of Latinas and Latinos. In order for culture to be authentic, it must be malleable to our conscious participation.[3] It is our stories that create culture as a civilization that provides us as a people with a total view of life.[4]

We and the stories of our lives have four faces: a personal, a political, a historical and a sacred face.

The sacred face of our being consists of actual living underlying patterning forces which shape the structure, meaning and purpose of all the stories within which we and our culture are grounded. If we remain unconscious of these underlying forming forces they will possess us. The presence of these underlying forming forces points to far more sacred and deeper sources than our allegedly secular culture is willing to acknowledge. These sacred forces are also called archetypal not because they are perfect and eternal but because they are the necessary underlying forming sources for all of concrete reality.[5]

As described in chapter 1, we enact all of the relationships and dramas of our life within the service of deeper underlying sacred ways of life. We need to know more about the dynamics of these deeper dramas so that we can free ourselves of the most powerful of living, underlying, patterning forces.

Allow me to summarize what I have said earlier about ways of life: there are four archetypal underlying ways of life, in the service of which we concretely enact the stories of our culture. The three ways of life of emanation, incoherence, and deformation are actually failed and truncated fragments of the core drama of transformation. The fourth drama, transformation, unlike the first three, needs our conscious, critical, and creative participation because it constitutes the core of the cosmos of being human. The core drama of life is constituted by a three-act drama that we are all called upon to travel again and again in order to achieve wholeness in all aspects of life. We call the story of transformation the fulfillment of the core drama of life because each time "we move ourselves and advance with our neighbors successively through the three Acts of the drama, we reach the heart of life—a wholeness of all four faces of our being that leads to love and justice for the problem at hand.''[6]

But many of us do not know how to practice transformation. We have been wounded and continue to harm ourselves as partial selves by remaining arrested in the incomplete ways of life of emanation, incoherence, and deformation. We remain partial beings, partial because no matter how much power we may accumulate as a fragment, we are left fragile and anxious. In these three overarching but truncated ways of life, we cannot personally intervene to face fundamentally new kinds of problems, and so we are rendered politically impotent to change a society, and we become subject to the past as an ahistorical repetition. The sacred sources, the lords, which are the underlying forming cause of these stories, invite apathy because the culture that is the result of their power will remain outside our participation, except as willing practitioners who carry out their will. The three partial ways of life will be contrasted with the way of life of transformation in this chapter in the context of our discussion of creating a new culture for la comunidad Latina.

THE LATINO STORY CONFRONTS THE EUROPEAN-AMERICAN STORY IN THE CONTEXT OF U.S. SOCIETY: THE STORY OF TRIBALISM

The majority of our foremothers and forefathers were already wounded in Latin America by the story of tribalism. This story is always in the service of deformation, because it diminishes our humanity. In this story a group of people take a fragment of life, skin color, or ethnicity and turn it into a total fantasy. Those who have the required or favored skin color or ethnic heritage are considered to be the chosen, the insiders, the superior. We know from the historical record that the Spaniards were obsessed with *la limpieza de sangre*, the purity of blood, during the Inquisition in Spain. This search for purity followed the conquistadores to New Spain, where there was established a new hierarchy based on race and ethnicity. Bartolomé de las Casas had to fight long and hard to convince the Spanish monarchs that Indians were human beings in order to protect them from the colonial authorities. There are five ways by which the allegedly superior can relate to the others, people of color or members of a different ethnic group: The excluded are treated as if they are *invisible*, they are nothing. If they insist on being seen and heard, they are allowed to participate, but only insofar as they accept their *inferiority* in all aspects of life: housing, employment, health care, and social relations. The only escape from this exclusion is *assimilation*, a strategy of self- and group hatred, stripping oneself of one's background in order to be more like the allegedly superior, one of the ''better'' Mexicans, Puerto Ricans, or Latinos. To awaken from this nightmare of self-denial and to begin to question those who would exclude and to demand participation for one's community results in *excommunication* for daring to be

disloyal. Finally, the allegedly inferior can be *exterminated*, since they are considered nothing.

In the United States la comunidad Latina continues to suffer from this same
story. We did not choose not to participate; we were made invisible. The dominant turned us into pariahs, allegedly inferior people who were allowed only
to do the menial in life and thus fulfill the prophecy of those who stereotyped
us as less than the powerful; those of us who were judged to be like the superior
were adopted as "honorary" members of the elite and so allowed to assimilate
as a reward for not being like the rest of "those people"; if we began to question
the system, we were considered to be disloyal to the dominant who gave us
privileges, and we were cast out, excommunicated; finally, as the allegedly inferior, we as Latinos and Latinas were faced with extermination by war, exploitation, and forced exile, especially following the wars with Mexico and
Spain. For example, the Treaty of Guadalupe Hidalgo, signed by the Mexican
and U.S. governments in 1848, attempted to protect the land rights of Mexicans
who chose to become American citizens. In all of the ceded territories the pattern
was the same: exorbitant taxes; legal trickery; outright violence; lengthy court
battles, which in New Mexico, for example, took on the average seventeen years
to decide land claims, and legal fees that led to bankruptcy.[7]

This creation of the archetypal drama of tribalism in the service of deformation began as an attempt to preserve the ways of life of emanation and incoherence. Of their very nature, these ways of life cannot accept fundamentally
new kinds of consciousness, creativity, new forms of justice, linkages to outsiders, or any new inspiration from the depths. To prevent these eruptions of the
deepest sacred and demands for a different kind of justice, more force and
violence must be used to protect the one "truth" in the service of emanation
and the power of the few in the service of incoherence.

The archetypal drama of tribalism results in ongoing *cultural* extermination,
the destruction of one's stories, which means annihilating one's past, one's
memory, one's history, one's very self. The irony is that many European Americans at different periods in American history also experienced this deadly story.
The Irish, Italians, Jews, and Slavic peoples, among others, were victims who
often became the victimizers.[8] Once again in our history, we are feeling the
deforming wounds of this story as the nation undergoes its periodic xenophobic
reaction to migration, especially from Asia and Latin America. This helps us to
understand that if we as a people do not empty ourselves in Act II, Scene 2, of
the core drama of the underlying patterning forces that give the story of tribalism
its mysterious hold over us, it will remain a part of the American story and
culture that permeate our body politic and wreak its vengeance again and again.

Since coming to the United States, or being absorbed and conquered, as in
the case of the Puerto Rican people following the Spanish-American War of
1898 and the Mexican people as a result of the U.S./Mexican War of 1846–48
who lived and continue to live in the former Mexican states of the United States
Southwest, Latinos have experienced the story of tribalism at the hands of Eu-

ropean Americans. Currently, Latino children have a devastating poverty rate of 39 percent. Prior to 1940, only 1 percent of Mejicano children in the Southwest were in school.[9] They were not allowed to go to school because the powerful made a decision to cripple a whole people by keeping them uneducated so that they could never walk away from back-breaking agricultural work. This is also an example of the story of capitalism at its worst that colludes with the story of racism in the service of deformation. What is the effect that this story has had upon the four faces of our being? In regard to our personal face, we have self-doubts, even self-hatred; we cannot see or love who we are; our personal face is erased. Our political face is confronted with the politics of exclusion, hatred, and violence; and so, out of sheer survival many of our people in different communities, especially in the Southwest, for generations were forced out of politics. Our historical face was plunged deeper into the abyss of despair. An avenging lord of deformation broke our bones and spirits in the name of the superior.

THE OFFICIAL STORY OF AMERICAN SOCIETY: THE ARCHETYPAL DRAMA OF CAPITALISM

The story of capitalism is based on the assumption that all are equal and therefore have a fair chance when competing with others for benefits. The state exists in order to guarantee the "fairness" of this competition. But the actual story of a capitalist, or market, society is a brutal one. In this drama all of us are forced to become immoral and insincere in order to survive; our relationships are based on competition; nobody can afford to be intimate for fear that it will be seen as a weakness; people are the cheapest commodity on the market; we live in constant anxiety that the person behind us will overtake us; all of our energy is used to acquire more and more; we feel no personal responsibility for others; all of us are bound to an impersonal system that keeps us running.[10]

Many well-meaning people get caught in this story since it is a sacred story with underlying roots we cannot see or control; it controls us. It is Luis in *La Carreta*, René Marqués's prophetic play that tells of Puerto Ricans as they struggle for self-identity both on the Island and on the mainland, who speaks of something *misterioso en la máquina*, a mystery in the machine,[11] by which he means not only machinery and technology, but the American system that would allow him to make *chavos*, money, and be someone. The story of capitalism had an emanational hold on Luis; it is such a powerful attraction that it becomes a competing emanation and overwhelms his love for the land, which the Puerto Rican *jíbaro*, farmer, always considered to be sacred. It is this competing emanational force of the story of capitalism in Act I, Scene 2, that inspires Luis and so many others like him to leave the island in search of a better life. What Luis, like so many of us, fails to do is to test the inspirations that come to us from the depths to see whether it is in fact a new and better voice urging us toward transformation. Luis remains enthralled and entangled in the new story of capitalism, unable to analyze what it does to him and to his family. The new inspiration gives him the impetus to rebel against the peonage of the past and to enter Act II, Scene 1, and to leave behind specific conditions of exploitation; but he became a new kind of *peón*, a person still owned by the powerful, but now in the form of an impersonal machine. One of the most poignant lines in the play is when Doña Gabriela says of Luis: "Es como un cabrito buscando a su mama."[12] He is like a little kid, or child, looking for his mother. This statement expresses Luis's profound sense of loss as he tries to assimilate into the value system of capitalism. His journey ends tragically when *el hombre quedó atrapado*, Luis is trapped in the machine at his place of work and it tears him to pieces.[13]

Like all other groups, we want a better life and for many this means to assimilate into the official story of United States society. Why? We are told that if we want to make it, we must learn to play the game, that is, the story of capitalism, because it is the only game in town. In terms of the core drama, this means arresting life in Act II, Scene 1, a permanent polarization of competition against potential rivals after which none of us can afford to be who we are. This story locks us all into a constant rebellion against the powerful. We cannot rest; we are driven to rebel again and again in order to grasp for power because without it in this society we are considered to be failures. There is no end to the desire to acquire more and more. Our young people and newly arrived Latino immigrants are encouraged to assert themselves by taking advantage of a new life. But rather than being encouraged to create something fundamentally new and better, people get caught as partial selves believing that freedom means being released from responsibility toward others. Thus, in the story of capitalism in the service of the way of life of incoherence, we build fortresses in a world of organized insecurity and power.[14]

Yet many say there is no alternative to this official story. American history books tell us that every other group after several generations made it by assimilating (obviously, not African Americans, American Indians, or many Asian Americans), so why not us? Yet Puerto Ricans, who are American citizens, and Mexican Americans, some of whom can trace their ancestry in this country back seventeen generations, are still not making it. But some of us are successful and achieve status, notably the Cuban community in Florida. And yet all of the latest statistics on Latinos are very alarming. Whether it be educational levels, unemployment, health, or other indices, the situation is serious and deteriorating. We are caught up in a story that we inherited from the dominant American society, the story of capitalism, but we are not getting ahead.

Of its very nature, the way of life of incoherence is fragile. It cannot respond to fundamentally new kinds of problems precisely because those issues demand a consciousness and an insight that are undermined by this way of life. The story of capitalism in the service of incoherence is inherently undemocratic, hierarchical, and authoritarian; it is always on the verge of violence since the powerful treat human beings as means, as tools to their ends. This drama stands in contradiction to a liberal democratic society with which it is in constant conflict. The powerful know that the system is calculated to tilt in their favor.

The most powerful authoritarian constraint in a democratic liberal society upon most men and women—and in most of the world even children—is the drama of capitalism. For most people, it determines who works, who is not hired and who is fired. It sets the working conditions, however hard or intense, without flexibility or adequate time for employees to participate in other dramas, including family life and community life. It pays most workers as little as possible—unless unions or the state set higher standards. Capitalism decisively shapes the conditions and quality of most lives. . . . The capitalist market constitutes part of the drama that depersonalizes—reduces the being—of the less powerful just as much as it does that of the powerful.[15]

The dominant live in constant fear, as they look over their shoulder, that their power will be taken from them. Power (and fear) is all they have; their own story as human beings is for them fulfilled in the pursuit of self-interest. So they live on the edge of the abyss, ready in a moment to use "legitimate" means or extralegal violence to protect what they have. In this way grasping for power becomes destructive death.

Since the drama of capitalism permeates our society, all of us are in danger of being caught by this sacred story and of believing that there is no other way. In this way even the poor in la comunidad Latina collude with and in their own oppression. They begin to believe the official story. If you are poor in such a marvelous system, it is your own fault, and so they hate and blame themselves. Yet it is fear of losing their power to the disinherited in collusion with the story of racism that compels the dominant to exclude the poor from a better life. The very logic of power at the heart of capitalism means that it cannot be shared, only judiciously distributed to keep people in line. This is the meaning of distributive justice: Give out benefits, but never allow the recipients to participate in the decision-making process of that distribution.[16]

The powerful want the poor to fail and remain the object of their largesse. To justify the failure of the excluded, the dominant point to allegedly inherent gender, racial, and ethnic deficiencies and thus practice sexism and racism. To hang onto power, the racist and sexist ploy is inevitable. Thus we have the alliance of two stories and of two ways of life: racism and sexism in the service of deformation and the story of capitalism in the service of incoherence, which, because of its fragility is increasingly turning toward deformation. Together these stories in the service of deformation and incoherence devastate our community.

Those of us who do succeed are tempted to believe that the system works, that the dominant are fair, that problems are due to our own people remaining culturally inadequate. In this way some among us practice the story of racism against our own people, urging them to assimilate. Other upwardly mobile Latinas and Latinos truly want to help the community. Yet they believe that as long as Latinos stay in their inherited culture, the community will not make it in the market society. In fact, even if all of us accepted the dominant story of capitalism as the way to a better life, given the very dynamics of competition, only some, often only a few, would make it. But many of us as middle-class professionals cannot see what is at stake since we get caught in the power of this sacred story that mutes our consciousness and moral courage. It is for this reason that others of us oppose assimilation. Assimilation means becoming like the dominant because they are allegedly superior. But the deeper meaning and danger of assimilation is that we believe that we can make it in the story of capitalism. Thus what we really assimilate into is not some kind of mystical skin color called white, but the underlying sacred story of capitalism in the service of incoherence that arrests us as partial selves in the first scene of the second act of the core drama of life. We are possessed by sources that prevent our being who we are. This is the real tragedy of assimilation, for us as well as for the dominant.

We need to reject as a fantasy and a lie the belief that the archetypal drama of capitalism is the answer to all of our problems. This story fails us all, Latino and European American alike. Because we live this story in a truncated way of life, wherein our humanity is obscured in the service of incoherence, we cannot respond to problems that involve a radical transforming of our society.

What effect does this story and way of life have on the four faces of our being as members of la comunidad Latina? If we are arrested in Act II, Scene 1, in the service of incoherence in the story of capitalism, we put on a personal face that is cagey, seeking to market ourselves by hiding our deeper self. Our political face, that is, what we can and need to do together, is impoverished and reduced to seeking to attach ourselves to the powerful, which means abandoning the powerless. Our historical face becomes one of struggling over time to become a more powerful fragment, getting ahead by acquiring degrees or skills. Our sacred face is inspired by the lord of incoherence who whispers that power is the only thing. The consciousness inherent to capitalism really cuts us off from any deeper, radical, and compassionate analysis or solution. For this reason those of us who practice the story of capitalism in the service of incoherence remain partial selves in a fragile way of life anxious to suppress any criticism or rebellion from within our own community lest it erode our privileges.

THE INHERITED LATINO CULTURE: THE STORY OF UNCRITICAL LOYALTY

Our forebears brought with them to the United States a very powerful and self-wounding drama that I have begun to identify as the story of uncritical loyalty. But even prior to our Latin-American experience, our Spanish ancestors were deeply influenced by the story of uncritical loyalty. This story was enhanced and deepened by the Counter Reformation of the sixteenth century, in which Spain was the leading force. As a result, the Spaniards emphasized a

Catholicism that was dogmatic, hierarchical, and ahistorical. When we look inside the story of uncritical loyalty, we discover the following characteristics: an
inability and even refusal to analyze or be critical; a profound personal repression, a repression so deep that even the repression is repressed; the forbidding
of new consciousness and creativity because they represent a fundamental questioning of the final truth and are therefore sinful and heretical; a hierarchical
determination of the flow of truth and authority; love as obedience to others;
and, finally, excessive and unquestioning obedience and selflessness.

But not all conformed; there is also the Spain of the Renaissance that led
many to raise fundamentally new kinds of questions, often under very dangerous
circumstances. There has always been a counter tradition, created by individuals
and groups who practiced dissent from the official story in a subversive manner.
There is evidence that Ignatius Loyola covertly practiced transformation in his
famous *Spiritual Exercises*, which have been used for centuries to prepare new
generations of Jesuits to confront the world. Subversion as a strategy of transformation will be further discussed in the last chapter of this book.

The majority, but by no means all, of our ancestors in Spain and Latin America remained arrested in the way of life of emanation in Act I, Scene 1. Conflict
and change were discouraged in favor of continuity and cooperation with a
justice that provided a seemingly unlimited security. As a result, this way of
life injured us by maintaining us as a people in a fragile container that makes
it dangerous and almost impossible to respond to fundamentally new kinds of
problems. Most of us were raised never to show disrespect by questioning authority. Everything was God's will, *la voluntad de Dios; cariño*, affection, was
coopted as a reward for being totally obedient. If we dared to be disloyal, we
were warned about the inevitable *castigo de Dios*, God's punishment.

This inability, this woundedness, is quickly seen when we see what this story,
arrested in Act I, Scene 1, of the core drama, does to the four faces of our
being. Our personal face is repressed because you and I do not count, only the
Church, only our father, only the family. In regard to our political face, we
practice unquestioning loyalty to those in official capacities of authority. There
is no history in the sense that you and I can participate, only a past that is
repeated generation after generation. The sacred face of our being is not our
deeper self connected to the deepest source, but we are dominated by a lord of
sin, shame, and guilt who will punish us for any deviation.

This story of uncritical loyalty, practiced for centuries by most of our foremothers and forefathers, is now everywhere being questioned and overturned.
But powerful fragments of this story remain, so that it is still one of the principal
stories in our community. Increasingly Act I, Scene 2, erupts as our inner voice,
and the deeper self is inspired by the deepest source to leave this collapsing
story and continue on the journey. But what strengthens the tradition of uncritical loyalty in the service of emanation is the assault on our community and
culture in this country. Newly arrived immigrants, who also have faced the story
of capitalism and racism in Latin American urban settings, find themselves once

again facing *el choque de las culturas*, living in two competing, conflicting cultures, between clashing stories and ways of life. As a result, many of us are caught in a double consciousness, living as fragments running between one story and way of life at home and another story in the public realm of our lives.

This dilemma leads to a great deal of anxiety. At home as the story of uncritical loyalty is daily questioned, partly because of the influence of the wider society, there arises a reactionary politics to save the old story because it upholds inherited relationships of authority and power. As the story of uncritical loyalty is endangered, it exposes and thus places at risk another story at the heart of our culture: the archetypal drama of patriarchy.

THE ARCHETYPAL DRAMA OF PATRIARCHY AND THE FOUR FACES OF OUR BEING

To better understand the four faces of our being in regard to our culture and one of the most serious problems that we face in la comunidad Latina, let us consider the drama of patriarchy, an inherited story that has played a crucial role in our heritage. This is a perennial cultural story that all of us have experienced that continues to haunt us.

Patriarchy legitimizes the systematic subordination and domination of women by men. The daily practice of patriarchy is a concrete manifestation of an archetypal drama. To wrestle with individual, concrete patriarchal fathers, rulers, or other authority figures is necessary, but not enough. We have to confront the deeper story, the archetypal roots of the story in underlying sacred sources. Almost always we confront the archetypal story of patriarchy only on the concrete level, defining the struggle in terms of our actual fathers. Because we fail to engage the story on the deeper, sacred level, it continues to manifest itself generation after generation.

This story can only come to an end when we refuse to continue to give it our allegiance. For example, when Cleófilas in ''Woman Hollering Creek''[17] refuses to continue the story of patriarchy in her life, as a Latina, Mejicana, Chicana, she takes on the ahistorical tyranny of the inherited past and initiates the most fundamental story of her and our lives, the core drama of life, the story of transformation. In resisting the physical abuse of her husband that the tradition had told her was her personal fate, her political duty to uphold, her historical heritage, and the will of the lord of emanation, Cleófilas leaves Act I, in the service of the way of life of emanation, and enters Act II, Scene 1, whereby she rejects this particular man. Cleófilas is moving toward transformation as she painfully comes to the realization of the need to confront patriarchy, with all of its roots connecting it to a deeper sacred realm represented by the *arroyo*, creek, that she has to cross, to break with her past. By saying no and leaving her husband, Cleófilas moves toward transformation by manifesting a new self, a woman who dared to be a person; she practices a new political face by rejecting the social and political structures that gave a man the right to assault her; by

leaving she creates a new turning point for herself and other women that decisively states that they will take responsibility for a new *herstory*; the sacred is
no longer found outside herself but within.

NEOPATRIARCHY IN THE SERVICE OF DEFORMATION

But something more deformative happened to patriarchy as it was practiced
by our fathers in this country. Because patriarchy and uncritical loyalty as stories
in the service of emanation were always fragile, there was always present the
move into deformation, that is, the threat of the use of violence to enforce these
stories if they were threatened by rebels. Conflicts were inevitable, given the
demands for loyalty at home and the necessity of learning aggressive behavior
to survive in the wider society. Capitalism did much to undermine the authority
of the inherited stories of la comunidad Latina, thus creating a great deal of
incoherence in the family. The fragmenting of the emanational container in the
home gave rise to a new version of patriarchy, neopatriarchy.[18] Neopatriarchy
is an extreme form of patriarchy that was born as an attempt by males to hold
on to their ego identity as formed by the tradition of patriarchy. But this is no
longer possible since the wider cultural, and especially the legal, structures in
the United States, even though patriarchy is still very much alive here, can no
longer be openly supportive of blatant male supremacy. Thus neopatriarchy, in
order to reassert male authority, turned more and more violent in an attempt to
prevent the death of the emanational hold of patriarchy over its members.

As the inherited traditional relationships of emanation, subjection, buffering,
and direct bargaining in the service of emanation that connected parents to
children were being broken, the ninth relationship, of deformation, was used to
prevent rebellion. This use of force was in the service of deformation. Although
a beating or constant verbal violence may not actually kill someone, the violence
moves us toward destructive death. Any use of violence that diminishes a person's humanity puts that person and the perpetrator on the road to deformation,
the exit from the core drama of life. For many threatened males, the downturn
into the politics of the abyss often takes the form of battering women and
children.[19]

In this regard a new archetype emerged for Latinas and Latinos, the disappointed male, who became more abusive. In order to compensate for the collapse
of their world, many men turned to physical violence. The archetype of the
disappointed male is an expression of neopatriarchy, a more virulent form of
the drama of patriarchy. The disappointed male is another expression of the
partial self. He is dangerous because he cannot respond to new issues with love
and openness. There is only a partial self present, a repressed, fearful self, too
loyal to the ahistorical past and too afraid of the unknown future to be able to
develop the new consciousness necessary to move beyond the collapse of the
old stories.

Laura Esquivel's *Like Water for Chocolate* is a novel, later made into a highly successful movie, that provides us with an excellent example of seeing how the various Latino stories hang together to create a web of meaning, a whole cultural context.[20] The novel also demonstrates how we as Latinas and Latinos can intervene in our cultures to practice transformation. But it is also a work of art that shows us the need for continuous transformation in all aspects of our life as members of la comunidad Latina.

The novel is permeated by the stories of matriarchy/patriarchy, romantic love, and uncritical loyalty in the service of emanation. Pedro and Tita's relationship is dominated by the story of romantic love that has colluded with the stories of uncritical loyalty and patriarchy. But as the tradition is threatened, especially by Tita, violence is used to preserve the power of these sacred stories. As the novel develops, Tita's life, and by extension the lives of women as a whole, is increasingly diminished, and thus these stories are now enacted in the service of deformation. Specifically, romantic love turns the lovers into projected fantasies so that they might possess each other. Nobody is home in this drama because the two have lost their unique selves in each other. In this story of possessive love, when the relationship breaks or is threatened, violence is often present. What is always found in this drama on both sides is a suicidal sense of loss: I cannot live without you. You are my only reason for living.

This sense of loss and despair in the story of romantic love is also experienced by María in Demetria Martínez's *Mother Tongue*.

When no phone call came, I curled up like a shrimp until midnight cast its nets and hauled me to sleep. Another time I held my finger above the flame of my Guadalupe flame and held it there to see how long I could take the heat. When he didn't call, my world shriveled. Fetal position. . . . Or when he called and didn't say, I love you, I shattered, then mistook a piece of myself for the whole, a mistake that disfigures women's lives time and again.[21]

Both of these novels are politically important because the message for Latinas is that romantic love is a story that leads women to repress their own personal desires and needs, to practice a politics of unquestioning loyalty to men, which leads them to repeat the personal and historical lives of their mothers while they fail to see their own lives as sacred since the lives of men are allegedly more valuable. Because the four faces of women's being are so undermined, there is a deep sense of loss that tells Latina women that rebellion and resistance are ultimately futile, since these acts cannot fundamentally change women's lives. This tragic sense of life gives too much power to the tradition and fatalistically turns women—and all of us who struggle against an emanational past—into permanent walking victims. The story of romantic love, together with that of uncritical loyalty, renders Latino men and Latina women powerless and turns us toward a deadly fatalism that ends in a loss of self.

THE ARCHETYPAL DRAMA OF TRANSFORMING LOVE

There is an alternative story by which to intervene and radically change the relationship between Latina women and Latino men. First, it is necessary to empty ourselves of the story of romantic love in the service of emanation and to send this story and way of life into the abyss at the exit from the core drama in Act II, Scene 2. In the first scene of Act III, we are filled with a new inspiration that urges us to create the story of transforming love, wherein we meet real men and women who are fully present. The archetypal drama of transforming love affirms the sacredness of men and women equally. We love in order to find out who we are as unique persons *in order to be able* to love others as ourselves. In the story of romantic love, we do not find out who we are; both persons lose their own personal and sacred faces through a desire to fuse themselves into the other for the sake of security. This leads them to take on a political and historical face that excludes others from their relationship while the need to create a new and better story grounded on a politics of equality and justice between men and women passes them by.

In contrast to the utter devastation and suicidal violence that may come when a relationship of romantic love ends, in the story of transforming love when the relationship ends, each partner is hurt but not destroyed, since both have an authentic self that was discovered in the relationship. Both persons can walk away because what the relationship provided for each other was the gift of their own selves. In the story of transforming love, each person is enabled to live fully their four faces of being. The two living their own stories can help each other to discover their own uniqueness. Only then can they create a new and better story together. They are fully present to their own needs, those of the other, and those of the wider society; their ability to find out who they are frees them to see and bring into being new and more loving possibilities in the political and historical faces of their being and that of others. These two fundamentally different kinds of love and the stories of matriarchy/patriarchy and uncritical loyalty will be fully explored as we follow Tita and Latina women through the core drama of life in chapter 3 of this book.

CRITIQUING BOTH CULTURES

It is necessary to critique the stories of both Latinos and European Americans because the answer for Latinos is not to condemn European-American culture and romanticize a Latino past. Nor is the answer to reject our heritage and assimilate into the official story of U.S. society. And above all, any alternative based on revenge against the dominant is no answer at all. This means that any response in the service of the truncated ways of life of emanation, incoherence, or deformation is totally bankrupt.

Many of the angry writings of the early and late sixties by authors like Juan Soto, Oscar Zeta Acosta, José Antonio Villareal, Arturo Islas, Rodolfo Acuña, the early writings of Cherrie Moraga, and Gloria Anzaldúa, among others, were necessary to awaken us from a kind of personal, political, historical, and sacred amnesia.[22] But then they stopped. They didn't take us beyond the anger; there were no strategies of what to do next. So we were left dangling in our *coraje*, anger, lost in rebellion, not sure what to do next. Like individuals, whole communities can get caught up in a prolonged adolescence that began with such promise. Adolescents experience a surge of youth: "it is a time of enthusiasm, idealism, and commitment. It is a time of courage and openheartedness, of genuine warmth, kindness, love, creativity and a love of life . . . of opening to a new world, and loving the world one opens to."[23] This is the kind of exhilaration people felt in the Chicano, Puerto Rican, and other Latino liberation movements when they first began as rebellions against the emanational container of European-American society. This rebellion was necessary to reject the attraction to the story of power prevalent in the wider society, as well as the web of emanation of our fathers and mothers. We left the worlds of emanation and assimilation and opened ourselves to the journey of transformation. But many of us, because we lacked a theoretical perspective, became involved in one-act dramas of rebellion that identified one issue, such as education. But because we couldn't see the relationship between the stories and how they hung together, we dedicated ourselves to incremental change, reform that often ended by strengthening the system. Sporadic forays into violence were acts of despair that demonstrated that we were not sure what to do next.

Our current situation is urgent. The economic pressures currently experienced in U.S. society expose the inability of those taken over by the story of capitalism in the service of incoherence to respond to the needs of others. Workers lose their jobs as corporations downsize in order to maximize profits. As many as 22 million workers in 1995 were working part-time, and 2.1 million were only able to find temporary jobs in most cases with lower pay, no health insurance, and no other job benefits. As of 1993 32 percent of all men between 25 and 34 years of age earned less than the amount necessary to keep a family of four above the poverty line.[24] The actual income for 90 million private sector employees in 1995 was 5.5 percent lower than in 1987.[25]

Social programs are cut back in order to save the economy, that is, save the system on behalf of the powerful, which means saving the story of capitalism and the way of life of incoherence. These tactics cause despair and suffering. Greed becomes destructive death and, thus, leads us as a society into the politics of making life fundamentally worse. The story of tribalism in the form of racism, ethnocentrism, and xenophobia is becoming more prevalent as a justification for labeling citizens of color and new immigrants as inadequate or incapable of being citizens.

LA COMUNIDAD LATINA AT RISK: THE POLITICS OF DEFORMATION

The stories of patriarchy, romantic love, and uncritical loyalty enacted in the service of emanation, arrested in Act I of the core drama, is of little help to la comunidad Latina. As Latinos encounter the brutality of capitalism, the increasing madness of racism as a form of tribalism, and at home the violence of neopatriarchal males seeking to assert their authority, how will entreaties for greater loyalty to the family and established authority help us, especially since the old institutions and stories are crumbling?

In the search for new sources of family and identity, Latino gangs emerge that symbolize a return to what is really an old form of the patriarchal *cacique*, chieftain, the conquering hero of the barrio who will allegedly restore pride in the community. This is a search for emanational substitutes to provide security and a web of life and meaning. It is a pseudoemanation, a fake, because it is an attempt to restore the old world of emanation in which everyone knew who they were because everyone was loyal to the same stories and values. The presence of patriarchal *lideres*, leaders who are really another incarnation of the *patrones*, the bosses of times past, is a symptom of our hanging onto stories that hold out no hope of helping us with our problems.

There is nothing new here. It is return of the old emanational stories of uncritical loyalty, patriarchy, and romantic love, although with different faces. These stories continue to fail us because, as Latina women and Latino men, we cannot be fully present as real persons with creative imaginations, only as caricatures of what others want us to be.

Despair is leading us daily to more and more self-wounding as a people. As the stories of our heritage become more problematic and as the dominant society refuses to give us access to the means for achieving better lives, many of our young are turning to forms of violence. In order to succeed in the story of capitalism, because they are denied access and participation, some Latino youth become adept at buying, distributing, and making drugs. Drug production is the leading form of underground capitalism in the world, reaching the phenomenal level by 1994 of $400 billion per year.[26] So what began as a capitalist endeavor to gain power in this society in the service of incoherence leads to the death of our community in the service of deformation as the victims become the victimizers and exit the core drama.

Others seek to do harm to the Anglos or European Americans because they are considered the enemy. Such a response, based on skin color or ethnicity, is racist, and the story of tribalism takes us over. Latinos who choose revenge become rebels. Why rebels? A rebel is a person whose consciousness is controlled by the story of the oppressor. Thus when the rebel acts, it is really a *reaction*, a *reformation*, that is, more of the same, and not a transformation. Rebels know only the story of the dominators and, with a vengeance, do to others what was done to them. Nothing has really changed except the skin color or ethnicity of the oppressor, since the story of tribalism has won once again. If we as a community fail to empty ourselves in Act II, Scene 2, of the story of racism/tribalism on the deeper, archetypal level, we are doomed to repeat it in our rebellion.

Other Latinas/Latinos turn to the self-wounding of gang violence, drugs, sexually transmitted diseases, alcohol, and crime. This self-destructive behavior fulfills the logic of the story of tribalism, because Latinos begin to believe and act out the stereotypes of the dominant.[27]

CHOICES FOR LA COMUNIDAD LATINA

It is up to us, from within the context of our sacredness as selves, to critique and analyze the stories of the culture with one criterion in mind: what is conducive to transformation. We are free to discontinue those stories of the culture which have been discussed, the dramas of uncritical loyalty, patriarchy, and romantic love, as well as the official stories of U.S. society, capitalism, and the story of tribalism/racism, which have wounded our people of both cultures. None of these stories allows us to respond to fundamentally new kinds of problems with love and justice. We can now choose to create and nurture the stories of participatory democracy, transforming love, the guide and the story of the self as concrete expressions of the deepest source. These stories in the service of transformation protect our humanity and affirm the political imperative of discerning what it is that we can and need to do together.

A community and culture resting on the foundations of transformation will be strong because the individual members who comprise the body politic are each valued in their uniqueness. Such a community will be strong, because each group respects the other without giving up the right to be critical of each other. We need one another in order to be fully who we are in our individuality and fully who we are in our common humanity. Robinson Crusoe, after degrading Friday, came to realize that he owed his humanity to Friday.[28] Thus in Act III, Scene 1, we are filled with a new vision; and in the second scene of Act III, we treat this new experience no longer as only a personal and sacred conversion, but we reach out to the other two faces of our and everyone else's being: the political and historical. We test our fundamentally new understanding of love and justice together with others to discover whether it is in truth a fundamentally new and better turning point in our history with respect to the problem at hand.[29]

The four faces of our being and of Latino culture in the service of transformation are dramatically changed. Our personal face comes forth in wholeness as a participatory, compassionate self; the political face of our being reaches out towards others to help enact political strategies of what it is we can and need to do together to include, to share, to build, to heal anew; in regards to our historical face we go beyond the sin of ahistorical living to create a history that is truly transformative because we as Latino men and Latina women participate in creating new and better turning points in our lives here and now.

CONCLUSION: SPEAKING WITH OUR OWN VOICES

Once we have faced ourselves, vomited out the poison of living unconsciously the destructive stories of our own inheritance and those of the wider society, we feel so strong, so free, to discover and practice a new story, a new culture. At the heart of this new culture are people with creative imaginations who are now free to enact the four faces of our being as we practice transformation in all aspects of our life.[30] What we need today is a transforming culture. A transforming culture is a personal, political, historical, and sacred creation in continuous and continuing creation of those who participate in it.

But is this practical? Yes. We can as Latina women and Latino men begin today to practice transformation. Let me give an example. For the past several years I have been teaching a course called Latina/Latino Politics in the United States. I challenge myself and the students, after discussing the various alternatives available to us, to be *in* the story of capitalism, but not *of* the story. We have had many lively discussions on this strategy. What we learned was this: This is the only world we have. We need to take responsibility for it now. We are not powerless victims. As members of la comunidad Latina, we have the right to acquire the necessary skills by which to gain the leverage necessary to change society for the better. For example, we can acquire the relationship of autonomy, which makes us competent in every possible field of human knowledge: medicine, law, engineering, education, computing technology, math, and science. What counts is that we use all of our relationships, especially autonomy and direct bargaining, in the service of transformation. This means being *in* the university, yet refusing to be *of* the university, because too often to be *of* a university is to agree with and exploit the privilege, power, and status of an elite institution.

To refuse to use our educations to become more powerful fragments is to reject the story of capitalism in the service of incoherence that arrests us in Act II, Scene 1, of the core drama of life as partial selves unable to respond to fundamentally new problems. Thus we learn to be simultaneously insiders and outsiders. An insider/outsider is someone who has learned the meaning of and practiced transformation in regard to an aspect of life and does the best she or he can in a society permeated by incoherence and deformation to bring about fundamental systemic change. This kind of resistance is only possible when we are able to link with others in a countercommunity, an affinity group wherein we are able to trust and care deeply for each other. In this kind of community, we can together test new strategies of transformation. In addition, an insider/outsider knows how to subvert the current system so that institutions can be used to protect and enhance the needs of people. For example, an administrator can use the resources of her office to experiment with new ways to shape an environment in which workers are respected *as persons for themselves* as well as for their skills. Such an administrator rejects the violence of domination inherent in all hierarchical elitism that is repugnant to true democracy.

In the final analysis, we all know as Latinas and Latinos that there is no one Latino story or one cultura Latina or comunidad Latina.[31] Latinas from the urban centers of Chile are different from Latinas who come from the rural areas of Guatemala. Latinos born in this country are also different in attitude and outlook from recently arrived Latinos. My mother warned me never to associate with Mexicans from *la frontera*, the northern part of Mexico bordering the United States, because they were not "real" Mexicans. We as Latinos come from different class origins, with varying degrees of racial mixture, of great variety in regard to complexion, stature, and facial features. Some of us are Catholic, others Pentecostal, some agnostic or atheist, others are Jewish or Muslim. And yet as we have seen, we do share common stories even if at times there are different concrete expressions of these stories.

When someone says to me that he/she is a Latino or Latina, I know very little, even if the individual tells me their national origin, class status, sexual preference, and educational level. These are only statistical indices that tell us little about who we really are on the deeper level of our lives. We cannot build an identity on race, class, gender, religious allegiance, or national origin. But as Latinas and Latinos on the deeper level we also live and practice different stories in different ways of life, and each of us has a personal face that makes us different and unique. How then will we ever be able to create a new Latino story and culture in this country?

I can only know what kind of Latinos and Latinas we are and the quality of the stories that we are living by asking the decisive question: *In the service of what way of life are you a Latino or Latina?* To be a Latino in the service of emanation living the story of uncritical loyalty, romantic love, or patriarchy reveals a person unable to respond to fundamentally new kinds of problems, because to question existing masculine authority is unthinkable. Latinos who assimilate into the story of capitalism and practice life in the service of incoherence simply cannot include the whole community, because the consciousness of this way of life expressed in the story of capitalism precludes sharing, justice, compassion, and love. There is only power and domination. Latinos caught up in the service of deformation as victimizers destroy themselves and the community. Whether it be drug dealing or nationalistic fanaticism against European Americans, deformation ends in exiting from the core drama of life where there is violence and destructive death. We must not become victims of deformation who repeat the story of the oppressor by living the same story of tribalism.

SAYING NO TO BEING VICTIMS OR VICTIMIZERS: GETTING OUT OF THE ABYSS

As a community, we can become living examples of how it is possible to get out of the abyss of deformation and to put an end to its vicious cycle by refusing to participate in it. This is the great power that victims have once they decide to end their victimhood. Archetypal sources, in order to remain alive and thriving, need our participation. Our capacity rests in our ability as human beings to say yes and no on the deeper level. By saying no, we can help to put an end to those sacred stories and ways of life that are destructive. By refusing to seek revenge, we deny destructive stories and ways of life any further sustenance. Having paid attention anew to the deepest source of our being in the second scene of Act I, we break with these stories in Act II, Scene 1, by entering into rebellion with those who practice them, and on the deeper level of underlying sacred sources, we say no again and break with the stories and ways of life, in Act II, Scene 2. We send these destructive dramas and not others and ourselves into the abyss. It is this kind of emptying of ourselves on the deeper level that prevents us from becoming sterile rebels caught by the lord of deformation who inspires us not to get mad but to get even. And by saying yes, we can, together with the deepest sacred source, bring about the creation of fundamentally more loving and compassionate stories.

The most authentic Latina women and Latino men, who are creating a new cultura Latina in this country, are those who live and practice life in the service of transformation by caring deeply about the members of our community as well as members of all other groups; they look for ways to make life fundamentally more human and just, now, here, today. Transformation is a continuous choice and creation on our part. We always need to be ready to risk ourselves anew and to take the next step in creating the fundamentally new and better.

In the service of transformation we can as Latinos and Latinas, together with American Indians, European Americans, African Americans, Asian Americans, gays and lesbians, and women as women help to bring about a new American culture, firmly grounded on uniqueness and diversity. Each of us as we struggle to transform our cultural story and ethnic uniqueness continues and enriches the American experiment that held out the promise of a fuller humanity for all of us. Yes, we are members of La Raza, which means not the race but the community, the people. But we are Latinos and Latinas of a particular kind of Raza, or community, because we live and practice the story of transformation that awakens us to the deeper humanity in all of us.

NOTES

1. Margaret Craven, *I Heard the Owl Call My Name* (New York: Dell Paperback Books, 1962), p. 103. See also in this regard David T. Abalos, *Latinos in the United States: The Sacred and the Political* (Notre Dame, IN: University of Notre Dame Press, 1986), chapter 2.

2. Manfred Halpern, "Why Are Most of Us Partial Selves? Why Do Partial Selves Enter the Road into Deformation?" (paper presented at the annual meeting of the American Political Science Association, Washington, DC, August 29, 1991).

3. Juan Gómez-Quiñones, *On Culture* (Los Angeles: University of California Los Angeles, Chicano Studies Center Publications, 1986).

4. Octavio Paz, "Reflections: Mexico and the United States," *The New Yorker*, Sep-

tember 17, 1979, 99, 138–44; see also his critique of Aztec culture, *The Other Mexico: Critique of the Pyramid*, trans. Lysander Kemp (New York: Grove Press, 1972).

5. Manfred Halpern, "Toward an Ecology of Human Institutions: The Transformation of Self, World and Politics in Our Time," (paper presented at the symposium Beyond the Nation-State: Transforming Visions of Human Society, College of William and Mary, Williamsburg, VA, 1993), pp. 7–8.

6. Ibid., p. 11.

7. Richard Griswold DelCastillo, *The Treaty of Guadalupe Hidalgo: A Legacy of Conflict* (Norman: University of Oklahoma Press, 1990).

8. Ronald Takaki, *A Different Mirror: A History of Multicultural America* (Boston, New York, Toronto, London: Little, Brown and Company, 1993).

9. Alan Pifer, *Bilingual Education and the Hispanic Challenge* (New York: President's Annual Report of the Carnegie Corporation of New York, 1979).

10. Marshall Berman, *The Politics of Authenticity, Radical Individualism and the Rise of Modern Society* (New York: Atheneum Press, 1972), pp. 113–44.

11. René Marqués, *La Carreta* (Rio Piedras, PR: Editorial Cultural, 1971), p. 99.

12. Ibid.

13. Ibid., p. 169.

14. Manfred Halpern, "The Archetype of Capitalism: A Critical Analysis in the Light of a Theory of Transformation" (paper presented at the Annual meeting of the American Political Science Association, San Francisco, 1996), pp. 18–19. This is the best analysis of capitalism that I have seen. It is a truly original and brilliant piece of work that shows us the devastating cost of this drama in the service of a partial and wounded way of life.

15. Ibid.

16. Iris Young, *Justice and the Politics of Difference* (Princeton, NJ: Princeton University Press, 1990), pp. 15–38.

17. Sandra Cisneros, *Woman Hollering Creek* (New York: Random House, 1991), pp. 43–56.

18. Hisham Sharabi, *Neopatriarchy: A Theory of Distorted Change in Arab Society* (New York, Oxford: Oxford University Press, 1988), pp. 3–25.

19. David T. Abalos, *The Latino Family and the Politics of Transformation* (Westport, CT, London: Praeger, 1993), 103–7; see also David T. Abalos, "Applying the Story of Transformation to Practice: Images of the Sacred and the Political in Literature," in *Strategies of Transformation Toward a Multicultural Society: Fulfilling the Story of Democracy* (Westport, CT, London: Praeger, 1996); and David T. Abalos, "Latino Female/ Male Relationships: Strategies for Creating New Archetypal Dramas," *Latino Studies Journal* 1, no. 1 (1990): 48–69.

20. Laura Esquivel, trans. Carol Christensen and Thomas Christensen, *Like Water for Chocolate* (New York, London, Toronto: Doubleday, 1992).

21. Demetria Martínez, *Mother Tongue* (New York: Ballantine Books, 1994), p. 96.

22. In my understanding of the anger and frustration due to an inability to go beyond the fight to choose among cultural resistance, assimilation, romanticizing the past, and violence against the dominant, I am indebted to John Moran González, "The Politics of Ethnicity: Cultural Hegemony and Cultural Liberation in Contemporary Chicano Novels" (senior thesis, Department of English, Princeton University, 1988). In his thesis González provides a very fine critique of the early Chicano dilemma of finding alternatives to domination. In this regard, see especially Oscar Zeta Acosta, *The Revolt of the Cockroach People* (San Francisco: Straight Arrow, 1973); Arturo Islas, *The Rain God*

(Palo Alto, CA: Alexandrian Press, 1984); Rodolfo Acuña, *Occupied America: The Chicano's Struggle Toward Liberation* (San Francisco: Canfield Press, 1972); Gloria Anzaldúa and Cherrie Moraga, co-editors, *This Bridge Called My Back: Writings by Radical Women of Color* (Los Angeles, CA: University of California Press, 1980); José Antonio Villareal, *Pocho* (New York: Anchor, 1970); and Sandra Cisneros, *The House on Mango Street* (Houston: Arte Público, 1988). In regard to the Italian community, Robert Anthony Orsi explores the same issues of cultural resistance, assimilation, and persisting in a romanticized past: *The Madonna of 115th Street: Faith and Community in Italian Harlem, 1880–1950* (New Haven, CT: Yale University Press, 1985). Ada María Isasi-Díaz, a feminist Cuban-American theologian, moves beyond the anger of breaking away to creating a better alternative for Latina women: "Ethnicity in Mujerista Theology" (paper presented at a national conference on religion and Latinos in the United States, Princeton University, Princeton, NJ, April 16–19, 1993).

23. For a brilliant analysis of the archetype of the adolescent ego that reveals for us the relationship between the personal and political faces of our being, see Cynthia L. Perwin, "The Ego, the Self, and the Structure of Political Authority" (Ph.D. diss., Princeton University, 1973), p. 645.

24. Lester C. Thurow, *New York Times*, September 13, 1995, as quoted in Halpern, "The Archetype of Capitalism," p. 25.

25. Businessweek, July 17, 1995, Citing Bureau of Labor Statistics, as quoted in Halpern, "The Archetype of Capitalism," p. 25.

26. Halpern, "The Archetype of Capitalism," p. 19.

27. John Staples Shockley, *Chicano Revolt in a Texas Town* (Notre Dame, IN, London: University of Notre Dame Press, 1974), pp. 1–41.

28. Carlos Fuentes, "Writing in Time" *Democracy* 2, no. 1: (1982): 69.

29. Halpern, "The Archetype of Capitalism," p. 6.

30. Henri Corbin, *Creative Imagination in the Sufism of Ibn Arabi* (Princeton, NJ: Princeton University Press, 1969).

31. Kwame Anthony Appiah, *In My Father's House: Africa in the Philosophy of Culture* (New York, Oxford: Oxford University Press, 1992), pp. 3–27.

3

Latinas Overcoming Personal and Political Inequality: Matriarchy in Like Water for Chocolate

In this chapter I would like to go beyond the usual interpretation of such terms and concepts as patriarchy and matriarchy, masculine and feminine, to consider how from the perspective of a theory of transformation we can speak about a way of life in which a woman or man can achieve wholeness, that is, a human being capable of participating in persistent transformation.[1] We do not know the meaning of terms like masculine and feminine. Even when we try to discuss the feminine within each of us, we are so burdened with the masculine interpretation that permeates all of our language that we are left feeling dissatisfied.

To be a whole person is to be both masculine and feminine, for both men and women. Virginia Woolf put it very succinctly when she wrote, "It is fatal to be a man or woman pure and simple; one must be woman-manly or man-womanly. . . . Some collaboration has to take place in the mind between the woman and the man before the act of creation can be accomplished. Some marriage of opposites has to be consummated."[2] For gays and lesbians as well as for heterosexuals the masculine and feminine are necessary for wholeness. By "feminine" or "masculine," I do not mean some human trait that we can arbitrarily designate as feminine or masculine. There is no single or monolithic way, and not even just a few ways, to express the masculine or the feminine. As I understand these two terms, they represent two archetypal forces within each human being that have been radically deformed through the politics of gender roles that attribute to women certain social, personal, and political roles and others to men. Thus, the masculine and feminine, which make sense only as complementary aspects of our being that coincide in wholeness, are both crippled when separated into fragments. On a deeper level, the words "masculine" and "feminine" represent underlying archetypal forming sources that shape the patterns of our lives. Thus, we are in a process of continuous creation as we seek to give new and creative concrete forms to the feminine and masculine in our daily lives. For this reason all of us, both men and women, are in the process of growing the feminine and masculine aspects of our being. As a result, the masculine and feminine will no doubt be expressed differently by actual women and men.[3]

Historically, men have monopolized all connections to those masculine archetypal forces which are useful for their dominance and in the process have limited *both* feminine and masculine archetypes, which are not conducive to male domination.[4] As a result of the dominance of impoverished concrete manifestations of the masculine, not only were men and women in la comunidad Latina cut off from other creative manifestations of the masculine, but we were all deprived of the experience of the feminine archetype of our being. Not to be both masculine and feminine is to have our personhood deeply wounded and fragmented as we become partial selves, cut off from the creative tension within us.

I raise this critique from the perspective of transformation because transformation in our being cannot proceed without the full participation of both masculine and feminine archetypal forces in all human beings. . . . The liberation now being initiated above all by women to free the fullness of the masculine and feminine capacity of being thus inescapably challenges the legitimacy and power of all fragments that seek to arrest and contain people.[5]

This means that Latino men, like all men, need to develop their own feminine selves; similarly, Latina women and women from all ethnic and racial backgrounds must seek the masculine in themselves. Men cannot give birth biologically, but both men and women can be pregnant with new selves. In the archetypal drama of relationships based on mutuality, men and women awaken in one another the desire to be whole and to embrace our complementary sexuality. Yet our society and la cultura Latina often militate against this mutual fulfillment. Therefore, our choice must be clear; to go home is to enter into our deepest source within and to recreate wholeness.

Carl Jung attempted to move us beyond the chasm separating the sexes, but in spite of his contributions, he was too much influenced by cultural filters in addition to the politics of a male-dominated society. Present-day Latina writers and feminists, like Gloria Anzaldúa, Leslie Marmon Silko, Rosa Martha Villareal, Cherrie Moraga, Demetria Martínez, and Sandra Cisneros have performed a great service by contributing a voice that was excluded from the conversation.

We have remained so caught up in the language of the struggle between men and women, however, that we have lost sight of the deeper sources of the dramas that have arrested us in power positions.

Our actual experiences of patriarchy and matriarchy have had real and, more than often, destructive effects upon us. But the concrete reality is only the outward face, since all of our relationships and stories have their roots in underlying sacred forming sources, the world of archetypal dramas and ways of life. When we ask the question In the service of what ultimate way of life am I enacting the archetypal stories of matriarchy/patriarchy? what we are after is both the concreteness *and* the underlying source. In the context of this chapter I will demonstrate that only in the service of transformation are we free as Latina women and as Latino men to participate with the fullness of our being in creating new and better relationships between men and women. In the core drama of life, the journey of transformation, the other three ways of life leave us arrested in a fragment of the core drama of life, as partial selves. If we remain arrested within these fragments of the core drama, then all of our stories and relationships will prevent us from responding to any fundamentally new kinds of problems.

Realizing that our stories and relationships are not only the concrete, lived realities that we share but also manifestations of underlying archetypal sources makes meaningful change more difficult. Many of us thought that change for the better meant becoming aware of those stories that hurt us and fighting against them. Change very often became another version of the same thing or something worse. For people who were caught in destructive stories, any kind of change seemed to be positive. But the underlying sacred roots of these dramas and relationships remain if we free ourselves only from their outer manifestations. Furthermore when we remain unconscious of them, they possess us and take over our lives. Thus when the Bolsheviks got rid of the tsar they replaced him with Joseph Stalin, the new tsar. The names changed, but the underlying archetypal story remained, the story of the tyrant. Too often we say, "I'll never be like that," and then we find that we have become what we hated.

AUTOBIOGRAPHICAL WITNESS

The struggle with the masculine and feminine archetypes and the story of matriarchy/patriarchy and how they can take over our lives on the deeper level I know only too well from my own experience. I was raised as a male in my own Chicano/Mexican tradition that gave me permission to dominate women. In addition, my Catholic training reinforced the patriarchy by teaching me to transcend the body and to use will power and prayer to dominate my own desires by resisting the temptations of the world, which meant sexuality and women. "Priest: The Spirit and the Flesh" by Freddy Rodriguez artistically made this point.[6] This repression, and as Adrienne Rich describes it, the psychic split between the masculine and feminine seeking for reunion,[7] denied the feminine within me. But it also led to the disabling of the masculine as well. I was so polarized living in the masculine patriarchal drama, that I had no awareness that the goal of transformation was to heal the split within me. I fought to survive in a very dangerous world, filled with racism and violence against women. Ironically, I was afraid of the physicality of the Mexican/Indian heritage, which was much more accepting of the feminine and of the body than was the Catholic/ Spanish/European part of me.[8] I believed that I could get away from the past by repressing my sexuality and that of others. I identified sexuality itself with male dominance.

In my attempt to split myself off from the tradition and the stories in which I was raised, especially patriarchy/matriarchy, which I experienced daily, I suffered a profound wounding within my own body and psyche. I did not know how, or even thought it was essential, to bring together the masculine and feminine contraries, as William Blake speaks of the struggle for wholeness.[9] I felt that it was necessary to obliterate the masculine in me since this part of me was the enemy. With a sense of profound fear, as a child I had seen Mexican males express violent rage against women. I felt that my very lifeline was being severed. How could I possibly become such a man? I knew nothing of the conflict raging within me between two worlds, one the European conqueror, the other, the Indian humiliated. In the United States I experienced daily the rejection of my ancestral past as inferior. Thus I was conflicted by my Mexican past, considered a stigma in this country, male violence, sexuality as temptation, fathers as dominators, women and the feminine as victims; all of these issues became terribly confused for me. My response was to romanticize women, choke my sexuality, refuse to be a penetrating, dominant male and to live a life of discipline that would make me acceptable to the powerful around me, especially the magical priests of my home parish.

This was a recipe for self-wounding. I was not reconciling anything, only alienating myself in a deeper way, as a partial self. I was filled with self-denial and a fear that I would give in to the sexuality that I identified with sin, shame, and violence. I became one of those sincere males, sensitive and caring and especially dedicated to preserving the honor of women. It was all a fake. I had no clue as to what to really do to heal the split within me. Rather than face the terror, I went further into the "good" masculine/patriarchal world of the Catholic priesthood. Why was this the answer? It was a world without all of the pain that I identified with passion (violence?), sex, the body, temptation, and domination of others, especially women. How did I prove myself in this new arena? By becoming more patriarchal than they, my fathers, through intense study and learning that allowed me to prove my worth to them, the others, the better, the best. I became one of the best by outbettering them as I studied and worked for most of the day. Another irony was that I thought that patriarchy was only a story that belonged to my Mexican past and not to European white males. In this way the war between my Spanish and Indian roots raged on, without my knowing it.

I met some deeply caring priests who stepped into my life as guides at a crucial point. If I had not discovered through them a different kind of drama of patriarchy, which has a creative side in nurturing care and self affirmation, I would never have made it out of the world of violence and the gangs that we formed in order to survive. I owe a great debt to these men, who were able to rise above the stories of their own training and reach out to me as the father that I never knew. But I held on to the repression inherent in patriarchy long after it had served to rescue me from the possessiveness of my mother and the violent streets of Detroit.

But there was something else; priests were special not only because they were males, but they were also pure, that is, they didn't have sex. This made them heroic figures in a world filled with sexual and other demons. This appealed to my sense of adventure and challenge as I sought to separate myself from my own matriarchal mother. I knew nothing of the world of underlying sacred sources, and so I replaced the story of matriarchy with that of patriarchy with my adopted fathers. What I also did not know was that matriarchy was really the same story of patriarchy with a feminine face. My mother had said often that now that my father was dead, she was in charge. There are clearly other forms of matriarchy, some which are positive, but for our purposes I shall be defining matriarchy as another face of the story of patriarchy whenever both stories concern themselves with domination and control.[10] Thus I had not really experienced change for the better. I, however, believed that I had put myself in a situation in which I could silence the issues of my identity and sexuality by fusing with others who confirmed me in the battle against my sexuality.

But fortunately our bodies and the deepest sacred within us give us no such false peace. Again and again the source of transformation intervened to upset my denial. This experiment in repression did not work; it constantly collapsed as I found myself against my will feeling a violent rage, experiencing sexual desires, and flirting with danger—my Mexican identity. I was painfully split at the root of my person. Repression wants nothing to do with the resurrection from death or transformation, but with maintaining a web of life that is given a life of its own while it consumes the life of the contained.

One of the reasons that I left home was because I seriously disagreed with the domination of women legitimized by the story of patriarchy. I did not like the way that my father had controlled my mother, and I objected to the manner in which my older brother and godfather related to women. My parting shot was that I would never be like them. As a result of education and travel, I thought that I had left the story behind me. But at that time I still believed that it was enough to become an intellectual revolutionary. I knew nothing of the world of archetypal, underlying sacred forces that constituted the grounding of stories that possessed us when we remained unconscious of them. Because I had merely broken with the actual concrete actors of this story in Act II, Scene 1, but had failed to empty myself on the deeper level in Act II, Scene 2, of the story enacted in the service of emanation that gave them their power, I woke up one day and realized that I was one of them.

I had failed to empty myself in Act II, Scene 2, of the underlying story and the ways of life that gave ultimate justification to the domination of women. It was necessary for me to reject the stories of patriarchy and romantic love on the deeper level in order to be filled anew by the deepest source in Act III. The way of life of transformation provides the only context within which we can express the capacity, freedom, and wholeness of being human both in our concrete creation and in our sacred depths and thus fully realize love and justice. The source of sources is free to continuously recreate the world only when we are prepared to participate in its transformation. In this way we incarnate the sacred source that inspires us, that actually breathes within us. Participation in persistent transformation belongs to each of us, of the very nature of our humanity. Each of us has the responsibility and joy of living the story and journey of transformation in all aspects of our lives.

I have returned once again to this very personal tone in order to show that the writing of this book is for me at once a personal, political, historical, and sacred task. I want to know how and why I as a Latino male have been badly wounded by the archetypal stories of patriarchy/matriarchy and romantic love and how these stories contribute to a culture wherein Latina women are unable to overcome the politics of inequality. I also want to show how these kinds of stories, because they prevent our personal wholeness, cripple our political capacity to shape a more just and compassionate society, deny us the right to create new stories, and cut us off from our own sacredness, which is rooted in the deepest of sacred sources, the source of the fundamentally new and better. But I want to go beyond mere understanding to see how we can transform our lives so that the wholeness we seek as men and women becomes a reality in all aspects of our lives.

LITERATURE, THEORY AND POLITICS

For years I have taught all of my courses with literature, primarily novels. Somehow I intuited that the authors that I used were doing more than narrative; they were writing the stories as they came to them from deeper sources. They were telling our stories, and as Leslie Marmon Silko has taught us, we should never be fooled into believing that they are just stories. If we do not have them, we have no way of warding off illness and death.[11] In telling the story, every writer was living a personal story that reached out to all of us so that together we could test the reality of the world in which we lived. All writing is political. In addition, the stories opened up new ways for us to see our past, our present, and intimations of how to create a new story, that is, a different history; the personal, political, historical faces of storytelling are ultimately grounded in the depths of sacred sources. But, once again relying on Silko, we have to be able to tell the differences between the stories of witchery and destructive death and those of life and transformation.

To be able to discern on the deeper level the meaning of the stories that these authors were writing, I read and taught them from the perspective of our theory of transformation. In this way, together with my students, I could apply theory to practice. We were able to test the theory and to see whether we gained a much better understanding of the novel. And of course, since these writings have a personal, political, historical, and sacred face, then we could test both the theory and the literature with our own four faces. We gained the right to legitimize our own personal views, since our experience was called upon by the author. We learned that we always had a political face, since our personal views shaped the dynamic of the classroom. We were giving contours to a historical face by telling a new story, our story, that had been denied under the guise of being "subjective" and therefore unworthy of "objective" discourse. Finally, we discovered that there had to be some deeper source from which this creativity came to bless our faces.

For so long we have lost our way in the realm of theory. We have all been turned into abstractions by the structures and functions of so much of our theory, or else into quantified abstractions in the search for certainty. In rebellion, many chose the postmodernist, deconstructionist school, which sought to dismantle the all-encompassing theories that failed to explain what was happening to us. But in deconstructing, we are left without good theory that allows us to address the quality of change in our lives. We need theory, good theory, that gives us the capacity to understand our choices and the deeper meaning of what we decide on. On this matter of the current suspicion of theory among academics there is an excellent article[12] in which the author speaks of the dearth of good theory and mentions that perhaps we can find a theoretical basis in the literature of women and people of color. According to the article, in these writings we encounter people who were marginalized and, so writing from the other side of the boundaries of power, they might be able to tell their story and our story with much more insight and integrity. But the author saw this writing as perhaps the only viable alternative for theory. Yes and no. I agree with the substance of his argument regarding the superb scholarship and creative works that are being published daily by the previously excluded, but I do not share his pessimism regarding the lack of theory; we can have both, that is, combine theory and the stories from the margin to tell again for our time the drama of transformation.

APPLYING THEORY TO PRACTICE: RE-VISIONING *LIKE WATER FOR CHOCOLATE*

What so many Latina women continue to experience and the choices that are available to them can be fruitfully discussed by analyzing a remarkable novel, Laura Esquivel's *Like Water for Chocolate*, from the perspective of the theory of transformation. We can best do this by following Tita, the protagonist, through the three acts of the drama of transformation. The most important stories that we will see Tita living are the stories of matriarchy/patriarchy, in collusion with the dramas of possessive, romantic love, and uncritical loyalty; these arrest her in the way of life of emanation in Act I, Scene 1, of the core drama of life.

THE ARCHETYPAL DRAMA OF MATRIARCHY

I will define matriarchy as an archetypal story that is a rebellious response to the story of patriarchy. Matriarchy is a reformation, not a transformation, of patriarchy; it is patriarchy with a female face: "I am a woman; I am in charge now"; "Now that your father is gone, I am both your mother and your father." In this scenario, women wield power and accept the inevitability of domination. But this is another form of the archetypal drama of patriarchy, in this case with a woman's face. By not attacking the very heart of patriarchy, which is rooted in the assertion of the superiority of one gender over the other, women help to perpetuate the tyranny of gender by becoming matriarchs. To continue this story, with women now in charge, means that women become rebels; that is, they now exercise the same power that men held and so are caught by the consciousness of the story of the oppressor.[13] There are creative forms of matriarchy,[14] but as long as it becomes or remains another aspect of domination based on gender, it cannot be in the service of transformation. As we go through the novel, the issues raised here will be further elaborated by giving an actual description of the story of matriarchy/patriarchy in action.

TITA AND THE CORE DRAMA OF TRANSFORMATION

As the novel begins, Tita's life is arrested in the first scene of Act I of the drama of transformation. All children need to be loved and provided for in order to be able to grow into mature women and men. Why then do I say that Tita is arrested in the first scene of Act I? Her mother, Mamá Elena, has no intention of using their life on the ranch in northern Mexico as a merciful, temporary container providing a stepping-off point for Tita's journey into her own life. Mamá Elena declares that, as the youngest daughter, Tita's duty is to take care of her mother until the older woman dies. Even in the womb, Tita has sensed that this would be her fate, which is why she instigated her own birth by shedding such a torrent of tears that it brought on her mother's labor. Furthermore she was born in the kitchen, crying because she knew intuitively that she would never be allowed to marry; this room was to be her domain for life.

Like Julie in Rousseau's *La Nouvelle Héloïse*,[15] Mamá Elena has to hide her own repression by repressing everybody else lest any show of passion would threaten the deadly order that comes from the strangling of sexuality. As a young woman, Tita dares to fall in love with Pedro Múzquiz. Mamá Elena moves quickly to remind Tita that her life belongs to her mother. Tita is reminded of the family tradition that since she is the youngest daughter, it is her duty to take care of her mother until the day of her death. But Tita cannot accept this tradition and for the first time in her life begins to protest:

"But in my opinion . . ." "You don't have an opinion, and that's all I want to hear about it. For generations, not a single person in my family has ever questioned this tradition, and no daughter of mine is going to be the one to start."[16]

Within this quotation we can see from the perspective of our theory of transformation the following: Tita is caught by the story of matriarchy in the service of emanation in the first act and scene of the core drama of life. According to tradition she has no right to question. By so doing, she creates conflict and change which threatens her security. As long as she surrenders her self and doesn't cause any problems, Tita is safe. But Tita is resisting; she is responding to something very new in her life: sexual passion. This is, of course, Mamá Elena's greatest fear. We also see in this quotation the inherent fragility of the way of life of emanation. It is heresy to question established authority. As the guardian of this way of life, which also protects her from herself, Mamá Elena is always on the verge of violence to ensure its maintenance. But Tita has listened to her inner voice in Act I, Scene 2, and speaks up in order to respond to this new voice and story that arises as a competing sacred source out of the depths. But she is suppressed since she refuses to dutifully repress herself.

The four faces of Tita's being are also evident. Tita has no right to her own personal needs or desires; her life is not important. It is her duty to practice a politics of unquestioning loyalty to her mother. Her historical face is shaped only by repeating the stories of the past. The dominating sacred in Tita's life is the force within her, the lord of emanation, that collaborates with her mother by legitimizing Tita's repression. Wounded as she is, Tita still fights back; doubts and anxieties continue to spring to her mind. But it is no use. As Tita moves toward rebellion in the first scene of Act II, there is nobody there to assist her, not even Pedro. To remove the threat of rebellion and the possibility of sexual passion as a chaotic force on the family, Mamá Elena moves quickly to marry off her daughter Rosaura to Pedro. In this way Mamá Elena can cut off Tita's rebellion and assure that Pedro and Rosaura's marriage would be a negotiated business venture and, therefore, neutralize the danger of sexual passion.

LOOKING INSIDE THE STORY OF MATRIARCHY/ PATRIARCHY

The novel is divided into chapters that correspond to the months of the year. At the beginning of each chapter, there is a recipe for food that gives us an insight into the relationship between various dishes and the Mexican fiestas celebrated throughout the year. Even more importantly, we see the intimate relationship between sex and food in the traditional world of the Mexican household. The kitchen and the bedroom were the only two realms in which a woman was allowed to work her magic, that is, some emanational attractiveness that gave women a temporary relief from drudgery. Concessions were granted by men, when they felt that their needs as masters had been satisfied.[17] But there was often no passion, no feeling, no real depth to the love. It was really about power through covert manipulation. A deadly kind of submissiveness permeated the lives of women and kept them saying: "I'm here to please." In the stories of patriarchy/matriarchy, romantic love, and uncritical loyalty, this meant that food and sex strengthened the stories.

Tita cannot accept the coldness that descends upon her when Pedro is promised to her sister. She resists going under for good and giving in to the cold that comes with repressing one's passion. Even against her conscious will, she fights back. In February it is Tita's job, together with Nacha, the family servant who taught her the mysteries of the kitchen, to do all of the cooking for her sister's wedding. As Tita castrates chickens for the meal, she knows that it is really she who has been victimized. Mamá Elena slaps Tita, using violence to keep Tita in her place. Still Tita rebells; as she makes the chabela wedding cake, Tita cries into the batter so that it can't thicken, and later her tears fall into the meringue icing. That night, after Tita has gone to bed, Nacha tastes the icing and begins to cry, as memories of her own past flowed over her. She remembers that, like Tita, she had not been allowed to marry the man she loved because the mamá of Mamá Elena had run him off.[18] Good servants, who were hard to come by, were cherished as part of the family, so much so that heads of households gave or withheld permission for their servants to marry and often arranged their servants' marriages.[19] Their life was an emanational possession of their masters and mistresses. But what is important to note here is that Mamá Elena is part of a history of domineering women; she is repeating the history of repression that has been practiced by her own matriarchal mother. Tita is but the latest victim of this story.

The following day, at the wedding, a most amazing phenomenon occurs. As people eat the wedding cake, they are overcome with sadness, and they soon begin to cry uncontrollably for lost loves until they get so sick that they begin to vomit: "But the weeping was just the first symptom of a strange intoxication. . . . that seized the guests. . . . all of them wailing over lost love."[20] This extraordinary scene exposes the hidden lies of repression. Nobody is happy because, like Tita, whose tears have awakened in them their sadness, they are suffering from a life without love and passion. That night Nacha dies, clutching her fiancé's picture. Once more Mamá Elena's response is violence; by beating Tita, she is trying above all to break her spirit[21] and to keep her in the container of emanation in the first act of the core drama of life.

Later in the novel we learn the reason for Mamá Elena's cruelty and more about the historical face of the story of matriarchy/patriarchy. As a young woman, Mamá Elena had loved a young mulatto man, of African and Mexican blood. Given the hierarchy of race, class, and gender of the period, there was no way that Mamá Elena's parents would give her permission to marry. The honor of the family was at stake. She was forced into an immediate marriage with Juan De la Garza. Mamá Elena has gone on seeing her lover. As she is about to run away with José, he is killed. Following his death, Mamá Elena resigned herself to a loveless marriage with her legal husband.[22] Because Mamá Elena has settled for less and decided that there is no longer any reason to fight for herself, she surrenders her life to the inherited stories of her traditional past. She continues the tradition by wounding her family in the same way. It is the only way that she can get her revenge on life. And this is how archetypal stories become *ahistorical*; that is, she has a past in which she is no longer an actor, but a passive recipient. This kind of unchallenged tradition freezes our historical face once and for all, in a permanent mold. These stories are carried from one generation to the next, and the persons caught in them continue to wound themselves and others. There is a sense of victimhood with a smell of finality.

Pedro marries Rosaura and thereby coldly uses her, turning her life into an instrument in his self-interest; now he can be near Tita. As they settle down to daily life, Tita cooks for the whole family. In the month of March, she prepares a sensuous feast that is sexual in its intent and in its effect. In this way, through food, she is able to carry on a passionate relationship with Pedro: "That was the way she entered Pedro's body, hot, voluptuous, perfumed, totally sensuous."[23] Her sister Gertrudis is so consumed with passion that she sets the wooden enclosure of the shower on fire and sends off a perfume so permeated with sexual desire that it reaches all the way to the camp of a revolutionary officer. Juan comes for Gertrudis, lifts her onto his horse stark naked and off they ride, making love in the saddle. Both Pedro and Tita watch this with great sadness and anticipation. From the second scene of Act I, inspired by the aching in their own bodies, their move into rebellion in the first scene of Act II is quickly defeated by the story of matriarchy, which pulls them back from their desire.

At this point Pedro and Tita begin to cry. They have been reduced to spectators within a drama in which others act out the love that is forbidden to them. But Pedro has a choice; for a brief instant Pedro can change their story. Taking Tita's hand, Pedro is on the verge of rebellion against their fate. But he is forced back to grim reality. He has heard Mamá Elena shouting. Tita is prepared to enter into rebellion with Pedro against her mother if Pedro asks her to run away with him, but he fails to act.[24]

The grim reality that pulls them back was the story of matriarchy in the service of emanation. This goes far beyond the power of one woman, Mamá Elena. What gives her power over the lovers was deeper underlying forces, the story of matriarchy in the service of emanation, of which she is a concrete manifestation, and which possesses them all, including Mamá Elena. Everybody here is a victim of this story in the service of emanation. As we have seen, Mamá Elena too had been frustrated in her love for José Treviño. To maintain the status quo based on repression, Mamá Elena has to act as if Gertrudis has never existed; she burns her birth certificate and all of her pictures and forbids any mention of her name. The violence that Mamá Elena uses against Gertrudis in this instance and against Tita on other occasions, as we have seen, points out the inherent limits and fragility of the way of life of emanation. Emanation as a way of life prevents us from responding to new kinds of problems. We cannot ask new kinds of questions that threaten to undermine the legitimacy of truths given once and for all. It is the anxiety created by this sense of vulnerability that exposes the violence lying just below the surface of the way of life of emanation. Why violence? Because rather than to respond to new issues openly and with risk, the guardians of this way of life are prepared to use violence against heretics, who could bring down the whole structure upon which their security is grounded.

Thus in the way of life of emanation there is the shadow of the abyss, which awaits those who would dare to defy the truth, established for all time. Since it is only a fragment of the core drama of life, those living within emanation cannot respond to fundamentally new kinds of problems. Thus conflict and change are sacrificed for the sake of cooperation with and continuity of the inherited stories of tradition, such as matriarchy, which provide a numbing security. Tita is limited to an inherited consciousness that forbade new forms of creativity, new kinds of relationships to others, any new forms of justice for herself or others and the deeper alienation from her creative unconscious. As we can see, Tita constantly tries to subvert this orderly repression by testing its limits, especially with her culinary experiments.

Not even in the kitchen can Tita practice transformation. In this realm, she is able to relate to herself and others in a rebellious mode through the very fact that she can experiment. But this too is coopted by the stories in the way of emanation because they prevent her confronting the real issue, her mother and the deeper, underlying sacred stories of matriarchy, uncritical loyalty, and romantic love in the service of emanation that legitimize the whole enterprise of repression. The sexual connection that Tita has made between herself and Pedro with food helps them to live with repression, so that it ends up prolonging the stories that held them bound in the service of emanation.

Tita realizes through the passion that she feels in her body how fire transforms the raw elements, how a lump of maize becomes a tortilla, how a person who hasn't experienced the passion of love is really dead, like a lifeless ball of corn flour.[25] So she turns to the preparation of food so that she can keep alive the passionate connection that she has felt for Pedro since they first met.[26]

In April there is an event that will lead to Tita's open rebellion against her mother, the birth of her nephew, Roberto. Initially, Tita is content to have helped Rosaura to give birth and to feel that life was good, because now she has not only Pedro but also his son, who she believed was just as much her child. So powerful is this child in her life that she was able to breast-feed him even though this is supposed to be impossible. What could have driven them apart brings

Pedro and Tita closer. But always there is the presence of Mamá Elena and the story of matriarchy, which overwhelmed the competing drama of romantic love.

Dr. John Brown has been called in to assist with the birth but, by the time he arrives, Tita has delivered the child, with the spirit of Nacha helping her. Tita's competence and beauty arouse in Dr. Brown feelings that he has not felt since his wife died five years ago. These feelings of sex and passion stir up fear in Mamá Elena. She could sense that something is going on between Tita and Pedro, but she can't see it. If she had known that Dr. Brown would be so taken with Tita, she would not have welcomed him. But it is evident that Tita, at this point in the novel, is a participant in the story of matriarchy. When Dr. Brown speaks of the possibility of Tita having her own child, Tita is visibly shaken: "I can't marry or have children because I have to take care of my mother until she dies."[27] Even though Dr. Brown exclaims that this is absurd, Tita consoles herself by taking the child in her arms and feeling that her fate does not matter with such a child to love. Mamá Elena caps off the day of Roberto's baptism by responding to Father Ignacio that in spite of the dangers due to the outbreak of the Mexican Revolution, she has no use for men: "I've never needed a man for anything; all by myself, I've done all right with my ranch and my daughters. Men aren't that important in this life, Father."[28] This is an excellent statement for a concrete example of the story of matriarchy as the other face of patriarchy.

TOWARD TRANSFORMATION: ACT II, SCENE 1

Knowing that something is going on between Pedro and Tita, Mamá Elena arranges for Rosaura and Pedro to take Roberto to live in San Antonio, Texas. Tita is devastated by this; she loses interest in everything around her. Her only escape is to feed her pigeons and to knit more of her ever-growing bedspread, which she began when Pedro married her sister. She cannot overcome the constant cold that she feels. On the surface there is peace in the household, but it rests on a persistent undercurrent of violence: "Unquestionably when it came to dividing, dismantling, dismembering, desolating, detaching, destroying, or dominating, Mamá Elena was a pro."[29] All of this reactionary behavior on the part of Mamá Elena is done in the service of emanation in collusion with deformation: the insistence on loyalty and the use of violence are devoted to preventing the unraveling of the container of emanation that kept the whole family arrested in the first act and scene of the core drama of life. Mamá Elena is prepared to send Tita into the abyss at the exit from the drama in Act II, Scene 2, just as she has expunged the memory of Gertrudis in order to keep intact the repressive womb of the ranch.

Tita's life in the container of emanation shatters, and she enters into the first scene of the second act of the core drama of life when the news comes that Roberto is dead. After Tita's care and cooking, Roberto couldn't hold down the food that he has been given in San Antonio. Tita explodes in anger. Mamá Elena is threatened by any kind of passion and so forbids Tita's crying. Tita is furious; she stares at her mother in anger and then begins to tear apart the sausages that she is preparing, screaming at her mother in open rebellion and defiance. Mamá Elena attempts to end the rebellion through violence, striking Tita across the face with a wooden spoon.[30]

Tita runs from her mother and goes up to the dovecote, where Mamá Elena cannot pursue her because she is afraid of heights. Dr. John Brown is sent for to take Tita to an insane asylum in Brownsville, Texas.

A RECIPE FOR MAKING MATCHES: GUIDES OF TRANSFORMATION

Under the care of Dr. John Brown, Tita is not sure if she wants to live or die, her mental state symbolized by her refusal to speak. She is overcome with depression, with nothing to live for. Yet Tita is conscious that for the first time in her life she is free. But she doesn't know what to do with this freedom. This is symbolized by her looking at her hands and not knowing what to ask of them because all they have ever known all of her life were her mother's commands.[31]

The chapter entitled "June" is remarkable because it captures the heart of the matter for people who move into rebellion. Tita knows that she can never go back home on her mother's terms. That part of her life is over. But in her prolonged convalescence she is also tempted to give up and, thereby, slowly kill herself. This would mean that the story of matriarchy as manifested in her mother in the service of emanation would have defeated her. In fact, at this point in the story Tita is faced with the challenge of proceeding on to the second scene of Act II, precisely where she could confront the deeper story. Either she can exit the core drama in a kind of living death or she can empty herself, vomit out the story of matriarchy and the web of emanation into the abyss.

At this crucial point in her life, feminine guides appear: Nacha, Morning Light, Chencha, and Gertrudis. Morning Light is Dr. John Brown's grandmother, who was excluded because she was an Indian until she performed a miracle of healing for a family member. Morning Light has often sat with Tita; but like Nacha, who has guided her through the delivery of Roberto, Morning Light is also dead. However, for Tita, Nacha and Morning Light, both strong indigenous women, are very much alive, serving as internal guides. Morning Light also lives on in her grandson, Dr. Brown. As a boy he had been greatly influenced by her knowledge of medicine and by her willingness to experiment. After medical school, his first desire was to prove scientifically all of the miracle cures that she accomplished.

A turning point in the novel comes with the making of matches. Morning Light has said that each of us is born with a box of matches inside us. But we need others to strike them, just as fire requires oxygen. Morning Light has taught her grandson that it is up to each of us to find out what will ignite the matches, since the combustion that occurs provides food for the soul. Fire is what nurtures the soul. Tita is afraid that for her it is already too late because her matches have grown damp and moldy and once they did, they could not ever be lit again.[32] Tita is also given a warning that the matches should be lit one at a time. If a powerful emotion were to set them all on fire, it would lead to death. But Tita's concern is that she might never again feel passion, and she wonders whether Dr. Brown is the one who could kindle her desire.

Tita slowly decides to live but she doesn't know how. She is helped in her desire to live by Chencha, her mother's maid, who feeds Tita oxtail soup. The soup awakens all of Tita's senses and the memory of all the good times in the kitchen with Nacha. They laugh, talk, and cry together until the stairs are flooded with Tita's tears. Tita learns the news of Gertrudis, how she has ended up in a brothel because even the revolutionary officer, Juan Alejándrez, could not satisfy her passion. Morning Light, Nacha, Chencha, and Gertrudis represent for Tita different ways of being a woman and her search for passion, love, bonding, freedom, experimentation, and sensuous cooking. Tita's decision to start a new life is sealed by her engagement to John Brown.

When Chencha returns home, bandits rob them and rape her. Mamá Elena, in her attempt to save her honor, is struck down and paralyzed. Tita knows that she must return home to care for her mother. But it is not the same Tita who comes home. She refuses to allow Mamá Elena to intimidate her. Tita defeats her mother's attempt to stare her down. It is Mamá Elena who lowers her eyes in a kind of submission and admission that she needed Tita. This is the first time that Tita has succeeded in holding her own with her mother. "There was a strange light in Tita's eyes."[33]

Tita knows that she is still in danger in spite of her resistance to her mother's attempt to suck her back into feelings of obligation based on sin, shame, and guilt. The small and fragile flame of her passion that John has coaxed back to life is threatened by her mother's chilling presence. Tita feels that she will not be free of her mother until she dies. It is John who keeps her from freezing in this environment of repression. Once her mother is recovered, Tita decides to marry John. John, on his part, decides to marry Tita whether Mamá Elena agrees or not since he had always felt that Tita's life sentence of caring for her mother is absurd. While in John's presence, Tita wonders whether his love, characterized by peace and security, weren't preferable to the agitated love that she has experienced with Pedro.

Mamá Elena dies. Her secret life is now discovered by Tita, who opened a box belonging to her mother. It reveals her forbidden love affair with José Treviño, whom she was forbidden to marry because of his racial background. It is also important to note that Gertrudis, who was the child fathered by José Treviño, is the one who in her wild life has lived out the sexual passion that her mother abandoned for the sake of the stories of uncritical loyalty, matriarchy, and patriarchy. This frustrated love helps to explain the cruelty of Mamá Elena. Tita mourns for the Mamá Elena who might have been and promises herself at her mother's grave that she will never renounce love.[34]

At every moment of our lives we are somewhere in the core drama of life, enacting archetypal stories in the service of a deeper way of life. With her mother's death, Tita has come to a turning point in two ways: her mother, even though dead, is still with her in the story of matriarchy rooted in the service of the container of emanation; Pedro is also still present. He returns for the funeral and is intent upon repossessing Tita in the story of romantic love that had been Tita's compensation for the chilling repression of the stories of uncritical loyalty and matriarchy that have frustrated both Mamá Elena and Tita.

THE ARCHETYPAL DRAMA OF ROMANTIC LOVE

When Pedro's love first manifests itself, it sweeps Tita away as a new inspiring force in Act I, Scene 2. With Mamá Elena's refusal to allow them to marry, Pedro and Tita carry on a clandestine and feverish love affair, at least through food and furtive glances and embraces. They never really get a chance to let it mature. But from the beginning Pedro shows cowardice in his inability to confront Mamá Elena and the story of matriarchy in the service of emanation. This is because Pedro is also part of the problem. He is a willing participant in the story of matriarchy; he accepts its inevitability. There is no evidence in the novel that he ever questions anything. He doesn't like what happens but makes no move to challenge his fate. Thus when Mamá Elena decides that he cannot marry Tita, but only Rosaura, Pedro sheepishly agrees. For his compensation he lives the story of romantic love with Tita. Rosaura is unfairly stereotyped as the long-suffering wife, helpless as her husband gives his love to another. But Rosaura also accepts her life as fate. She too has acquiesced in her mother's command, although she has no love or passion for Pedro. It is also her way of humiliating Tita. Nobody wins; these stories in the service of emanation wound and violate everyone. The story of romantic love, in which Pedro, Tita, and Rosaura are caught, is in collusion with the stories of uncritical loyalty and matriarchy. These stories enhance and feed one another.

THE ARCHETYPAL DRAMA OF TRANSFORMING LOVE

John Brown's love for Tita is a profound threat to the stories of matriarchy, uncritical loyalty, and romantic love. He relates to Tita as an equal, with a sense of her own mystery and freedom. He sees Tita as a woman in the spirit of his grandmother, Morning Light. All of the characteristics of transforming love are present in John Brown's love for Tita. What separates these two kinds of love is that in the story of transforming love there is no possessiveness. Nor is there the domination of romantic love. Two people are present, each with a story of transformation to live. Transforming love frees each to find and live this story by becoming a self. When two people meet each other in the story of transforming love, they seek to grow within themselves what the other inspired in them. In romantic love, by contrast, you lose your self in the other; you want to live only for the lover. You are not important except as an extension of the other. You don't find out who you are; you seek to fuse yourself in the other, who you believe is the more important.

When Pedro hugs Tita at the funeral, she quivers like jelly. In the second scene of Act I, a new inspiration arises from a sacred source that competes against those that presently hold us. But we have to test these new sources, or else they will end by possessing us in place of the previous force or strengthen the old forces by entering into collusion with them. The story that inspires Tita and Pedro is that of romantic love. But this story, like that of matriarchy and patriarchy or uncritical loyalty, does not allow us to step forward as whole persons. Thus both Pedro and Tita are further disabled in their ability to question their fate. Even though Pedro has been away and Mamá Elena is dead, at the funeral the stories of uncritical loyalty, matriarchy, and romantic love intertwine to keep Tita repressed in the container of emanation. Pedro watches Tita and John through jealous eyes. Tita has been his woman, and he doesn't like the familiar way in which John relates to Tita. Tita belongs to him, he feels, and now that Mamá Elena is dead, he is back to claim Tita as his own.[35]

THE PERSISTENCE OF ARCHETYPAL STORIES AND WAYS OF LIFE

Even though Tita is engaged, she remains very vulnerable to Pedro, who is furious that Tita is planning to marry John. He feels that he has to repossess her, so he looks for an opportunity, pulls her to a bed, and forces himself upon her.[36] What in reality takes place here is sexual violence; Pedro in effect rapes Tita so that he can reclaim her as his property. Once again this reveals the inherent incapacity of emanation as a way of life and the story of romantic love to respond to new problems. Pedro uses the relationship of deformation in order to return Tita to the container of emanation. This places their relationship on the way to destructive death at the exit from the core drama. The other issue to note is that Tita does not fight back; she accepts this attack as if it were her fate. This demonstrates once again the power of these underlying sacred stories to possess us and to take over our lives, especially if we are unaware of them.

When Chencha sees the plumes of phosphorescent colors caused by the sexual passion of Pedro and Tita, she thought that the smoke represented the haunting presence of Mamá Elena. Chencha cries out to the Virgin Mary to help Mamá Elena's soul to stop wandering in purgatory. But in reality it was Mamá Elena, or the story of matriarchy, who was still present. And the story of matriarchy manifests itself in another way; Rosaura has borne another child, a baby girl, Esperanza, which in Spanish means hope. Because of complications at birth, she will not be able to have any more children. Rosaura declares that, as the only and youngest daughter, it will be Esperanza's fate to take care of her until the day she dies. Tita is beside herself with anger and determined that Esperanza will have a life of her own. But Tita's own life is now further complicated;

she is engaged to John Brown, has missed a period, and is afraid that she may
be pregnant. The stories of romantic love and matriarchy in the service of emanation are very much alive. Mamá Elena may be dead, but the story of matriarchy, of which she has been a concrete manifestation, continues to haunt Tita.
Thus it is really the underlying story that is present, punishing Tita with guilt.[37]
Tita's mother continues to harass her, appearing behind doors and throwing her
furious looks.

Through Gertrudis's intervention Pedro discovers that Tita is pregnant. For
Pedro this is a stroke of good fortune, because now he knows that Tita belongs
to him and that she will never leave the ranch with John Brown, who has been
away since the engagement.

ENTERING INTO ACT II, SCENE 2: EMPTYING OURSELVES

Unless we enter into Act II, Scene 2, and empty ourselves of the stories and
the way of life in which we have enacted them, we will repeat them and continue
to cripple our lives. Even after Tita no longer has a mother, she lives with the
constant fear that she is about to be punished because of the continuing presence
of her mother.[38]

As Pedro, in a drunken state, serenades Tita, Mamá Elena appears for the last
time to try to return Tita to the first scene of Act I, wherein she would accept
her shame and agree to repress herself in a shroud of sin, shame, and guilt.
Now, for the first time, Tita breaks with her mother on the deeper level of
underlying forming sources. Tita demands that her mother leave her in peace,
once and for all.[39] Her mother tries to make Tita feel guilty, but Tita resists by
declaring, "I know who I am! . . . I won't put up with you! I hate you, I've
always hated you!"[40]

With these words, the story of matriarchy in the way of life of emanation and
not just Mamá Elena are exorcized; Tita has succeeded in ridding herself of
Mamá Elena forever. The power of her mother over her life is now reduced to
a tiny light, but a light that still has the power to lash out and cause trouble by
burning Pedro.[41] Tita feels such a relief come over her that it relaxes the muscles
at the center of her body, resulting in a menstrual flood. She is not pregnant.
This release can be interpreted as symbolic of Tita's success in emptying herself
on the deeper level of the sacred source that has possessed her soul. Tita also
earns the title of the novel, *Coma Agua Para Chocolate*. She has generated the
anger necessary to empty herself on the deeper level, not only of her mother,
but of the story of matriarchy and the way of life of emanation in which she
has arrested her life. Tita, like water for chocolate, has boiled over.[42] This is
the alchemical process of transformation. The formula used by the alchemists
was *solve et coagula*, dissolve and reform, break and reconnect. Both were
necessary for participation in the process of sustaining life, dissolving it and
then creating new life. If either the one or the other dominated then there could

be no transformative change. The practitioners of alchemy symbolically sought to dissolve heavy metals and recoagulate them into gold. What they were really after was the process of transformation, by which one takes the scattered aspects of the personality and finds the pearl of great price, the self.

For generations chocolate has been made in Mexico in hard round disks. They become so hard that it takes a considerable effort to break them while dry, and so to dissolve the chocolate, it is necessary to use boiling hot water and constant stirring. It takes this kind of boiling anger on Tita's part to dissolve the stories of her tradition which, in their hardened, coagulated state have become unbearable, untenable, and unfruitful. The culture has frozen into an emanational web of life and turned the other necessary ingredients, change and conflict, into a heresy, thereby frustrating the process of transformation.[43] Tita, in the countertradition of transformation, seeks to dissolve the story of matriarchy and the underlying way of life of emanation that have hardened into arresting all of their lives in the first scene of Act I in order to free herself to create a fundamentally new and better story.

Once we have emptied our soul in this way, we are free to be filled with the fundamentally new and better in Act III, Scenes 1 and 2. The story of transformation that Tita is able to bring to life as a new kind of *coagula*, was that of the guide on behalf of her niece, Esperanza. In regard to the four faces of her being in the service of transformation, Tita's personal face has come forth: she is a strong woman, capable of nurturing herself and others. With her political face, she raises her voice not only against Mamá Elena, but against the story and way of life that have made not only her but Esperanza and all women possessions of others. With her historical face, Tita has stepped forward with urgency to bring about a new turning point, a new story, a new history for herself and other women. And with her sacred face she has discovered the deepest source of transformation that blesses her own life as sacred and invites her to participate in the continuous creation of the world.

Both Pedro and Tita do everything they can to prevent Rosaura from raising Esperanza in the tradition practiced by her mother, as another child of matriarchy.[44] In order to preserve the honor of the family and to give the impression that her marriage and family life are going well, Rosaura agrees to share Esperanza with Tita as long as Tita and Pedro do nothing to cause others to question the image of a happy family. According to Rosaura, Esperanza is sent to the best schools to meet the right people. For Tita and Pedro, however, Esperanza's education is intended to develop her mind. Tita teaches her the secrets of love and food as revealed in the kitchen. But as was not the case in her own life, Tita wants to make sure that Esperanza has the opportunity to experience the secrets of love openly and honestly and not be condemned to live a life of manipulation and secrecy.

The biggest battle comes when Esperanza falls in love with Alex Brown, Dr. John Brown's son. Rosaura is determined to hold on to her right, a daughter who will stay with her until she dies. Soon afterward Rosaura dies from severe digestive problems. Tita has succeeded as a guide of transformation since she has led Esperanza to her own selfhood. Tita is proud to see Esperanza step forward as a self-confident, intelligent, capable woman. She is beautiful as she dances with Alex to "The Eyes of Youth."[45]

During the wedding dinner passionate love is the biggest ingredient of the chile in walnut sauce. The wedding party breaks up because the guests rush to find a place to make love. What a contrast with the wedding of Pedro and Rosaura, with the guests overwhelmed by the sadness of repressed love.

CHOOSING BETWEEN ROMANTIC AND TRANSFORMING LOVE AND WAYS OF LIFE

Tita has successfully broken with her actual, concrete mother and on the deeper level she rejects the story of matriarchy and the way of life of emanation in the second scene of Act II. She comes forth as a transforming self in Act III, Scene 1, and in the second scene, as a guide of transformation, she is able to escort her niece to a new and better life. Once we have experienced transformation in one area of our life, it is necessary to practice it again and again in all aspects of our life. Tita has refused to accept the story of matriarchy as her fate or as that of Esperanza. She has intervened against their fate, the story of matriarchy and the way of life of emanation, and creates a destiny that is open and filled with new possibilities. But transformation is a persistent process; we never transform once and for all. Whenever we experience transformation, it is always in regard to one aspect of our life at a time. For Tita there is still the unresolved issue of what kind of love she will choose.

As stated earlier, Pedro did not question the legitimacy of Mamá Elena's claim to possess Tita's life in a matriarchal embrace that is part of their emanational tradition. Furthermore, he sees his love for Tita as his right and possession. He only knows one thing, and that is that Tita can belong to no other man. For a time Tita goes along without questioning this fantasy. But there arises in Act I, Scene 2, a competing emanation that brings into question the story of romantic love that binds her to Pedro. John Brown loves her in a radically different way, which gives her a sense of peace. He nurses her and waits for her to respond when she is ill. When Tita tells him that she has broken their engagement by having sex with another man, John is not upset. He loves her and wants to marry her. He demonstrates no jealousy, no possessiveness, no angry impatience with her. He is a remarkable man, not angry even when Tita reveals that she has been sexual with another man. When Tita speaks of her inability to make up her mind, he does not pressure her but respects her need for time to make a decision.[46]

"What you've told me hasn't changed the way I think. . . ."[47]

"I don't want to put any pressure on you, I just want to assure you that you would be happy with me."[48]

After Rosaura's death and at the wedding of Alex and Esperanza, we learn that Tita had chosen Pedro years ago. But until the very end Pedro continues to be jealous. At the wedding, Pedro is not pleased when he sees John take Tita's hand in his and hand her a box of matches to light the oven. This is significant when we recall the experiment with making matches that John's grandmother taught him long ago. The matches represent passion. It is as if John is celebrating the fact that Tita has the right to live her own passion with whomever she chooses: "Tita looked splendid. . . . At thirty-nine she was still as sharp and fresh as a cucumber that had just been cut."[49]

Tita and Pedro had once agreed to be discreet about their relationship. With the death of Rosaura there is no need to hide. Now Pedro and Tita can love each other openly and freely.[50] It is Nacha who prepares the room with 250 candles so that they can release their love. As Tita is experiencing sexual climax, a bright tunnel opens in front of her. It is then that she remembers what John has taught her about the tunnel that appears to show us the way. *"Tita checked her passion. She did not want to die. She wanted to explore these emotions many more times. This was just the beginning"*[51] (emphasis added). But in the midst of this passionate embrace, Pedro dies, and with his death Tita despairs of ever again being able to light her inner passion.[52]

Tita refuses to go on alone, without Pedro. She is beginning to feel the cold that she has experienced during the many years of lost love. She now takes the matches that John has given her and begins to eat them one by one. But she knows that she has to have someone to help her to ignite the matches, so she fantasizes about Pedro's first caress and the first time she made love with him. The passionate images work; her passion is on fire and she sees the tunnel open again, with Pedro standing at the end, waiting to consummate his love with her again and for all eternity. Tita rushes to Pedro; they embrace and experience once again an amorous climax. They have regained their lost Eden and will now be together for eternity.[53] As they embrace, they let off fiery sparks that ignite the room in flames and consume the entire ranch. The fire continues for a week. Only a layer of ash several yards high is left. The legend begins that under this ash every kind of life flourished, making this the most fertile land around.

In this powerful way the stories of uncritical loyalty and of romantic love that have been in the service of emanation end in deformation. Tita commits suicide. She gives up on her life, her matches/passion, her desire to experience these emotions many more times, her youth and her chance of experiencing love with someone else.

Tita has a choice. Tita had succeeded in sending the story of matriarchy and the way of life of emanation into the exit from the core drama in the second scene of Act II. Once again she could have sent not herself in this act of self-immolation, but the stories of uncritical loyalty and romantic love, together with the way of life of emanation, into the abyss. But Tita cannot see any other way as long as she is possessed by the logic of these stories in the service of emanation. And this is precisely the fragility of the way of life of emanation. As this story and way of life crumble, Tita fights to restore it to the point where she uses violence against herself. Thus in her attempt to save the past, she enters into a fundamentally worse way of life. Since she belongs body and soul to Pedro, she now has no right to a life of her own. Since she feels that she is nothing without Pedro, she has to die to be with him. Once Tita acts as if she is nothing, she turns her life from emanation to deformation. The four faces of her being in the service of deformation are profoundly altered for the worse: Tita erases her own personal face for that of Pedro. She practices a politics of violence against herself and others by telling them that neither she nor they are worthy of her love, only Pedro. Historically, she makes life worse because she is living and helping to perpetuate a story that gives men the right to possess the lives of women even in death. Her sacred face is inspired by the lord of deformation, who tells us that we are nothing without the other, the master, the warrior, the lover, the leader, who is more valuable than we.

CONCLUSION

One of the major conclusions of the novel is that the lives of men are more valuable than those of women. Because Pedro dies, Tita's life is considered to be over. Tita had many other choices. She has already demonstrated for herself and all women that she is not a permanent victim. She has defeated the story of matriarchy and freed herself of the web of emanation. She has intervened in the story to create a new destiny, a new story. When she raises her gaze and her voice to Mamá Elena, this is more than a personal rebellion; she is making a political statement that no society has the right to shape life so that women are the possessions of others; Tita is creating a new turning point, her story, as the basis for a new tradition, a new and more human history. These new faces of Tita's being boil to the surface, like water for chocolate, because she dares to listen to the deepest source, who tells her that her life is sacred. Because she has freed herself, Tita is also able to enact the archetypal story of the guide in the way of life of transformation by intervening on behalf of her beloved niece, Esperanza, who represents the hope for the next generation of men and women.

When Pedro dies Tita is a beautiful, young woman. She is intelligent, strong, courageous, competent, an extraordinary cook, and full of life. After a respectful period of mourning for Pedro, Tita could have married John Brown; she could have taken several lovers; she might have gone with Alex and Esperanza and opened the best Mexican café in Boston to nurture true love in Harvard students; she might have sold the ranch and traveled around the world; Tita, as the proprietor of the ranch, could have established a school of culinary arts, which could have educated Mexican women so that they were able to support themselves; she could have eventually established a chain of Tita's Restaurants throughout the Southwest, using the profits to open schools where boys and girls would be given the same opportunities to excel. When the Albuquerque *Times* came to review the restaurants, it would be sure to recommend the delicious oxtail soup and the exquisite quail, topped off by a cup of steaming hot chocolate. But none of this was to be. We are all robbed of a marvelous human being who has only begun to share who she was. There are no sadder phrases in the realm of transformation than "I should have," "I could have," "I would have," "I might have," and "If only." All of these phrases represent lost opportunities for practicing transformation.

The following conclusion by a reviewer fails, despite its attempt, to go beyond the usual interpretation of masculine and feminine.

Each of the female characters has an individual identity that does not necessarily fit into the rigid dichotomies imposed by patriarchal thought. . . . In short, *Como Agua Para Chocolate* portrays women and men as individuals, not as allegorical others. Real women, the novel shows us, may have "masculine" attributes such as strength and courage, just as real men may show "feminine" nurturing sides.[54]

The analysis of *Like Water for Chocolate* from the perspective of transformation allows us to go beyond the usual meaning of the terms "masculine" and "feminine," "matriarchy" and "patriarchy," and to ask the questions, In the service of what way of life are the characters enacting their lives? What difference does it make if Tita is more masculine in her courage than Pedro or if Nacha practices a kind of nurturing maternal side if they live these qualities in the service of stories and ways of life that wound them? When Tita decides to kill herself for the sake of love, does it make any sense to call this a masculine kind of bravery or a sign of feminine loyalty?

To analyze novels from an archetypal perspective tells us that even an author may not have been aware of the power of the stories that she is telling except on an intuitive level. All works of art have four faces; they are personal statements with political, historical, and sacred consequences. It matters greatly if a work of art is done for profit in the service of incoherence, or in the service of emanation to uphold a traditional view, or to act as an apologist for stories in the service of deformation. My conclusion is that Esquivel is a brilliant writer who exposes the inner reality of the dramas of matriarchy/patriarchy, uncritical loyalty, and romantic love. She realizes that patriarchy and matriarchy remain as powerful, living, emanational fragments of the Mexican tradition. It is possible that she has freed herself of these stories. But in regard to romantic love and uncritical loyalty, Esquivel loses control of the story as it carries her and her characters down in a blaze of glory. It is true that Gertrudis lives a full and joyful life; not only was she a lover, a married woman filled with passion, and a mother, she even serves as a general in the army. But she is not the heroine. As a character she is minor in relation to Tita. It is Tita who carries the burden and who leaves us with the most powerful impression of the author's intent.

The message for many people who have seen the film and read the novel is that love is beautiful and that love conquers all. In her attempt to keep her promise to herself at her mother's funeral, never to renounce love, Tita chooses love, but a romantic, possessive love that cancels out and erases her personal, political, historical, and sacred faces and is therefore in the service of deformation. Even most reviewers failed to mention the tragedy of Tita's self-immolation, and one reviewer who does quickly dismisses the suicide by declaring, "Tita does follow her man even into death, but her story and her recipes serve to supplement the traditional role of the romantic heroine. Her text also confers a higher status and power to the traditionally devalued personal sphere of the kitchen."[55] The argument that the kitchen can become a liberating space for Latina women is a seductive one. If their freedom in the kitchen leads them to recognize their *unfreedom* in the other aspects of their lives and to rebel against this systemic tyranny, then the kitchen is indeed the beginning of a process that can lead to a greater liberation. But if their experimentation is restricted to the culinary arts, then the dutiful, even if cheerful, acceptance of the daily preparation of food co-opts the true creative imagination of women and becomes a kind of self-immolation.

From the perspective of the politics of transformation, the novel ends in deformation, as Tita tries to preserve the stories of uncritical loyalty and romantic love and the way of life of emanation that is dying. This is significant for Latina women, both in Latin America and the Latino community in the United States as well as for all of us. Our nations are struggling to let go of stories such as the politics of inequality inherent in current male/female relationships, the violent battering of women and children, and the authority of fathers and mothers over us when these very important relationships become distorted as the stories of romantic love, uncritical loyalty, matriarchy and patriarchy. All of this has consequences for democratic citizenship. Latino men and Latina women who are unable to break with inherited stories and ways of life that disable them in the political realms of the family and in relationships with the opposite sex will be incapable of confronting the fragments of emanation wielded by the matriarchs and patriarchs of the state and other institutions, such as religious organizations that seek loyalty above all. We are not fully present in the stories of matriarchy/patriarchy, uncritical loyalty, capitalism, romantic love, and nationalism. To remain wounded by these stories means that we will not be capable of healing the psychic split within us between our feminine and masculine selves and thus failing to achieve the wholeness of selfhood. Stories such as patriarchy, matriarchy, romantic love, and uncritical loyalty continue the domination of the feminine and the inflation of the masculine to the detriment of our wholeness as persons. To create a new and better politics and history can only be achieved by persons like you and me who struggle to create a wholeness of being and who, together with the deepest sacred, can create fundamentally new and more compassionate stories and relationships. Latino men and Latina women in the service of transformation are free to analyze those stories and ways of life which have hurt us, to empty ourselves of them and to create fundamentally more compassionate, just, and loving stories in all aspects of our life.

NOTES

1. In the writing of this chapter, I am greatly indebted to my friend and colleague Manfred Halpern, Professor Emeritus of the Politics Department, Princeton University. Professor Halpern in his forthcoming book brilliantly links theory to practice by relating the four faces of our being to the realm of the deepest sources and to the basic choices we face in life: "Transformation: Its Theory and Practice in Our Personal, Political, Historical and Sacred Being."

2. Virginia Woolf, *A Room of One's Own* (New York: Harcourt, Brace and Co., 1929), p. 181.

3. David T. Abalos, *Strategies of Transformation Toward a Multicultural Society, Fulfilling the Story of Democracy* (Westport, CT, and London: Praeger, 1996), p. 20.

4. Manfred Halpern, "Why Are Most of Us Partial Selves? Why Do Partial Selves Enter the Road to Deformation?" (paper presented at a panel on Concepts of Self: Transformation and Politics at the annual meeting of the American Political Science Association, Washington, DC, August 29, 1991), p. 12.

5. Ibid.

6. Freddy Rodríguez, a Dominican artist, titled a recent showing of his works in the Jersey City Museum, December 13, 1995–February 17, 1996, in Jersey City, NJ, "Priest: The Spirit and the Flesh."

7. Adrienne Rich, *On Lies, Secrets, and Silence: Selected Prose, 1966–1978* (New York: W. W. Norton, 1978), p. 90.

8. In this regard, see Ramón Gutiérrez, *When Jesus Came, the Corn Mothers Went Away: Marriage, Sexuality and Power in New Mexico, 1500–1846* (Stanford, CA: Stanford University Press, 1991), pp. 3–36 and 46–94.

9. See in this regard William Blake, *The Complete Poetry and Prose of William Blake*, ed. David V. Erdman, with commentary by Harold Bloom (New York, London, and Toronto: Doubleday, Anchor Books, 1988), especially Blake's famous "The Tyger" and "The Marriage of Heaven and Hell"; and also the brilliant work on Blake by David V. Erdman, *Prophet Against Empire* (New York: Dover Publications, 1991).

10. David T. Abalos, *The Latino Family and the Politics of Transformation* (Westport, CT, and London: Praeger, 1993), p. 76.

11. Leslie Marmon Silko, *Ceremony* (New York: Penguin Books, 1977), p. 2.

12. Larry M. Preston, "Theorizing Difference: Voices from the Margin," *American Political Science Review* 89, no. 4 (December 1995): 941–53.

13. Abalos, *The Latino Family*, pp. 66–77.

14. In this regard see Erich Neumann, *The Great Mother: An Analysis of the Archetype* (Princeton, NJ: Princeton University Press, 1974), especially "The Matriarchal World of America," pp. 179–208; Gerda Lerner, *The Creation of Patriarchy* (New York: Oxford University Press, 1987); Adrienne Rich, *On Lies, Secrets, and Silence*, pp. 115–16; and Ann Belford Ulanov, *The Feminine in Jungian Psychology and Christian Theology* (Evanston, IL: Northwestern University Press, 1971), pp. 168–69.

15. See Marshall Berman's brilliant analysis of *La Nouvelle Héloise* in *The Politics of Authenticity, Radical Individualism and the Rise of Modern Society* (New York: Atheneum Press, 1972), pp. 231–64.

16. Laura Esquivel, translated by Carol Christensen and Thomas Christensen, *Like Water for Chocolate* (New York: Doubleday, Anchor Books, 1992), p. 9.

17. Gutiérrez, *When Jesus Came, the Corn Mothers Went Away*, pp. 227–40.

18. Esquivel, *Like Water for Chocolate*, pp. 24–34.

19. For a fascinating insight into the world of the Mexican hacienda, dealing with honor and virtue, issues of race, class, and gender, and the relationships between men and women in the northern provinces of pre-Revolutionary Mexico, see Gutiérrez, *When Jesus Came, the Corn Mothers Went Away*, pp. 176–270.

20. Esquivel, *Like Water for Chocolate*, pp. 37–38.

21. Ibid., p. 39.

22. Ibid., p. 134.

23. Ibid., p. 48.

24. Ibid., p. 53.

25. Ibid., p. 65.

26. Ibid., p. 67.

27. Ibid., p. 77.

28. Ibid., p. 79.

29. Ibid., p. 93.

30. Ibid., p. 96.

31. Ibid., p. 105.

32. Ibid., p. 112.

33. Ibid., p. 126.

34. Ibid., p. 135.

35. Ibid., p. 136.

36. Ibid., p. 155.

37. Ibid., p. 169.

38. Ibid., p. 192.

39. Ibid., p. 193.

40. Ibid., p. 194.

41. Ibid.

42. Ibid., p. 147.

43. For a scholarly discussion of the process of alchemy as transformation, see Titus Burckhardt, *Alchemy* (Baltimore, MD: Penguin Books, 1971), pp. 133–38. For an application of the theory of transformation as it relates to the caduceus as symbolic of the alchemical process, see David T. Abalos, "Strategies of Transformation in the Health Delivery System," *Nursing Forum* 17, no. 3 (1978): 284–316.

44. Esquivel, *Like Water for Chocolate*, p. 209.

45. Ibid., p. 234.

46. Ibid., p. 217.

47. Ibid., p. 218.

48. Ibid., p. 219.

49. Ibid., p. 230.

50. Ibid., p. 237.

51. Ibid., p. 238.

52. Ibid.

53. Ibid.

54. Kristine Ibsen, "On Recipes, Reading and Revolution: Postboom Parody, *Como Agua Para Chocolate*," *Hispanic Review* 63 (1995): 143.

55. Cecilia Lawless, "Experimental Cooking in *Like Water for Chocolate,*" *Monographic Review/Revista Monográfica* 8 (1992): 268. The following reviews and articles also failed to deal with the significance of Tita's death but do highlight the personal and political meaning of the kitchen, which has a potential for women's creativity and for freedom from the daily drudgery of their lives. In this regard see Heidi Schmidt, "La Risa: Etapas en la Narrativa Femenina en México y Alemania. Una Aproximación," *Escritura* 6, no. 31–32 (January–December 1991): 247–57; Janice Jaffe, "Hispanic American Women Writers' Novel Recipes and Laura Esquivel's *Como Agua Para Chocolate (Like Water for Chocolate),*" *Women's Studies* 22 (1993): 217–30; Beatríz González Stephan, "Para Comerte Mejor": Cultura Calibanesca y Formas Literarias Alternativas," *Casa de las Américas,* (October–December 1991): 81–93; and María Elena De Valdés, "Verbal and Visual Representation of Women: *Como Agua Para Chocolate/Like Water for Chocolate,*" *World Literature Today* 69 (Winter 1995): 78–82.

Among those reviews that failed to discuss the meaning of Tita's death, see Marisa Jannuzi, review of *Like Water for Chocolate, Review of Contemporary Fiction* 13 (Summer 1993): 245–46; and Gabriella deBeer, "Mexican Writers of Today," *Review: Latin American Literature and Arts* 48 (Spring 1994): 8–9.

4

Teaching Latina and Latino Students Transformation: Its Theory and Practice

INTRODUCTION

Recently, I went through a painful period of time when I wasn't sure what or how to teach. This was also an ironic experience because I was involved with a group of K–12 faculty to whom I was introducing the theory of transformation and how to teach it. What I discovered was that there are no experts in the classroom and certainly not when it comes to teaching transformation.

I walked into my classroom believing that I knew my material cold. I had taught the theory of transformation many times, and so I felt that this would be another satisfying semester. What I discovered was that I might understand the material very well, but these students sitting in front of me were not just another group to be awed by a fascinating theory and good teaching. I had forgotten that the theory of transformation is not only taught but also lived by those who teach it. I forgot what I myself had written about being a living example of the reality of transformation. I became too concerned with students learning terms rather than experiencing the process of transformation. For example, in the beginning of the term I felt concerned about the difficulty that the class encountered in learning the language of the theory of transformation. In addition, my anxiety was increased when ten new students appeared as late registrants. I felt that everything was out of control, so I took command: "This is the theoretical language that you must learn so that you can apply it to practice. To get the course under way, your first paper is due in ten days.'' The class was surprised, to say the least. How could they possibly write such a paper when they didn't even understand the concepts?

That evening I began to reflect on what material I had already covered and, more importantly, how I had related to the students. From the first two weeks of lectures, they were at least expected to be somewhat familiar with the dynamics of the theory of transformation. They had been introduced to the core drama of life, a story and journey that consists of three acts, with two scenes in each act. I explained that at every moment of our lives we are somewhere in one of the three acts and six scenes of the core drama of life, living stories and relationships in the service of a particular way of life. I had also taught that when we arrest our lives in the first two acts of the core drama or exit from the drama in the second scene of Act II we are only partial selves; we cannot fully participate with our whole being in the creation of a new and better reality. Only in the service of transformation in Act III, Scenes 1 and 2, can the personal, political, historical, and sacred faces of our being experience the wholeness of our lives and thereby participate in creating a more loving and just society.

What I now understood was that I had tried to impose transformation on these students as if it were information that they simply had to ingest. On further reflection, I realized that I had projected on them my own story. Allow me to explain. I shared the following understanding with my class at our next meeting. As a child I had experienced a great deal of chaos. My father had died when I was only two years old. We never knew where the resources would come from to meet the needs of the family, my mother and six children. I remember not having a dresser or a closet to store my clothes in, so they were placed on an armchair. When it came time to dress, I had to search through a bundle of clothing. As I got older, at times I missed school because I had nothing to wear. In addition, I was afraid of the violence that surrounded me. As a result, as an adult I did everything I could to put things in their proper place, to organize, to establish order to the point where it was easy to lose sight of what I was doing. This story of organization and order carried into my teaching. It had always been there, but I had not discovered it with such clarity. I now saw that whenever I felt anxiety, I responded with a demand for order, as if that could solve difficult issues having to do with my life and the lives of students in the midst of living our stories.

It was clear to me that I was not able or ready to guide the students through the process of transformation by issuing commands rather than inviting them to test this theory with their own experiences. I saw the disruption and their resistance as a threat to my authority as a teacher who always gets good results. I myself therefore became arrested in the core drama of life in the first scene of Act II by turning my encounters with the students into a contest for power. In such a situation, transformation is never possible because there is no trust and, therefore, no willingness to make yourself vulnerable. I could not show the way since I hid my own personal face for fear of revealing my own doubts. I practiced a politics of power that really ended discussion, and with the historical face of my being, I lived a story that students have known only too well when it comes to schooling: "I am in charge here. If you want to make it, then just tell me what I want to hear." Finally, my sacred face was inspired by the lord of incoherence, to dominate for the sake of order.

By revealing my story in this way, I hoped to remind myself and to demonstrate for the class that there are indeed no experts in the classroom, only people like you and me who are trying to find their story, their deeper self, their way. I learned once again that I had to take the journey again with this group of students. Never mind that I had done it before many times; I had not yet experienced the core drama of life with these students, here and now. Transformation is not a blueprint, but a process, and each time we experience it, we come closer to the deepest source of our being.[1]

CREATIVITY

> In order to work, in order to be excited, in order to simply be, you have to be reborn to the instant. You have to permit yourself to feel . . . to be vulnerable. You may not like what you see, that is not important. But you must be attacked by it, excited by it, and your body must be alive.
>
> —*Martha Graham*[2]

ALL LEARNING IS PERSONAL: THE FOUR FACES OF OUR BEING

I ask my students: What pronoun were you never allowed to use since you first began to learn to write paragraphs in school? They all know the answer. From the very beginning of our formal education, all of us, almost without exception, were told by our teachers never to use the pronoun "I" when writing our papers—unless it was those silly essays we were asked to write every fall about what we had done for the summer. Any serious writing in preparation for scholarly work could not to be personal. To be personal was considered to be subjective, only our opinion and therefore not worth much. We had to be objective, quote scholars, use many references, and build an impressive bibliography. By the time we were in high school, most of us learned to write a research paper like sewing a quilt: we took several books, found appropriate quotes that we stitched together with commentary that was as neutral as possible, then wrote a summary as a conclusion. At times, we were asked to comment on what we had learned, but usually this was just a pro forma requirement that masked the loss of our authentic voices. Much of our education was flawed by a philosophy of specialization in which a body of knowledge somehow exists out there, independent of you and me, and which rules over us.

The absence of the pronoun "I" is no small matter. From our introduction into the academic world, the four faces of our being are obscured. Our personal face has been profoundly wounded. This has great political, historical, and sacred consequences. If we as Latina and Latino students have no personal face, then we cannot practice the political face of our being. Politics means asking ourselves again and again what it is that you and I need to do together to respond to the issues that confront us as a society. But if our personal faces are not present, how or on what grounds will we be able to ask fundamentally new kinds of questions? Since our views have been reduced to mere opinions that don't count much, we agree to leave it to others, that is, professional politicians, to do our politics for us. In this way, our political face practices a politics of uncritical loyalty to those in charge, or we seek to join the powerful or to respond to our powerlessness by following those who promise us absolute power over allegedly lesser human beings. What we are deprived of is participation based on our needs as members of a community. But since we have no personal feelings, ideas, dreams, or intuitions of any worth, then we can only look to others to tell us what is best. In this way our historical face is predetermined to repeat those stories that enhance existing authority; we cannot create new turning points or new stories that constitute a new history. We are limited to repeating the past, using time to become like the powerful, or becoming victims of history as life becomes fundamentally worse. Our sacred face is linked to a deeper sacred source. There are three sacred sources that diminish our value: the lord of emanation requires us to accept without question its final truths; the lord of incoherence rewards us with more stocks and bonds or, if we are failing to become powerful, the hope of more power in return for our allegiance; the lord of deformation leads us into the abyss, either as victims or victimizers, and life is made fundamentally worse. Because we have a wounded personal face, we cannot politically, historically, or on sacred grounds resist any of these three deeper sources. It is only in the service of transformation as a way of life that we rediscover the four faces of our being in their wholeness. The deepest ground of our being, the god of transformation, inspires us anew to see new visions, to politically change the conditions of our life, to bring about new directions in our history and to see our own face as a sacred participant in the completion of creation.

The four faces of our Latina and Latino students were too often obscured and even canceled by the educational system, which turned them into invisible people with no culture and stories worthy of being included in the curriculum.[3] All education has four faces: personal, political, historical, and sacred. The problem is that the personal face of American education was that of a blonde, European American who saw her or his image in all of the textbooks and readings. This was a political face with a message: to be Anglo is to be the best. The historical face of this kind of education and curriculum showed forth only that of the powerful, so that the lie of history was not only what was said but also what was left out, the stories of students of color. This of course also carried with it a sacred face: since many of the Latina and Latino students were dark-skinned, dark-eyed, and foreign-looking, they were not as valuable as the students from the dominant group. This kind of exclusion is what led to the demand by the Chicano and Boricua movements for Puerto Rican and Chicano studies. The students demanded to see their own four faces in the curriculum. This struggle, along with the African-American push for black studies and the similar efforts by the American Indian and women's movements, led to a serious revision of American history. The battle of the books that began in the 1960s and continues to this day is essentially a fight over who will tell the story of this nation. For perhaps the first time in American history, we have more people telling and sharing their stories than ever before. This is a very positive conflict, because it really points to the heart of the matter, that people want to be part of a participatory and democratic movement to create a more open and diverse society.

I remember only too well sitting in a classroom and looking at a huge picture resting on the blackboard in front of me. It was that of a young boy, blonde and blue-eyed, dressed in a perfectly starched shirt with aviator's wings on the front lapel. He was eating the "ideal breakfast," a glass of milk, egg, bacon, a piece of toast, and an orange. I felt very bad about myself and my home. We had no such breakfast; I usually had a piece of bread with jam or a piece of cake or pie with milk, or we had a more traditional Mexican breakfast with *pan dulce*, sweet bread, or a tortilla. But what really made an impact was that this was the "ideal breakfast." Without knowing it the teacher, who was a Catholic nun, had made a very powerful political statement that rubbed out my personal face, my historical heritage, and made me feel not at all like a child of God. In addition, none of our books or lessons ever mentioned anything, even remotely, of my Latino, Mexican heritage. We were never encouraged to speak or write about our culture. As far as the schools were concerned, our history and culture simply did not exist. The hidden message, the hidden curriculum, was telling me and the other Latina and Latino students that we were only valuable to the extent that we became like the ideal students having ideal meals who lived in the ideal world of Anglo or European America.

CREATIVE IMAGINATION IN THE CLASSROOM

I was a Hidden Treasure, I yearned to be known.

—*Ibn Arabi*[4]

This is the prayer of each of our students. The fight over prayer in the classrooms misses the whole point. The silent, often unconscious, prayer of students is the desire to create; creation is the answer to prayer. Above all, students seek to create themselves, to discover the four faces of their being, to tell their own stories, to find their own sacred underlying source that inspires them. It was Karl Marx who prayed in a similar way when he taught us that each of us has an inner need to create, that all of us need to discover and excavate the artist within ourselves.[5] Our human creative imagination is a grace, a cooperative relationship between ourselves and the deepest source of transformation that brings about the fundamentally more loving and compassionate.

In all of my classes, I invite students to do archetypal analysis, that is, to do radical analysis by getting to the roots of all of our concrete stories and relationships. Archetypal analysis allows us to see the underlying forming sources that give to our concrete reality its ultimate meaning and purpose. I redefine the practice of transformation as our participation in the life, death, and resurrection of sacred sources. These underlying sources are always moving through us and determining the quality of our actions. We need to know how to identify and name these sacred forces. Otherwise, if we remain unconscious of them, they will possess us and take over our lives. We apply theory to practice first of all by reading and analyzing novels from the perspective of the theory of transformation. As we read the novels, I ask the class to see their own lives in the dilemmas faced by the various characters in the readings. Then I invite them to apply the theory of transformation to their own lives. Almost all students choose to do these personal papers.[6] At first, they are surprised that anybody would ask them to write an academic paper about their own stories and experiences. There is a certain suspicion and a feeling of threat. After all, most of us as students got to where we are by telling teachers what they wanted to hear.

The majority of students are looking for opportunities, in some cases desperately so, to tell their story. They are often amazed, but pleased, that they are receiving this invitation in an academic course. I have discovered that almost all of my students have suffered from or are presently in a situation in which they are experiencing one or several of the following traumas: alcohol abuse, sexual abuse, physical and psychological abuse, drug abuse, and the trauma of desertion due to the death of a parent, divorce, or abandonment. Because we live in the midst of the story of capitalism, which arrests our lives in Act II, Scene 1, in the way of life of incoherence, which grounds our lives ultimately in the pursuit of self-interest and power, students feel that they cannot afford to show anybody their vulnerability. So they hide the personal face of their being because they have been badly wounded and think that they have nothing to offer. As a result, they are reluctant to be political, that is, to ask what it is that they need to do together to change their school, campus, or curriculum or to exercise the historical face of their being by questioning their past; and they feel everything is the will of an all-powerful lord who will punish them with guilt, a loss of power, or victimization. They have learned how to play the power game and are prepared to dominate others so as not to be dominated.

We discuss as a class the story of the wounded self and how in the story of capitalism, because it is based on competition, we cannot afford to be ourselves. They know that they are often forced to be immoral and insincere in order to survive in a brutal competition for power. As a group, we analyze how we are given permission by the powerful to compensate for being kept as partial selves by living fantasies such as the story of romantic love. In this story, we fantasize that finally I have found a person who will live only for me and whom I can trust completely. In a world where everybody lives only for self-interest, this is no small treasure. If we are lucky, the other person will project the same fantasy unto us. The result is two people who are hiding their personal faces and project upon the other, this ideal person. They do not know the other, but only their projection. As time goes on, the projection will wear thin, since both are in reality obscuring who they are. The great fear is that if the other gets to know his or her weaknesses, they will be rejected. Nobody is at home; both are forced to wear masks. Because these persons are our shields from the world and from our own terror, we cannot live without them. Jealousy, possessive behavior, and mistrust corrode the relationship. When the relationship ends, as we have seen in the story of Tita and Pedro, either one or both feel suicidal and betrayed. Physical and mental violence is often used to force the relationship to continue. When it ends, both are devastated, since they now have to face their own wounded self. Soon afterward, since they have only broken with the concrete manifestation of this story and have failed to empty themselves on the deeper level, another is found, to keep the fantasy going. Nothing has changed except the actual subject of the fantasy; what remains is the underlying sacred source, the story and the way of life, which now possess us once again.

Every semester I introduce my classes to archetypal analysis by relating stories that they are presently living. And each semester several students have said that they felt as if I were speaking directly to them, revealing and putting into words what they are living. Once they understand that this is a theory that allows them to participate, most of them readily respond. I then see it as my task to guide them to understand how the personal face of their story is linked to the political, historical, and sacred aspects of their being, which are also at stake. At our great loss, we ignore any of these four faces. But especially if our personal face is repressed, hidden, or erased, we cannot experience our own creative imagination. All transformative change begins with a person like you and me asking new questions because something has moved us in our depths to doubt the reality that surrounds us. This is an awakening that has been described by people who felt these new feelings as the beginning of creative impulses that led them to breakthroughs in their own lives, as well as in the arts and science. It is not science or art that goes through revolution, but the scientist and the artist who see a new world with new eyes.[7] The powerful do not want us to uncover the relationship between the four faces of our being. They want to continue the debilitating split between our personal and political faces by stressing the private and the public domains as separate. To expose this disconnection and its implications, we discuss why the powerful encourage romantic love in our culture. When we are involved in possessive love relationships, nothing else matters, since the story takes us over. In this context, I introduce the term "depoliticization." The students put this in their own words and comment that such intense emanational relationships remove them from the scene; they couldn't care less about what is going on in the world around them. This allows people in authority to make decisions, knowing that many will not even realize what has happened. This means that history is being determined by the powerful, for the benefit of the powerful. The lord of the way of life of incoherence in the underlying realm justifies this accumulation of power; the powerful deserve it because they work so hard, and the powerless have only themselves to blame.

Once they are introduced to the process of relating theory to practice, using the language of the theory of transformation, I stress with them again and again to test it by applying it to literature and to issues that arise in our society and especially to test it with their own experiences, to make their knowledge personal.

CAPACITY, YES; POWER, NO

Capacity, not power, is what is involved when people like you and me seek to discover their underlying creative imagination. Power dominates and commands and ultimately kills; of its very nature, power cannot be shared because power *is* power because it is scarce and, therefore, always results in hierarchies of privilege and prestige. Capacity arises from within us as creative energy that we wrestle with in order to bring about the fundamentally new and better, together with others and the deepest sacred source. Capacity is a grace, that is, a relationship with others and the deepest creative source. It is a dialogue with the deepest source of our being. The deepest ground of our being needs us in order to be known; reciprocally, we need the deepest sacred as the ultimate ground of our being in order to exist. In this way each of us is a possibility, an epiphany who makes concretely real in the world around us the fullness of being. We become fully who we are by manifesting through our own being the source of creativity. In this sense, all of us who even implicitly long to be fully who we are utter a prayer in the search for our very being, our very capacity for being. Prayer in this context means the longing for and creation of our deepest self, demanding full realization and the desire to help others to realize in their own being this same fulfillment. For this reason, each of us, together with our students, comes to realize that our capacity for creativity can only be fulfilled by our desire in the midst of our unknownness to share together with the deepest sacred source of transformation the same prayer and desire: "I was a Hidden Treasure, I yearned to be known."[8] Our creative imagination serves as the hermetic vessel within which the deepest sacred source of transformation comes to know itself and us, and we see and know ourselves and our creator as friends in the same enterprise of transformation.

The capacity that comes from creative imagination emerges from the reciprocal relationship between ourselves and the deepest source of our being, shared as between two mutual and intimate friends, facing each other. The deepest source of transformation is our ultimate grounding, the source from within which we see and contemplate our self; and we are, as the manifestation of the deepest creative source, the creation by and in which the deepest source knows and contemplates its many archetypal expressions.[9] The deepest source and we are like antiphonal choirs that need and reveal each other, as beautifully stated by Shihābuddin Yahyā Suhrawardí: "You are the spirit which engendered me (my father in respect of the spirit that you formed), and you are the child of my thought (He who is engendered, who is created by my thought of you)."[10] Each of us therefore reveals the god of transformation in a unique way. The deepest of all sources is known and made present in the world, not by dogmas imposed by a collective belief or ideology, but by the vision that corresponds to each person's innermost being.[11]

This is why the four faces of each of our Latino and Latina students, beginning with their personal face, is so crucial for their participation in persistent creation. To erase the sacredness of anyone's personal face is to impoverish the deepest source to keep it from knowing itself in this way. Politically, it means that we deny ourselves the inherent creativity and unique contribution of each person in helping all of us to bring about a new and better history.

ARCHETYPAL ANALYSIS: THE UNDERLYING GROUND OF OUR DAILY LIFE

In applying theory to practice, in making their understanding personal, in experiencing their own creative imagination, in discovering their own unique voice, and in the telling of their own stories, students become involved in archetypal analysis. In this way, they are invited to share in the life, death, and resurrection of sacred stories and ways of life that have hitherto gone unexamined and unchallenged. They are asked to answer the following questions in their papers: what is the story that caught you, possessed you so that you could not be yourself? In the service of what ultimate way of life did you live and practice your story that disabled you so that you were prevented from creating a new and better life? Where are you in the core drama of life, and are you living arrested in one of its scenes and acts that leaves you a partial self? And finally, in regard to the four faces of our being, are you living a drama in the service of a particular way of life in an act and scene of the core drama that denies, hides, or erases your personal face? Do you find yourself practicing a politics of uncritical loyalty, domination, or violence? Have you reduced your historical face to being ahistorical, that is, only a recipient of the past, a spectator who observes the march to power and to violence rather than a creator of a new and better story? Is your sacred face connected to a lord that threatens us with sin, shame, and guilt or to a lord who urges you to pursue self-interest or to a lord who inspires the search for absolute and crippling power over others, or is your sacred face connected to the deepest sacred source, the god of transformation who invites us to join together in completing the creation of the cosmos in a more loving and compassionate way?

STUDENTS RE-VISION AND RETELL THEIR STORIES

My students begin the healing process of their wounded selves by seeing and telling their stories from the perspective of transformation. They have shared with me that they knew something was wrong, but they had no language or conceptual framework by which to explain to themselves where they were in their journey. The writing of their papers is more than a catharsis, a purging of the emotions. Many begin to take action to change their relationships, the stories, and the ways of life that held them. During the week prior to the due date for the papers, I hold extensive office hours. Students are free to make appointments or to come unannounced. It is during these encounters that I come to know my students, perhaps for the first time. I feel close to them and become vulnerable to their stories. I believe that they sense this openness and respond by revealing themselves in ways that surprise them and me. Often, they come in looking to find out how to proceed with their essays and end by discussing the pain they feel in their current situation.

With the guidance of the theory, they write about their lives in essays that flow with ideas and insight. It often happens that several students have difficulties analyzing novels but understand the theory only when they discover their voices in writing about their journey. What I find especially gratifying is the ability of students to see the linkage between the personal, political, historical, and sacred aspects of their being. This means that their papers are definitely personal, but now in such a way that their own experiences are seen in a broader and deeper manner. For example, one young man wrote about his struggle with racism. He had been the victim of beatings by African-American or black youth who were looking for revenge against anyone European American or white. Out of anger and a desire to punish black people, he had become a white supremacist. He now helped to organize raiding parties that sought out blacks for beatings. He was filled with anger and hatred and felt that only violence could quench his rage. It did not work. Violence led to more violence because he was now caught in the story of racism in the service of deformation. His paper was inspired by Alan Paton's novel, *Too Late the Phalarope*, in which the white, Afrikaner protagonist, Pieter, and his entire family are destroyed by racism.[12] What affected him so much was the discussion in which we spoke of the four faces of our being and how when you think that you are erasing or canceling out the personal face of the hated victim, you are also erasing and crippling your own face. Yet his story does not end with transformation. As he himself wrote: "finally, my sacred face which once worshiped the lord of nothing (Satan) is now moving toward the source of transformation. However, even though I'm working towards it my life is only in Act II, Scene 2, trying to empty the stories." He went on to write that he was still struggling with his painful past as he confronted black activism on campus. I discussed this paper with the author, and he said that he wanted to come to know himself better and to share his life with black students. What impressed me about this young man and his essay was that he fought the theoretical perspective from the beginning of the course. He only accepted it when he felt that it had truly explained his life to him. What his paper also revealed to me was that he could see the connection between events taking place in a historical, political novel situated in South Africa with events in his own life that he then was able to relate to the political situation on the campus and to the wider context of racism in American society.[13]

In another powerful essay, a young woman revealed that she had been absent from class for two weeks because she had been practicing what we were speaking about in class. She described in detail a romantic love relationship that had become violent when she questioned her lover:

One day I told my lover that I thought that I was slacking off in school. The result was he gave me a black eye. He said that I did not respect him because I was being selfish and putting my needs before his. After I had to look in the mirror at my face and saw the destruction that he had caused, I realized that I did not deserve this. I entered into Act II, Scene 1. In Act II, Scene 1 we break with the concrete manifestation of our earlier inherited form of emanation because that relationship has become unbearable, untenable and unfruitful. When I got up that morning I actually visualized me shooting him with a gun. I had a black eye, the semester was almost over and my grades were not good; and most of all I was addicted to marijuana. If I had gone through with the plan to kill him then he would have won. I would have thrown myself and him into the abyss instead of the story and I would have become the victimizer instead of the victim.

She went on to explain how she broke away from her lover and sought help for her addiction. She joined a group in which she is helping ''to create new and better stories every time I get up in front of them and share parts of my experience.'' Furthermore, she saw this kind of participation ''no longer as only a personal and sacred renewal, but we reach out to the other two faces of our being, the political and historical and we test our fundamentally new understanding and experience of love and justice with others.'' She concluded her essay with the following analysis:

Transformation is rejecting the inherited and assimilated stories of uncritical loyalty, power, of deformation in our lives so that we might choose the story of life creating and nourishing fundamentally new and better relationships. I found that after all this, when I look in the mirror I will find a young, beautiful, intelligent woman, who is worth being loved. I know that I am filled with a new and better alternative story of the new found sense of self. . . . My four faces of my being in the service of transformation have changed drastically. My personal face emerged into wholeness, my political face is one of compassion, love of myself and justice, my historical face is creating a better story as we speak, and my sacred face is in me, no one else and it allows me to participate with the deepest source of my being as a co-creator with the God of transformation.

Another student wrote:

When I first entered this class, I questioned the universality of the drama of transformation I was being taught. I had never heard of this theory before and I thought some aspects of it may be valid but overall it was not applicable in the world. . . . As the semester progressed and I started reading different novels, I found many similarities not only in what the characters were facing in their lives but what I have also faced. Stories like patriarchy and racism are alive in the world today and not something only read about in books. Through archetypal analysis I began to apply this theory to my own life and those around me. . . . Writing my personal paper, I reviewed so much that had happened to me and is still happening. I also began to look at the environment around me to see what is occurring in the world and right here at Seton Hall University.

Once again, I was pleased to see how this student applied the theory not only to her own life and the politics of her family, which she had written about at midterm in a personal essay, but to the wider world around her and to her immediate situation on the university campus. This helps me to realize that students do see the possibility of practicing transformation in all aspects of their lives.

One student had chosen not to write a personal paper but to analyze a novel and to comment on what she had learned in the course that was of value to her. The paper was beautifully written, with great insight into the novel. When she wrote about what she had learned, the following phrase jumped off the page at me: "When I look in the mirror I hate what I see." I immediately interpreted this as a cry for help. She is very shy, and I wanted to preserve her privacy. I asked if she would like to discuss her paper, and without hesitation she answered yes. As we spoke, she cried. I inquired as to why she had such negative feelings about herself. She was not sure. I had heard from a colleague that she had been so depressed in her first semester that she was failing academically. Now, this semester, she was emerging as a fine student. She went on to say that she feels that she has nothing to offer, and she is surprised when people speak to her at all. This was for me a deeply moving encounter. The conversation gave me hope, because by telling at least a part of her story, she was reaching out and trying to heal herself. She wanted to empty out the poison that we spoke so much about in class, the poison that teaches us that we are not valuable, and how to take this story of the wounded self and empty it out into the abyss and the way of life of deformation in the second scene of Act II so that we can choose a new and more compassionate story.

For the past fifteen years I have taught courses in sociology and politics at Princeton, Yale, and Seton Hall titled Latina/Latino Politics in the United States and The Personal, Political, Historical, and Sacred Faces of Latinas and Latinos in the United States. From these classes, I learned a great deal about our present generation of students. As I described above, I invited them to write personal papers in which they could identify where they got caught in the core drama, what stories they were living, the four faces of their being, the relationships they were free to enact, and in the service of what ultimate way of life and sacred source they were living their lives. We read Sandra Cisneros, Laura Esquivel, Leslie Marmon Silko, Frank Bonilla, Oscar Hijuelos, Demetria Martínez, Rosa Martha Villareal, Richard Rodríguez, Tato Lavierra, Octavio Paz, Gloria Anzaldúa, René Marqués, and other Latina and Latino authors. We explored the stories of the cultura Latina, especially romantic love, patriarchy, and uncritical loyalty.

The stories that I most frequently encountered were those of romantic, possessive love and patriarchy/matriarchy enacted in the service of emanation and deformation. This means that the Latina and Latino students were dealing with the breakdown of the way of life of emanation as they challenged the stories that held them. There was a lot of deformation because it was a reactionary response, especially against Latina women on the part of parents and lovers. They felt deeply threatened by the new freedom being expressed by the women. As a result, these women faced the full barrage of sin, shame, and guilt as an attempt to return them to a crumbling container of emanation.

Recently, I had a discussion with four Latinas. They were facing all of the difficulties of any other student: exams, papers, financial aid, cafeteria food, and suite mates. In addition, as Latina women, they also confronted discrimination and racism when professors questioned them regarding their written work, which seemed to be so well done that they could not have possibly been the authors. But then, on top of all these problems, they faced issues that were culturally specific. All of them had experienced a bad home life. They had seen their mothers betrayed by men and were deeply affected by this. Their mothers had lost faith in Latino males and raised their daughters to be careful of men because "they will ultimately hurt you."

Each of the Latinas had already or was presently involved in a romantic love relationship. They all felt that it was a bad situation, but they didn't know what to do about it. On the one hand, their mothers warned them that they would be hurt and not to trust a man. But they were caught in the story and so refused to listen to their mothers. In the course of the conversation, the women expressed a profound pessimism about their ability to have a good relationship with a man. They spoke openly of how they were beginning to protect themselves by developing a sense of contempt for men. They understood very well the tactics of Latino males, who would make a great show of loyalty to their woman while pursuing other women in their own lives. When discovered, the men would ask for forgiveness and manipulate the Latinas' cultural sense of loyalty and guilt until they took the men back. It never failed, and the women knew it; but they were frustrated in their inability to deal with how they were caught. To free themselves, the women began power plays in which they did everything to outlast the males; a woman would refuse to call until he did, and when he did call, would refuse to talk, even though, as the women revealed, they wanted badly to return to the relationship. They devised ways to make the men suffer: refuse them sex and affection, tell them you are too busy to go out, date other men, refuse to talk to them.

What these young women had in common was that they were angry with their mothers, who they felt were trying to control their lives while telling them how to relate to men. They believed that their own mothers had not done very well in this aspect of their lives and so resisted their mothers' advice. But something strange began to happen. The women, against their will, had been affected by their mothers, and they now, in effect, became their mothers. It was almost as if in front of me they had become matriarchs, prepared to live without men. They all wanted to marry and have children, but it would be on their terms. They agreed that they would not allow men to control them and that they would marry but not make the mistake of loving their husbands. They felt that in this way they could stay in control; by repressing their feelings, they could exercise power over men rather than be dominated by them.

From the perspective of the theory of transformation, what was taking place was the collapse of the inherited stories of patriarchy, uncritical loyalty, and romantic, possessive love in the service of emanation. The women listened to their inner voices in the second scene of Act I that told them that there had to be a better way to enter into a relationship with a man. They rebelled with anger due to betrayal; they were adamant that they would not return to "normal" as women suffering in silence. Thus they entered into Act II, Scene 1, wherein they openly defied their lovers. But rather than proceed to the second scene of Act II and empty themselves of the stories, they remained arrested in permanent rebellion against men. They wanted power over the lives of men. And, what was more disturbing, they spoke of wanting to get revenge on men. Again, as we have seen earlier, this response on the part of Latina women demonstrates the inherent limitations of the ways of life of emanation and incoherence. To remain in emanation was no longer possible, because this fragmenting way of life legitimized the domination of women by men. Yet they felt guilty. To overcome their confused feelings, they rebelled and wanted to dominate men, not realizing that this was no answer, but a reformation of the same story. All the power in the world could not alleviate their sense of loss. They were still possessed by the stories and substituted the story of romantic love and patriarchy in the service of emanation for the same stories of romantic love and matriarchy, but now in the service of incoherence and deformation. This turned the women into rebels, because they were living the same stories as they had before, but now they were in charge. Their lovers had not hesitated to turn to violence when they saw that their women were turning away from them. They often attempted to preserve the stories of romantic love and patriarchy through violence, which means that emanation, in alliance with deformation, crippled the four faces of the women.

The women were prepared to use their new-won freedom in this country as a means to power, so that they could become independent of men. But this is not real independence; it is incremental change, because the women are reforming an old story that will disable them in their search for wholeness. Each of them and each of us needs to be loved for who we are by others who care deeply about us as persons. To seek revenge on men or to want to dominate them means that neither they nor the men they relate to will be able to find out who they are. Both jealousy and domination drives us as persons underground; none of us can be who we are. Men often say "If I can't have you, then nobody else will." A strategy of revenge signifies that the men have won; now the women will belong to no other man, but ironically not even to their own selves.

In our ongoing discussion, we talked about how they had become their mothers, because now they would raise and wound the next generation of women and men with the same destructive stories. This has profound implications for the future well-being of the Latino family. How will a child be able to experience transforming love if she sees her father and mother daily hold themselves back from each other, hide their true selves, and hammer away at one another? How will young children be able to cope with the tension in the house caused by the infidelity of a father who believes that it is his right as a male to have lovers? And how will young boys feel when they are raised by mothers who still prefer sons but are ambivalent about them as the potential abusers of the next generation of Latina women? How will young boys and girls be able to develop healthy relationships with members of the opposite sex when they see their fathers and mothers locked in a competition for power?

This prolonged conversation with the Latina women is significant for another reason. More and more families in la comunidad Latina are headed by young women who often do not have the necessary education or skills to provide for their families. The men are absent. Some of this is due to the racism of the wider society, which makes it difficult for them to find good-paying jobs; in part, it is the failure of the schools to challenge and educate them; the anger and despair also place many Latino men in danger of confrontations with the law due to drinking, joining gangs, and the crime that usually follows. It is also the internal cultural collapse of the stories of possessive love, uncritical loyalty, and patriarchy.

There is no other way except to empty ourselves on the deeper level of the stories that cripple us and to send them and the ways of life of emanation, incoherence, and deformation into the abyss. Until we are able to do this, we cannot be fully present; we remain partial selves, unable to bring forth our creative imagination. Latina and Latino students know that they cannot breathe new life into the dying way of life of emanation, and they sense but are not sure if the assimilated way of life of incoherence is the answer to their search for wholeness. They are still unsure of what it means to void themselves of the dramas that hurt them so that they can create new and better stories in all aspects of their lives as whole women and men.

Other students wrote in their papers that they understood everything that was being taught in the theory of transformation but that they found it difficult to fight the ingrained stories of the Latino culture. As a matter of fact, the majority of the students who wrote about their relationships saw the answer only in reforming the story: we are no longer so possessive; we have agreed to give each other more space; we no longer demand to know where each other was last night; he doesn't tell me how to dress anymore. But the underlying stories of uncritical loyalty and romantic love, in collusion with the story of patriarchy, are alive and well here. Many students agreed that they were putting off the real issue, the underlying story that still held them enchained but enchanted. But they felt at least that they were on their way to transformation because now they were aware as to where they were in the core drama, the stories they were living, the relationships they were allowed to practice, the four faces of their being and what sacred source was inspiring their soul. My hope is that when they realize that their situation is unbearable, untenable, and unfruitful, that the core drama of transformation will serve as their guide as they move to transform their lives.

THE TEACHER AS GUIDE

The above excerpts from student papers and discussions flowed with an amazing, antiphonal response, interweaving theory and practice, concept and feeling, intuition and expression. These papers are for me always the best test for the theory of transformation. If students determined that the theory did not help them to re-vision their lives and prepare them for action, I would not be able to go on teaching the theory. It is they as practitioners who help me term after term to recognize weaknesses in the theory or in my teaching or both.

In regard to my teaching, I was dissatisfied with my response to questions being raised by students about my analysis of several novels. It required me to reevaluate my interpretation from the perspective of the theory of transformation. As a result after teaching *The Color Purple* for the past several years, I now teach it in a way that I had not previously done. This once more had much to do with the way that I was looking at my life. Because of painful memories of violence and abandonment during my childhood, I was hesitant to point out the deformation that surrounds us. I wanted to push the characters, meaning myself and my students, to transformation. At times I withheld myself, failing at times to see the extent and depth of the terror in life. In respect to *The Color Purple*, I now analyzed the novel as an example of a young woman who, from the very beginning of the story, is crippled in deformation and of how difficult it is to get out of the abyss at the exit from the core drama. In Celie's case, it takes about thirty years for her to fight back, to refuse to remain a victim, and to empty herself of destructive stories and ways of life so that she can experience the joy of transformation. But like Celie, we are not always ready to resist. Since we are gripped by sacred stories, we develop a certain security that lulls us to believe that there is nothing we can do. At one point, Celie advises her stepson, Harpo, to beat his wife, Sofia, because Celie is threatened by her. Sofia is acting out her womanhood in such a way as to make Celie's version, as willing victim, a farce. Celie's initial response to her inner voice, which we all hear from in the second scene of Act I of the core drama, represented by Sofia's defiance of male domination, is to silence the new inspiration by bringing Sofia into the abyss. Then she could say that all women are condemned to masculine control, even those who get uppity. In this way, Celie seeks to continue to erase her own personal face by canceling out Sofia's. Every time we choose to participate in destroying ourselves, we also cripple those around us. The remainder of the novel, especially with the arrival of Shug as a concrete manifestation of the archetype of the guide, is a meditation on how one frees herself or himself from the emanational stranglehold of underlying destructive sacred sources, in this case the story of patriarchy, practiced in the service of emanation and deformation.[14]

To begin the discussion of the novel with the question How do you get out of deformation so that you can be free to reenter the core drama of life and complete your journey? is to emphasize the great mercy at the heart of life. With Rainer Maria Rilke, I agree that even in the midst of the worst deformation, the deepest source of our being can reach us.[15] The god of transformation intervenes when we least expect it to provide us with an alternative sacred source that is more powerful than the lords of the other three ways of life. To ally ourselves with the deepest source, the god of transformation, is necessary because alone we are powerless against archetypal sources. The lesser lords and their ways of life and stories will do all that they can to prevent us from hearing the source of transformation. When we remove our concreteness from their underlying forces, they begin to die. This is the capacity that we have of the very nature of our humanity. Archetypal sources, even as we have seen, the god of transformation, need human participation in order to manifest themselves in the world. But we cannot be naive about the power of these sources. Just when we think that they have been emptied out into the abyss, they can return as powerful fragments in different guises. In the Gospel according to St. Matthew, we are told that when an unclean spirit goes out of a man, he is not safe, because when he returns to the house from which he came, he brings with him seven other evil spirits more evil than himself, so that the last state of that man is worse than the first.[16]

We have always, therefore, to be vigilant. This discussion of how we participate with sacred sources is crucial to many of my students, who are already well on their way to being cynical or feeling that there is nothing that they can do except succeed in the current story of capitalism in the service of incoherence as a way of life.

TEACHING IN THE SERVICE OF FOUR WAYS OF LIFE

Each semester I need to reexperience once again the core drama of life. As the students write their papers, I ask myself the same archetypal questions required of them: In the service of what way of life are you living the stories of your life? What is the dominant story for you here, now? Are you living in a fragment of the core drama, arrested in one of its acts and scenes? Are you able to live the four faces of your being in their wholeness? There is no other way to teach transformation except in this very personal, political, historical, and sacred manner. If we as guides do not know where we are in the core drama of life, then we cannot assist others to find their way. Each of us, and especially the teacher, has to discover not *the* lord, but his or her sacred source in order to find our deeper self and the story that holds us or frees us.

I want to share another example, related to the one that I wrote about at the beginning of this chapter that helped me to understand where I was caught and how this affected my personal, political, historical, and sacred relationship to my students. A student had broken her foot, so it took her some time to leave her previous class and get to mine. As a result, she was always late. As I saw her approach, I would make sure that she had a seat and rearrange an area where she would be comfortable. This went on for about four weeks. Another student approached me and commented that I really do live what I teach. He was impressed with what he considered to be care and concern on my part. This compliment helped me to realize how appearances cannot reveal the underlying meaning of the choices we make. I knew that when I was solicitous, it was because of my need to control the situation and not to allow the student to disrupt the class and, especially, the kind of mood that I like to establish from the beginning of a lecture. I was in charge when I provided the seat; I was in command as I opened the door and guided her toward a place. It revealed in me once again a deep fear of disorder, of chaos, of loose ends. This meant that in this situation with this student I was practicing the story of the teacher who exercised power in the service of incoherence arrested in Act II, Scene 1, of the core drama of life. I personally felt threatened by the seeming disorder and so moved politically to take control. I was allowing my history to lead me to get power, so that I would not again feel the anxiety of being out of control. And so I was inspired by the lord of incoherence to move quickly to assert my power as a teacher. In this way the four faces of my being were deeply affected. Because my personal face was threatened, my political face took action to dictate the situation, driven by the need of my historical face, which was justified and certified by my sacred face, which was dominated by the lord of power. This was a humbling experience that helped me to understand that we do not always succeed in practicing transformation because it is the name of our course. We have to choose it time and again. We do not become experts in transformation but, rather, risk ourselves to become vulnerable to the moment and choose persistently to be a new and compassionate teacher. The question In the service of what way of life are you making decisions to do what you do? is a constant guide and reminder that our lives are always manifestations of the deeper depths.

In order to explain the four different kinds of teaching, learning, and education in the service of four distinct ways of life, I would like to reexamine and recapture the root meaning of four Latin verbs: *seduco*, *reduco*, *deduco*, and *educo*. The root word of all four verbs is *duco*, which means to lead or guide. *Seduco* is a kind of teaching that by means of mystique or charisma leads a student only to be embraced in the enchantment of the brilliance of the teacher. This kind of education is really training students to accept uncritical loyalty to others; students are made into permanent disciples since the teacher and all authority figures have the answers. The verb *reduco* means that some teachers motivate their students along the path of actually reducing everything to the pursuit of personal power and profit. Instructors provide the power to students by teaching them to be competent with skills they can eventually use to dominate others. In the meantime, by accepting the power of the teacher until it is their turn to exercise control, students are learning the story of domination. This teacher prepares rugged individualists for the "real world," usually without any explicit philosophical justification except to assert that making it is what it is all about. In this choice of teaching, the archetypal source of incoherence, which is not even acknowledged, gives teacher and student alike the right to use each other to increase their power.

Then there is *deduco*, the worst kind of education. It is fundamentally new, but worse; it is education in the service of deformation. It is another kind of teaching that literally deducts, takes away, strips away the personal, political, historical, and sacred meaning of those considered to be lesser people. This kind of teaching leads the allegedly superior to take a fragment of life, such as skin color or ethnicity, and create a fantasy that elevates this fragment to dominate the whole of life. Women, blacks, Latinos, gays, welfare people are all stereotyped to create scapegoats. The allegedly superior cannot analyze the deeper meaning of his or her own hurtful actions because such training in fantasy never leads the allegedly superior individual to confront the cause of the wound. This type of teaching preserves and deepens racism, sexism, and classism. It violates to the point where many feel *nothing* when they are hurt by others or when they hurt others. This nihilism, the politics of violence in the classroom, has to be the deepest kind of wounding because when we feel nothing for others, we can also no longer feel our own personal face.

Those who practice this way of life and teaching turn Latina and Latino students and other students of color, women, or gays, or whoever may be the target, into invisible people in the class. There are no books or readings that represent their personal face; they are not called on; they are ignored. But even before they get to school, many students are experiencing the five faces of the story of tribalism in the service of deformation. In this story those who are allegedly superior treat the outsiders in a way that leads down a path of increasing violence and death. The powerful treat the powerless as if they are invisible and inferior; only "the better ones" deserve to be assimilated, exiled if disloyal and exterminated if they rebel. A whole political environment is constructed in the classroom by which the privileged are aware that they count, and the outsiders clearly know that they do not belong. Some teachers ignore the presence of deformation throughout our society, going on as if there were no racism or poverty or physical abuse that debilitates the energy and confidence of many of our students. Instead they just want to teach math or English, ignoring the issues daily faced by their students.

Educo is a fundamentally different choice from the other three modes of education. It means to guide a student out of herself or himself so that each in her or his own way can participate, together with their neighbor, in personal, political, historical, and sacred transformation. Teaching and education are always political. But what counts is to ask the question: In the service of what way of life am I being political in the classroom? Teaching in the service of transformation critically and consciously turns the classroom into a political setting wherein students are treated with respect for their person, not for their status. In such a context, the majority of students are free to choose to make themselves vulnerable by responding with trust. This kind of transformational politics in the classroom guides students into a radically democratic process, because it needs for its fulfillment the creative imagination and participation of each person. In this kind of education, it is necessary for the individual student to come forth, or else what is within them will die, and their contribution will be lost, thus depriving us all. This kind of educational endeavor demands that students and teachers eventually become colleagues who are embarked on a common journey together.

Since we are speaking of choices and of underlying sacred sources as the deepest ways of structuring and organizing life, we cannot choose once and for all teaching in the service of transformation. We have to continue to choose to live and act in the service of transformation. It is a permanent struggle. There are times when we as teachers become afraid, as in the examples provided above regarding my own teaching. So we might lose our way and exercise domination or feel threatened by dissent. This appeal to the lord of power or to the lord of loyalty and the temporary rejection of the source of transformation and risk is what students refer to when they say that the teacher is acting like the lord almighty. This is actually true, because a teacher responding to a student either in the service of emanation, incoherence, or deformation incarnates and serves a lord who possesses us. Only the deepest source of transformation invites us to participate in continuous creation.

The redeeming aspect of this conscious struggle is that a teacher can come to know the choice she has been making so that she can through humor, for example, acknowledge her own fears and choose again to risk herself as she pursues issues with her students. This is what the politics of the classroom is all about: always taking the next step, opting again and again to be honest and vulnerable, and refusing to stifle the emergence of the students. This kind of education, created by students and teachers together, prepares students to see politics not only as cooperation but also dissent, not only continuity but also change. The politics of transformation in the classroom sets the agenda for the politics of the wider community.

When we exercise authority in the classroom, we always have to ask the question: In the service of what way of life do I teach and guide? As we have seen earlier, we can relate to the sacred in four fundamentally different ways. Therefore, whichever sacred source we respond to is the source to which we will lead our students. In this regard, the four faces of our being are inextricably linked: the sacred forces that inspire us will determine whether we relate to students as disciples, as collaborators in the power game, as members of a group that make life worse, or as mutual friends on the journey of transformation.

Teachers are good teachers because they can touch others on a deeper level beyond the sharing of facts. Through their personalities they can attract others to themselves. Thus when students come to see the four faces of their own being because they were initially drawn out of themselves by the teacher, they begin to realize that what attracted them to the teacher is what the teacher awakened in them: the mystery of what it means to be who you are, a person, another incarnation of the deepest sacred capable of creating new turning points in their lives as they engage together with others to create a more compassionate society. The teacher as guide leads the student away from false sacred sources, destructive stories, and partial ways of life in order to initiate the journey to become themselves practitioners of transformation.

Teachers in the service of transformation as guides practice a particular kind of pedagogy; they escort students to the heart of the matter, actually leading them anew to their original roots, to their deepest sacred source, that is, their own selves. Many of us have repressed, hidden, or allowed the four faces of our being to be erased because we live in a dangerous world based on power and self-interest. Thus we are reduced to attaching ourselves to powerful others as our protectors. But good teaching and education have the capacity to restore us to our origins, enabling us to recognize the choices available to us. Any new re-creation of the world can only come from people rediscovering their personal faces and emptying themselves on the deeper levels of those sacred sources which preserve inherited stories of loyalty or power or destructive death and choosing to create fundamentally more loving and just stories and relationships.

In the encounter of teaching, the most detailed and planned course cannot avoid the presence of underlying forces. We can explain the process of transformation and the four faces of our being, but there are always the deepest depths, which demand that we let go, that we risk ourselves, that we never stop learning, and allow the process once again to take place in us. Even though the teacher as guide invites students to participate in this process, the students will not respond until they feel in their deepest selves the urge to depart from rote learning and memorization and risk faith in something new happening within them. Teachers, although they have taught the subject matter in many classes before, are asked to take the journey through the core drama of life once again. They know the process and yet not in relationship to this class, the new students sitting in front of them.

Only this willingness to reexperience the call into the depths of creativity and to participate in new birthing and transforming is what allows the teacher to be the authentic guide and prevents the whole process from becoming a repetitive story. This is not a power relationship—authority yes, but not power. To use power is to exercise control over the process, actually over the students, to actually manipulate their lives while teachers become the tyrannical lords who want to make students into clones. The creativity that comes forth when there is mutual discovery is not the result of power, but of capacity, or new linkages to our deepest source and to one another. The students and teacher in the crucible of transformation often entered as disciples or as partial selves. The alchemy of the classroom practicing transformational politics has metamorphosed them into colleagues, a learning community of equals.[17]

THE HEART OF THE MATTER: INCREMENTAL CHANGE AS REFORMATION OR TRANSFORMATION

One of my students did a fine job of articulating the inadequacy of incremental change. She addressed a tense situation at Seton Hall caused by racist comments that had been written on an African-American professor's door: ''The university cannot ignore this by cleaning off the graffiti and resuming with business because this is not just one student who is vandalizing the school. What the school is facing is the story of tribalism in the service of deformation which needs to be addressed on a larger scale.'' This was a very astute commentary that goes to the heart of the matter: incrementalism and reform cannot deal with the problem at stake. Reform and incrementalism are precisely what too many university administrators had in mind when they attempted to deal with the problem by offering dollar rewards for information leading to the arrest of the person or persons responsible. It was the students who immediately criticized the university by saying that the problem was systemic and that there needed to be structural changes at the very heart of the university: the politics of the curriculum and the hiring of faculty and administrators who represent communities of people of color. Also this student realized that what we were really facing was the underlying cause of the problem, the story and way of life that must be uprooted. Unless we get to the roots of the issue, everything else is only system-maintaining change, changes within the existing story and way of life that actually strengthen the story by giving the false impression that something is being done. What is required is not change *within* the existing story, which constitutes reform, but a change *of* stories and ways of life and the creation of fundamentally new and more just stories in the service of transformation.

Another student came to see the difference between reform, or incremental change, and transformation when she discussed with me a personal paper that she thought of writing. She spoke of a relationship that she felt was not healthy. It was a possessive relationship, filled with suspicion and jealousy, in which she could not share her personal face. She settled for a political face that succumbed to his need to dominate; she repeated her historical face by practicing this story over and over; and her sacred face was repressed. They established a pattern of breaking up and making up. She was trying to figure out how to change him.

In fact, according to her account, since their latest reconciliation he had already changed. When I inquired as to how he had changed, she responded that he gave her more freedom than before and that he restrained his jealousy. I answered by stating my belief that he had conceded a few details in order to preserve the story of romantic love, which still held both of them. To end the story, she could take the risk of staying away for months and exercise her right to meet other men. She thought that this was too heavy a price to pay. She wanted to stay in the story because the thought of not having him was unthinkable.

This was a good example of two people who wanted to reform a story but not give it up. It was clear from the discussion that the story was hurting them both, but they did not want to risk ending it. What they wanted was to keep the structure of the relationship but adjust it so that they could live with it. In reality, they did not have a relationship; the relationship had them. As a result of this conversation, she decided not to do a personal paper. She said that she felt it would be too painful to admit to herself that she was still caught in the same story, even though they had made changes that gave her hope. But I felt a strength in her that I believe would eventually bring her to confront the issues that she was experiencing.

During the semester, as mentioned, we analyzed *Too Late the Phalarope* as a study of organized and systemic racism, an official sanctioning of the story of racism by a whole society and government. The novel was written in South Africa in 1953, during the height of apartheid, when all publications were subject to censorship. Alan Paton, the author, who was an Englishman and a citizen of South Africa, wrote about the van Vlaanderen family, who represented the Afrikaner community. Even in this blatantly racist society, they were compelled to hide the real story and the cause of black unemployment and poverty by supporting social workers. In a scathing paragraph, Paton described the work of the local social worker, Jappie Grobler, as a "poor cheerful fool who went laughing through the town and the grass country, and tinkered in his merry way with this problem and that, and saw nothing of the greatest of them all."[18] What he failed to see was the underlying cause of the poverty, the stories of racism and capitalism in the service of deformation. He was a joke because nobody, unless ready to dismantle the structure of apartheid, could take seriously changing the condition of blacks. As we saw later, Nelson Mandela and the African National Congress would settle for nothing less than the total structural eradication of apartheid. Prior to the end of apartheid, the ruling National Party did everything it could to reform apartheid in order to make it acceptable to black people. It was a case of racism with a kinder face. There were measures to establish native homelands, abolish the hated pass system, set up a new legislature (still subject to white veto power), open up the white schools to blacks. But everybody knew that these were only rearguard actions that would not satisfy the drive for full equality. Racism was officially ended as the law in South Africa in 1990. Everything is now being done to reconcile the races and to build a new South Africa. The story of racism is still very much alive, but it no longer has official approval and is being courageously confronted.

But there remains still the story of capitalism, which has been embraced by the ruling African National Congress. The lives of most black people are still mired in desperate poverty. Whites still own most of the resources. Although capitalism at its worst, in the service of deformation in the form of slave labor, together with the hated company towns that owned all the homes and stores and controlled their economic well-being, have been abolished, capitalism itself has remained in another guise as a reformed story in the service of incoherence. This means that the ultimate grounding for many in South Africa is not human rights, but the pursuit of power. Changes will continue to be made, but always compromised by looking at the bottom line. There is certainly hope. Transformation is never total. But once we have experienced transformation in at least one aspect of our lives, the sheer joy and wonder of it inspires us to transform all other aspects of our lives. Not to continue to carry out the revolution of transformation is to deny the revolution and to frustrate the hopes of those who are still on the margins of the victory. The powerful will do all they can in South Africa to slow things down by attempting to reform the revolution to death. There is much to be done since transformation is a permanent revolution.

During one of our discussions, I asked the students to take two paragraphs that they had not seen before. I asked them to apply archetypal analysis to see whether they could identify the stories present and in the service of what way of life the dramas were being enacted. One paragraph was taken from a speech given by the current president of the Dominican Republic, Leonel Fernández.

As you can see the Dominican Republic is a country undergoing an important political and economic transformation. Our administration conceives development as an intelligent combination of the state and of the market . . . I believe that we can make our dream of a more prosperous nation come true by ensuring greater freedom and trust in the marketplace so that the ability and inventiveness of the private sector and labor can blossom. I truly believe that it is the courage and creativity of businesspeople, both foreign and domestic, that will provide the basis for real long-term development.[19]

A month later another speech was given by a Dominican man, also named Fernández, but that is all they had in common. Father Avelino Fernández gave the following presentation, at which I was present. (The quotation is based on my notes):

In the Dominican Republic 75 percent of the people live in poverty. In the past the Church went to the rich and asked them to give to the poor. Now we say let us begin with the poor, so that they can change their lives for the better. This means that we have to change the social structures that keep people poor. Faith and religion cannot be reduced to being dogmas and laws; faith lives in the midst of life to produce love, justice, and truth. The obstacles to love and justice are the lack of food, jobs, education, and medical care. Our passion for God means a passion for His people. So when we see people suffering, we must fight for and help them to acquire their rights.[20]

In their responses the students did very well recognizing that the president believed that the story and sacred source that would save the Dominican people were the story of capitalism in the service of the way of life and the lord of incoherence, whispering that those who pursue their own self-interest are on the path to salvation. In contrast, they recognized that Father Fernández was appealing to a different sacred source and story. They identified the god of transformation as the sacred source that, together with the people, would achieve the story of democracy both politically and economically. It was gratifying to know that many of the students understood the profound differences between these two men and their ideas regarding the future of the Dominican Republic. Again this class assignment was for me a test to see whether students could apply theory to practice in regard to material they had not seen or read prior to being asked to analyze it. I make it clear to my students that a very important goal of the course is to prepare them to do archetypal analysis wherever they find themselves. To be able to see with the guidance of theory what stories are being practiced, in the service of what way of life we are living these stories, to discern where we are arrested in the core drama of life, and how this affects the four faces of our being is to know not only concrete reality, but the deeper underlying causes. It allows us to make decisions to intervene so that we can bring about the fundamentally new and better.

Recently, I took students to the Dominican Republic for a course entitled Religion and Revolution in Latin America: The Case of the Dominican Republic. It was an extraordinary experience because we got to see firsthand a nation that was coming out of virtual dictatorship for the past sixty years and in which the same men held power or contested for power with one another. There was a passing of the torch to a new generation, symbolized by the young and energetic new president, Leonel Fernández. But the Dominican economy is in a shambles. Above all, the new ruling party felt that it had to establish credibility with the business community both domestic and foreign, especially the United States. As a result, old laws restricting foreign capital were abolished and new legislation passed to facilitate the three fastest-growing segments of the economy: tourism, communications, and free enterprise zones.[21] Of the seventeen students on the trip, about half were business majors. Dominican professors held discussions and gave lectures about the role of capitalism and whether the benefits being provided should be the priority of the country. Most of the students agreed that to give capitalism a free hand in the Dominican Republic and then, when enterprises are wealthy, to expect them to share their success with the Dominican people was probably a mistake. They understood that the government was trying to establish a tightened economy, with punishing cutbacks in social programs, for the sake of acquiring International Monetary Fund loans. But the question was how far could you push the people before they lost faith in the

system and went into the streets. For the time being, the government had as-
surances from union bosses to hold the workers back but even they could not
guarantee that the people would not take to the streets.

What affected the students the most were the free-enterprise zones that hire
young, uneducated Dominican women for low wages, no benefits, and no unions. This was capitalism at its worst, and the students criticized such blatant
exploitation. Yet they were concerned that if capitalism was not the answer,
then it was hard to know what could take its place. What was clear to them was
that the trickle-down effect of capitalism was not working. The rich were becoming wealthier, and the poor were slipping more deeply into despair. This
points out the fragility of the story of capitalism and the way of life of incoherence. Of its very nature, the story of capitalism in the service of incoherence
cannot resolve the issue of poverty because its main concern is profits and power
for the few. For capitalism to succeed, many people have to fail. In order to
legitimize this situation, the poor have to be convinced that if they work hard,
they will get somewhere, but if they fail, it is their own fault. There was ample
evidence that Dominicans were ready to try anything to set up small businesses
to succeed economically. But we were told by one of the Dominican economists
that every day more businesses fail than succeed. It was also clear to us that
the government was prepared to use force to protect the life and property of the
rich. In this way, capitalism in the Dominican Republic, as elsewhere, exits the
core drama of life and enters into deformation, wherein life is now fundamentally worse.

We also saw sugar-cane plantations and had lectures given by Dominican
scholars detailing the historical and political background of the sugar industry
in the Dominican Republic. Their lectures centered around the relationship between Haiti and the Dominican Republic. For historical reasons, the Dominicans
have been manipulated to believe that Haiti is their enemy. Although both pop-
ulations are primarily black, with more African features than European, the
Dominicans have been educated to feel superior to Haitians. The sugar-cane
industry highlights the chasm between the two peoples. Dominicans refuse to
work in the cane fields because it is "Haitian work," that is, below them. This
identification of Haitians and the sugar industry goes back to the time of the
1930–61 Dominican dictatorship of Rafael Trujillo. He personally owned most
of the sugar-cane fields and used almost exclusively Haitian workers. They were
not allowed to go home once they began working for him. Any Haitians found
in the country not employed in the fields were subject to arrest, imprisonment,
or even death. With the class I discussed how the story of capitalism often
colludes with racism and sexism to exploit workers. Whenever profits become
more important than human life, especially when people of color or women are
diminished as human beings, capitalism is no longer just competition for advantage in the open market in the service of incoherence but now becomes
something worse, capitalism in the service of deformation. Reform at its best in
this context would remove the most scandalous kind of abuses, such as the

virtual slavery of the Haitian workers in the cane fields, but leave the story itself intact, along with the ways of life that collude with each other in order to preserve the power of some at the expense of the majority.[22]

We have to remind ourselves that we are dealing here with men and women who are seized by the story of capitalism. They are not in control. They are taken over, possessed by the story of capitalism that drives them and makes them incapable of compassion. This story produces an emanational hold over people that is truly demonic. Yet we are not victims fated by our past history. We can free ourselves personally and politically from this story and become conscious of what it is doing to us and others. We can enter into incoherence with it, so that we break critically and consciously on the deeper level with capitalism and the ways of life of incoherence and deformation that wound our humanity and choose to create an economy that meets the human needs of all of its citizens.

CONCLUSION

Robert Coles, a child psychiatrist at Harvard University, wrote a short but provocative article on the occasion of Harvard's 350th birthday that reminded me why and what it is that we need to teach.

If only there were a correlation between the genetic endowment of intelligence and goodness. But is there? How many of us are all too smart, and yet also weird, snotty and selfish? In his novel, *The Second Coming*, the writer Walker Percy describes one of his characters as "one of those people who got all As but flunked life." How will we pass life? How will we learn to nourish one another and care for one another, and care for our children, and be good to them? How can we be good enough for our children to inspire them to be good to others?[23]

This statement highlights the importance that we as teachers play in the lives of our students. In the work that I do with K–12 teachers, I remind them and myself that our task is not to prepare our students to join the powerful. Our efforts to introduce multicultural diversity and gender into the curriculum must not be seen as assimilation into existing structures. Rather, our challenge is to ask fundamental questions about how and why we educate students. Do we prepare them to follow orders without question in the service of the dying fragments of emanation as a way of life? Do we train them to dominate and control others in the service of incoherence? Do we give them the tools to cripple others in the service of deformation? Or do we critically and consciously guide them to their deepest creative imagination so that, together with others, they can participate in practicing transformation in all aspects of their lives? How we answer these questions will determine the ultimate quality of our schools, colleges, and universities and the quality of our teaching. There is no escape from taking responsibility for such questions. In the final analysis we teach who we are and guide students not only to where we are in the core drama of life, but beyond, so that they can through the capacity of their own creative imagination give shape to their own life and story and assist others in their journey. Teaching in the service of transformation helps to free students from smothering dogmas that cannot be questioned, assists in liberating them from a sacred story that justifies competition for power, and above all guides them in emptying themselves of stories based on race, class, and gender that justify hurting others. Once we have vomited out the poisonous stories and ways of life, we, together with our students, can now turn to the task for which we are here: to guide people to the deepest source within themselves, so that they can persistently participate with their personal, political, historical, and sacred face in the transformation of self, other, the world, and the deepest sacred.[24]

NOTES

1. I have gained greatly from conversations with my colleague Manfred Halpern, Professor Emeritus of the Politics Department, Princeton University. For the past twenty-five years, we have been friends together, involved in developing ever anew the theory and practice of transformation.

2. Martha Graham, as quoted in the *New York Times*, December 19, 1994, p. B7.

3. See the fine book by Félix M. Padilla, *The Struggle of Latino/Latina University Students, In Search of a Liberating Education* (New York, London: Routledge, 1997).

4. As quoted in another work that sees the sacred as the underlying meaning of all of our relationships and stories: Henri Corbin, *Creative Imagination in the Sufism of Ibn Arabi* (Princeton, NJ: Princeton University Press, 1969), p. 257.

5. Shlomo Avineri, "Marx's Vision of Future Society," *Dissent* (Summer 1973): 323–31.

6. David T. Abalos, *Strategies of Transformation Toward a Multicultural Society Fulfilling the Story of Democracy* (Westport, CT, and London: Praeger, 1996), chapters 4 and 5.

7. Thomas Kuhn, *The Structure of Scientific Revolutions* (Chicago: University of Chicago Press, 1969). This work in an extraordinary way parallels the three acts and scenes of the core drama of life. As the scientific community moves from normal science to anomaly, as scientific discovery leads to crisis, and as crisis leads to the creation of a new scientific revolution, the changes of worldview that accompany them results in the understanding that science, in order to be science, needs, as a human endeavor, to continue to respond to the creative imagination. This process leads to continuous revolution or transformation. See also in this regard a wonderful book, edited by Brewster Ghiselen and titled *The Creative Process* (New York: A Mentor Book, published by The New American Library, 1963), especially Henri Poincaré, "Mathematical Creation."

8. Corbin, *Creative Imagination in the Sufism of Ibn Arabi*, p. 257.

9. Ibid., p. 271.

10. Ibid.

11. Ibid., pp. 232–33.

12. Alan Paton, *Too Late the Phalarope* (New York: Charles Scribner's Sons, 1953).

13. In my use of the comments and direct quotes from student papers, I received

permission from the students to use their papers in the writing of this chapter. I would also like to take this opportunity to thank all of my students in both of my sections of Rels 1502, Contemporary Moral Values.

14. Alice Walker, *The Color Purple* (New York: Pocket Books, Washington Square Books, 1982).

15. Rainer Maria Rilke, *Breife an einen jungen Dichter (Letters to a Young Poet)* (Leipzig: 1929), p. 48.

16. The Gospel According to St. Matthew, 12:43–45.

17. For a further development of creative imagination in the classroom, see Abalos, *Strategies of Transformation Toward a Multicultural Society*, chapter 5.

18. Paton, *Too Late the Phalarope*, p. 62.

19. President Leonel Fernández, "The Future of the Dominican Republic," speech given in Miami, FL, December 10, 1996.

20. Father Avelino Fernández, "The Role of the Catholic Church in the Dominican Republic: Religion and Social Change," lecture, APEC University, Santo Domingo, Dominican Republic, January 10, 1997.

21. President Fernández, Miami speech, December 10, 1996.

22. Lectures were given by Dr. Argelia Tejada on "Race, Class, and Gender in the Dominican Republic"; Lic. Carlos Cuello on "Economic Development of the Dominican Republic and the Caribbean Region"; Lic. Ruben Silié on "Haiti and the Dominican Republic"; and Dr. Hector Aristy on "Dictatorship in the Dominican Republic and the Civil War of 1965."

23. Robert Coles, "Educating for a Moral Life," *Harvard Educational Review* (May 1987):195.

24. During the 1996–97 academic year, I served as an academic advisor to the Brick Township School District in Brick Town, NJ. My task was to work with the whole of the school district, but especially the faculty, to integrate multicultural and gender issues into the curriculum. This was truly an extraordinary experience. The schools received me with a wonderful sense of hospitality and openness. I can't thank them enough. I want especially to recognize the outstanding courage and leadership provided for the project by Dr. Bruce Normandia, the superintendent of Brick Township School District. He cares deeply about children and about helping to bring the personal, political, historical, and sacred faces of their being to their fullness.

5

El Siglo XXI: Strategies of Transformation for la Comunidad Latina

INTRODUCTION

One of the most important tasks that we face as a community is to develop strategies of transformation to enable us to redeem our past, transform our present, and prepare our future in an ever-present now. One of the most important strategies needs to be to create a cultura Latina. In this final chapter, I want to return to issues raised in chapter 2 and to be more specific, especially as to how we can use a strategy of subversion to turn our culture around and free ourselves as whole human beings. Presently, all of us Latinas and Latinos are caught, suspended, and struggling between two civilizations as the Mexican philosopher and poet Octavio Paz has taught us.[1] We have a rich, indigenous past that beats in our blood as well as a European, an African, and a Jewish, Christian, and Muslim heritage.[2] But these various cultural, religious, racial, and historical strands of our *mestizaje*, mixed heritage, have never been reconciled.

Since the Conquest, we have experienced this *choque de las culturas*, clash of cultures, together with a loss of memory because we were denied access to our past. Our various Latino cultures were violently interrupted by cultural imperialism that rendered any but Western European culture as inferior and therefore not worthy of being taught. Two Latino communities, the Chicano/Mejicano and the Puerto Rican, do not consider themselves immigrants, but conquered peoples. Mejicanos were made to be strangers in their own land as a result of the Mexican/U.S. War.[3] For this reason many Chicanos consider the recent return migration of Mejicanos to be a peaceful reconquest of the American Southwest. With the passage of the Jones Act in 1917 Puerto Ricans were made U.S. citizens purely for economic reasons, without their participation or consent. Since that time many Boricua, a word taken from the Taíno word for the island, Borinquén, have found themselves displaced from their own land by the economic policies of the mainland and the island's elites.[4]

Many other Latinas and Latinos are here because of the displacement, both economic and political, brought about by U.S. foreign policy, which sought to dominate the Western Hemisphere ever since the Monroe Doctrine of 1823. Still other Latinos have come to seek a better life in the United States. What all of us have in common is the Conquest, a 500-year-old trauma that was never healed, and the confusion of identity that resulted from the coming of the Europeans. The Spaniards were ruthless in their determination to destroy the culture of the indigenos. Our *herencia indigena*, Indian heritage, which consisted of at least 500 different cultures, was tremendously rich and varied. When Hernán Cortés witnessed the beauty and engineering marvel of Mexico City, Tenochtitlán, he concluded that it had to be the work of the Devil since God was of course a Spaniard, a European, a Catholic, and on their side. They believed that they had the truth and came to the New World to evangelize and to find gold and silver.

The peoples of the Americas experienced cultural domination, cultural imperialism, and cultural extermination. What does ''culture'' mean? Culture is a total way of life consisting of values, feelings, and ideas regarding basic human issues such as love, food, old age, sex, family, death, and rebirth. But culture is also, and perhaps more importantly, the gathering together of all of these elements into a network of stories that provides for a people a cosmos of meaning.[5] In the confrontation between the cultures and stories of the two civilizations, the Europeans imposed their culture. As a symbol of their alleged superiority, the Spaniards destroyed pyramids and other Indian places of worship and built churches on top of the decapitated structures. But the culture was also superimposed by the forced marriage of the Spaniard and the *indigena*, the native woman. The story of La Malinche, Doña Marina, the Indian concubine of Cortés, is a constant reminder to the indigenous male that his power is gone.[6] Honor and family were undermined by the conquest. This historical fact still reverberates throughout Latino America and in la comunidad Latina in this country. It served and continues to serve as the justification for possessive relationships that are often characterized by physical retaliation whenever a Latina threatens a Latino's manhood.[7]

All Latinas and Latinos are the result of a *mestizaje*; we are a *mestizo* people, the coming together of different civilizations, different stories, different races. But it is important to point out that our Indian ancestors were not innocent victims. The Moche in Peru, the Aztecs in Mexico, the Maya in Central America all practiced human sacrifice, even cannibalism, conquered other tribes, and were dominated by a warrior culture. The point is that all cultures have a destructive, as well as a creative side. So it is up to us as the mestizo children of these cultures to discern which of the stories are worth continuing by choosing the stories of life and transformation and rejecting those dramas that diminish and deform our humanity.

INTELLECTUALS AND ACADEMICS IN LA COMUNIDAD LATINA

My mother knew the difference between a lot of nonsense and an intuitive understanding of the truth when she used an old saying, a *dicho*, "Ese no tiene educación," that person has no education. Our forebears understood the distinction between schooling and a deeper understanding of education. In the Latino community an educated person, *una persona con educación*, an authentic academic and intellectual should not be above it all, who uses big words to mystify others; on the contrary she or he is rooted in community, in a threefold manner. The intellectual is first of all grounded in the depths within herself or himself; all of us have a community of inner voices, interior guides, and a creative imagination that we need to express in order to find our deeper self. Second, the intellectual is connected to la comunidad Latina, family, friends and neighbors; through interaction with these significant others, intellectuals come to understand their own life and that of their neighbors, and they come to discern the stories that hurt or nourish the community. Third, intellectuals are connected to the deeper underlying, forming sacred sources from which our culture and stories draw their ultimate purpose and meaning. By means of this threefold connectedness, the intellectual in our midst serves as a guide, an interpreter, a prophet, a philosopher, and a participant ready to engage the issues that face us all. Thus the authentic intellectual is never a haughty, withdrawn person who passes judgment on the ability of others. No, the true intellectual identifies with the concerns and pain of others and is in touch with his or her own suffering and the search for the cause of this pain in the sacred stories and ways of life in which we are all caught.

The Latina or Latino intellectual, writer, or artist, guide us in their writings, teaching, and artistic creation and thus assist the community in understanding, conceptualizing, and reexperiencing the deeper meanings of life. They help us to become aware through their analysis of the connections that bridge us and those that are breaking; we are enabled through their creative work to recognize and act on the choices we have regarding our relationships, stories, and ways of life that presently connect us and whether they are destructive or to the good; they guide us in breaking or nurturing connections to our cultural stories and, finally, they, together with the rest of la comunidad Latina, participate with the deepest source of transformation in creating new and more loving connections that heal. This is the process by which culture is transformed.

As a Chicano/Latino academic, I teach a theory of transformation. The re-action to academics in general and especially to theory by some in the Latino community is often one of intimidation. Many in our community, like others, identify academics, intellectuals, and theorists with the upper class, who are looking for more ways to control the people. But the theory that I teach is an invitation to participate in the deepest story in all cultures: the core drama of life, the story and journey of transformation. In this way all of us are intellectuals because this theory asks of us that we look at the deeper meaning of our own personal lives and identities and ask Who am I? We can ask fundamental ques-tions regarding our relationships to ourselves, to others, and to the deeper sacred sources, and we can ask how these connections either disable us or capacitate us to deal with new kinds of problems. This is a theory that you and I can test with our own experiences. In this way we all need good talk, good theory that allows us to tell our story.

Theory is only authentic when it is fruitfully related to practice. There is a dialectical relationship between action and reflection. Theory and action are antidotes to each other, for it is action that tests and purifies theory and theory that does the same for action; we therefore need both theory and practice, words and deeds, to participate in carrying out the transformation of ourselves, the world, and the sacred. Theory without action becomes empty and useless rhet-oric; but action without theory as a guide is the activity of those who have no idea as to where they are going.

In summary, it is the best of our intellectuals and artists, connected to the truth in ways described above, who live this story and process of transformation and can serve as our guides. Good theory guides us as we reflect on who we are, where we have been, where we are now, and where we are going as a community. As the sun rises in this time of renewal and transformation, it is crucial to be able to discern what stories and ways of life are crippling our capacity as a people and how in fact we can practice transformation here and now. The Aztec empire was destroyed because it failed to read the signs of the time correctly. When reports came that there was a strange god who had come out of the sea in the east, the Aztecs believed that it was the return of Quetz-alcóatl, the exiled god of culture who was supposed to return in the year 1 Acatl. Disaster struck, for the return of Quetzalcóatl was in reality the coming of new but worse lords: war, invasion, slavery, and the destructive death of deformation. We have it in our capacity to make every day a year 1 Acatl, the return of the god that will renew us. Each day as the sun rises as a symbol of the victory of life over the death of night, we need to be vigilant and to discern between the forces of deformation and the new and more loving face of trans-formation. Every day becomes *Sun-day*, a *Domingo*, a new birth of the sun. It helps us to understand what our parents meant when they said to us: ''Aquí está tú Domingo'', Here is your allowance. Our new allowance for each *sun-day* is the right to daily participate together with our community in the life, death, and transformation of sacred sources. How do we do this? We can do it by testing our life and experience through new eyes that allow us to understand and participate in a beautiful story that has been told and lived for at least 2,500 years, the story and journey of transformation as the core drama of life. Each of us, of the very nature of being human, can participate in this drama, which connects us to our deepest self, to our neighbors, to problems, and to the deepest sacred. Through our participation in the theory of transformation, we can do archetypal analysis, that is, search out the deeper, sacred underlying meaning of life. This is radical work, (a word that comes from the Latin, *radix, radices*, the root[s] of things), because it enables us to get to our Latino roots, *nuestros raices*, and to discover the underlying causes of our rootlessness and how to grow new roots and plant a fundamentally more loving and compassionate culture.

CRITIQUE OF LA CULTURA LATINA

Our foremothers and forefathers often kept us arrested in the first scene of Act I in the service of the way of life of emanation, wherein we were forbidden to question their authority because it was a *falta de respeto*, lack of respect, for which we would receive a punishment from God, *un castigo de Dios*. The pyramid of privilege and power that had been blessed by the indigenous gods was replaced by the hierarchy of Spanish priests, warriors, and royalty. These authorities demanded uncritical loyalty and were prepared to use force to suppress any emerging new voices and ideas that represented Act I, Scene 2. The rebellions against Spanish rule in the nineteenth century, although it did much to end the age of emanation for the powerful, also kept the majority of the people on the bottom of the pyramid. The powerful freed themselves from the restraints on the pursuit of self-interest and became fully engaged in the story of capitalism, which arrested them in Act II, Scene 1. The people in the countryside remained for the most part caught in the container of emanation; it was therefore very difficult for them to resist the powerful, who were no longer inhibited by the threats of sin, shame, and guilt. In Mexico, during and after the Mexican Revolution, the peasants were betrayed by those who sought the return of the pyramid by institutionalizing the power of the Institutional Revolutionary Party (PRI), which in the elections of July 6, 1997, would suffer its worst defeat, but after wielding absolute power for sixty-eight years.[8] Time and again the people found themselves victims of the way of life of emanation allied with the ways of life of incoherence and deformation. The upper classes used the fragments of emanation to keep the people loyal to them while they pursued power at the expense of the nation. If there was resistance to their oligarchy, they did not hesitate to use violence in the service of deformation.

Our forebears suffered from the story of tribalism in the service of deformation. Since the Conquest, the Spaniards had held heated debates as to whether the Indians were human. Even though the Church and Crown sided with those who fought for the full humanity of the indigenous, racism was a reality in everyday life. The whole of the landholding system, the *encomiendas*, tied the people to the land.[9] They belonged to the land so that when the land was sold, their services were part of the deal. The Spaniards, and after them the powerful among the mestizo class, who always emphasized their Spanish heritage, created a fantasy. They took a fragment of life, either the purity of Spanish blood or skin color, and turned it into fantasies that dominated the whole of life. If you had one of these fragments, then you were considered one of the better ones. There were only five ways by which the chosen could relate to the outsiders: the dispossessed were invisible, inferior, forced to assimilate, exiled for disloyalty to the powerful, and subject to extermination.[10] The Indians to this day continue to suffer in Guatemala from this story in the service of deformation. The January 1, 1994, uprising of the Mayan Indians who call themselves Zapatistas, after the Mexican Revolution hero Emiliano Zapata, in the Mexican state of Chiapas represents a struggle for justice: they sought land and human rights that go back to the time of the Conquest. The victims of the death squads in El Salvador, Honduras, and Guatemala, *los desaparecidos*, the disappeared, in Argentina and Chile all represent the fragility of the ways of life of emanation and incoherence. When the ability of the stories of uncritical loyalty, patriarchy, and capitalism to silence the people begins to give way to analysis and critical action, the privileged have always turned to violence, at the second scene of Act II. Rather than empty themselves of the stories and ways of life that cripple the people and empty them into the abyss, they choose to send themselves and their victims into the exit from the drama, where life is made fundamentally worse for all. Why does this show the fragility of these ways of life? Because, as we have seen, the ways of life of emanation, incoherence, and deformation take us over and cripple us, so that we cannot respond to new kinds of problems. Since nobody is fully present because of the possession by sacred stories and ways of life that bind us all, our deepest self and our creative imagination are cut off from the deepest source of transformation.

But the god of transformation has always been present, from the beginning. One of the great mercies of the universe is the presence of the deepest source of transformation, which intervenes again and again on our behalf. We have evidence from our heritage that the *indigenos* understood the struggle between competing sacred sources. The Popol Vuh is excellent evidence of the awareness of the Indians that there was a loving sacred source that constituted the deepest ground of our being and wanted us to succeed in practicing transformation as the purpose of life. Whoever the author or authors of this story of creation were, they understood that life was a struggle of choosing between destructive sacred sources and the deepest source of transformation that created us to participate in finishing creation. Listen to the dialogue in The Popol Vuh between the gods and goddesses who had gathered to discuss the creation of a creature that would be worthy enough to honor them. They experimented and attempted to make human beings out of wood, clay, and monkeys but were dissatisfied with each of these attempts. Then they discovered the right material, maíz (corn), which was the food of the gods. There is a terrifying element here in the sense that the gods could now devour human beings made of maíz as food. But a subversive strategy was also present. Those who are eaten become necessary to the survival of the gods. Thus, in a sense, the human beings have also devoured the gods. They now need one another. As time went on, humans began to become sacred in their own right. The gods were surprised that human beings came to know everything; they could see and understand all. The lesser, jealous lords were alarmed that they would be surpassed by human beings who would no longer need them, and so they sought to undo them. Human beings were crippled by jealous lords, who blinded them and took away their ability to see and know everything.[11] Human beings were now wounded and therefore dependent on those lords who did not want their participation in the work of finishing creation. These lesser lords sought to arrest the transformation of human beings and to frustrate the core drama of life. They were free to do so, as I have said earlier, because this is not a puppet play. We and the sacred sources are free to arrest the drama of life and to settle for less.

This story from our Indian past, which has many parallels in other American Indian cultures as well as around the world, throws into sharp relief the choices that we have. We have the capacity of the very nature of our humanity to participate in the process of transformation as the core drama of life. But we are also free to arrest the drama together with lesser sacred lords in a fragment of the core drama that leaves us partial selves. Thus we can, together with the lord of emanation, declare that creation is finished, and we need no longer to practice transformation; or we can get caught in the first scene of Act II and turn our whole lives into the pursuit of self-interest and power and be inspired by the lord of incoherence; or we are free to make life fundamentally worse through self-wounding and the wounding of others as we listen to the lord of nothing at the exit from the core drama in the abyss, where life becomes fundamentally new but worse; or, finally, we are capable of choosing to respond to the deepest source of transformation, which invites us to join in the continuous creation of the cosmos.

These four sacred sources correspond to the four ultimate ways of life, emanation, incoherence, deformation, and transformation. Whenever we respond to an inspiration, it comes from one of these sacred sources. At every moment of our lives, we are somewhere in the core drama of life, living in one of its acts and scenes particular concrete stories and relationships. These stories, such as capitalism, patriarchy, democracy, possessive love, the guide, the family, and others, derive their deeper meaning and ultimate value from the sacred source that inspires them and the way of life in which we enact them. As discussed above, all of our concrete stories and relationships that are practiced in the first three ways of life are only a fragment of the core drama of life; therefore they leave us fragmented and incapable of being able to respond to fundamentally new kinds of problems. We know only how to reform and stay with what we have and know. Now that we are aware of the stories and the ways of life that have harmed us, we are also free to empty ourselves on the deeper level of destructive stories and ways of life and to choose transformation as the only way of life that allows us to step forward with the fullness of the personal, political, historical, and sacred faces of our being.[12]

LATINAS AND LATINOS IN THE UNITED STATES

Many of our Latin American foremothers and forefathers were already badly wounded by the stories of tribalism, capitalism, uncritical loyalty, possessive love, and patriarchy in the service of truncated, partial ways of life that arrested them in a fragment of the core drama of life and prevented them from practicing transformation. These stories and ways of life kept our foremothers and forefathers arrested in the core drama in either Act I or Act II, often as victims of others who practiced deformation by diminishing their humanity. To escape their suffering, many left their native lands and sought to make a new life. To achieve this, many had to pay a heavy price in American society: repressing their past and assimilating into the ranks of the powerful, who usually conspired to keep them out, as they were potential competitors and threats to their power. Assimilation signifies hatred of one's self and of one's community, a stripping away of what the powerful consider unacceptable. Many of us in this society, especially the second and third generations, became, or were made, ashamed to speak Spanish and were embarrassed by our Spanish-speaking, often poorly educated parents and *abuelos* and *abuelas*, grandparents.

To become like the Anglos, the whites, the European Americans, was really to accept the story of capitalism that arrested and held U.S. society in Act II, Scene 1, in the service of the way of life of incoherence. In this partial story and way of life, we above all join white males in their permanent adolescent rebellion.[13] Why permanent? Because after rebelling against those who held us in the container of emanation in Act I, rather than breaking away not only from our concrete antagonists but of going on to the second scene of Act II wherein we empty ourselves of the stories and ways of life that render us impotent as partial selves, we turn Act II, Scene 1, into the way of life of incoherence. Here we are caught by the lord of incoherence who inspires us to seek more and more power. Since we can never have enough power, we live always on the edge of insecurity. In the realm of emanation we share common values with others; when we leave the container of emanation, we consider others potential enemies, who cannot be trusted. The powerful and those looking to become powerful are doomed to look perpetually over their shoulder for fear that they will be overcome in the race to power. The powerless are equally caught by this drama. They believe that the only option open to them is to rebel against the current distribution of power, so that they can become a success. If they fail, they blame themselves, rationalizing that this is an open society that gives everybody a chance to make it. Even the powerful—especially the powerful— continue to rebel against their previous accumulation of power and seek to deprive others so that they can accumulate and concentrate more power. This story drives everybody to distraction. Nobody can get out of the rat race for fear of falling further behind. If some threaten the whole system by their refusal to participate according to the rules, then the legitimized violence of the state is used to punish them. Threats to the whole system can also be deflected by reforms and incremental change such as establishing welfare systems that buy off the poor.

Any attempt to make capitalism into a kinder and gentler system or to make capitalism work for us is only a reformation in which we add and subtract benefits depending on who got elected. What is never at stake is the story itself, the story of capitalism in the service of incoherence and/or deformation. We cannot ask nor expect capitalism to finance its own demise by supporting transformation. These two stories are mutually exclusive. In any efforts to support community groups, what is always involved is self-interest. There is no other reality for capitalism. There is no concern for the humanity of the poor; all of the community involvement is ultimately motivated by a desire to save the system and those who profit from it. Drastic steps are taken against those who pose a real threat to the power of the few. In order to protect what they have, the powerful are willing to go outside the law and to collude with the way of life of deformation by the use of violence.

Some of us Latinas and Latinos rationalize our participation in this story and way of life by promising to give back to our communities when we are successful. We therefore settle for less and arrest our lives in Act II, Scene 1, in which we join the powerful. The impact of this arrest on the four faces of our being is dramatic. We hide our personal face because we cannot afford for people to get to know us, lest we become vulnerable in a dangerous world of competition for power. With our political face we look to attach ourselves to those in power so that we can become more powerful fragments. Our historical face sees the past, present, and future only from the perspective of power—a powerless past, a promising present, and a grounding in power to secure the future; our sacred face is obscured by the lord of incoherence that whispers in our ear that self-interest and getting ahead are all that matters. With the story of capitalism holding us in an emanational embrace, we deceive ourselves in saying and believing that we want to serve the community. We now give back only what serves our self-interest. We begin to see our community as a threat to our advancement. The powerful want us to become spokespersons for the people in the barrio so that they will not be able to speak for themselves. This is what it means to be a token; we represent the community only to the extent that the corporate and government agencies that hired us allow it. This means that we in reality represent the needs of the dominant and serve as fronts for their public image. In this way we as educated and professional Latinas and Latinos can be co-opted by the powerful to help control and police our own people.

We wear our *sarapes* and *sombreros* on the appropriate fiestas, but we have really lost contact with the spirit of resistance that many of our people demonstrated, especially in the earlier decades of the twentieth century. For example, the Chicano miners, Los Mineros, in Clifton and Morenci, Arizona, fought for fifty years to win the rights of equal pay and health benefits. Many were imprisoned, shot, killed, and deported in the struggle to win their rights. This is an extraordinary story that was just recently told,[14] one filled with collusion between capitalism and racism that deprived the Mexican miners of these and other basic human rights. They were brutalized by a corporation that divided the workers along ethnic lines, paying the Anglos two to three times the salary paid to Mejicanos. This is the kind of story that needs to be told, along with the stories of other Latino groups who are currently being treated in the same way as these miners: low pay, no benefits, no unions, no promotions, no respect. It is time once again to step forward and to protect the rights of the exploited workers in our midst, usually *los recien llegados*, the newly arrived. Because many of us do not know the stories of resistance from our past, we continue to practice accommodation rather than a politics of resistance and transformation. We suffer from an amnesiac condition, *los pasos perdidos*, the lost footsteps in our journey of transformation. Because of a school curriculum based on the supremacy of the dominant groups, we learn almost nothing of *nuestro antepasado*, our past. As time goes on, the second and third generations in this country lose their cultural memory. Although we were told to forget our past and become Americans, too often we were excluded precisely because we are members of la comunidad Latina. This leads to a great deal of hurt and loss for our young people. On the one hand, they know neither their history nor their culture, and they are not really fully accepted here. To assimilate is not to find out who we are, but to allow others to define our story for us. Thus in spite of what the European Americans tell us, none of us as people of color or whites in this society can really pursue our self-interest because we cannot know who that self is or what our best interest consists of.

With our emanational connections to our past breaking in Act I and our inability to make it in the story of capitalism in Act II, Scene 1, which dominates American society, many of us are tempted to turn to stories of underground capitalism, that is, crime, or to organize gangs, or *cliqas*, as alternatives to the loss of identity and family. Our communities in many of the urban centers of our country are being victimized by drugs and violence that are sometimes controlled by members of our own community. Currently, we know that Mexican drug lords are in competition with Colombian cartels to determine who will control the drug trade in this country. In the barrios of Los Angeles, New York, and Chicago, Latino gangs are involved in the local drug trade. Trying for a piece of the American dream, to become an ''American Me,'' the drug business leads many Latino and Latina youth to forms of deformation that make our people's lives fundamentally worse. The gangs that turn to violence to establish turf and substitute families are looking for new forms of emanation, a container, something to which they can belong and give their loyalty. The gang members get caught by a pseudoemanation and are willing to follow anybody who promises them not just power, but absolute power over the lives of others, those others who have hurt them and made them feel bad by excluding them. This search for revenge is always in the service of deformation. It is really a form of rebellion that catches the rebels in the story of the oppressor. Just as the Anglos hurt them, now they will get back at them. The struggle is still one based on race and ethnicity, but now the victim becomes the victimizer. Nothing has changed to make life better; we are still caught in the same story, the drama of racism/tribalism in the service of deformation, which keeps us all in the abyss.

Now why do communities that have been traditionally so law-abiding turn to crime? The system, the sacred story of capitalism in the service of incoherence and deformation, would not let them in. Incoherence as a way of life, as I have mentioned, is based on anxiety and insecurity because power can be so easily lost. This makes the way of life of incoherence very fragile. It cannot deal with new problems that threaten its power except by resorting to reforms that are only incremental changes that strengthen the status quo; it is system-maintaining change. When reforms fail, the system can resort to forms of violence. The practitioners of the story of capitalism, once they feel threatened, are in danger of no longer being only in the service of incoherence. Now they are tempted to enter into collusion with deformation. "Why won't we let you in?" asks the dominant group. Among the answers given are: "Because you are not as intelligent; you don't have enough experience or education; you are too emotional; you people like to party too much; you are not a team player; you are too loyal to your own people; y'all are good workers but you don't know how to administer or manage and you don't speak good English." These are the kind of responses, whenever European Americans are open enough to express them, that many of us have heard all of our lives. In this way the story of capitalism in the service of incoherence enters an alliance with racism in the service of deformation because the dominant feel that their power is threatened.

This means that people in power choose to prevent the powerless in la comunidad Latina from acquiring enough food, jobs, access to health care, housing, education because they are systematically excluded from participating in the wider society. This is not the fault of the Latino community; it is largely due to the fear of the dominant society of the competition that will come from an educated and well-prepared community. To preserve their power, the powerful do more and more to cripple the ability of others to compete. This is the root cause of the attacks on Affirmative Action and immigration in Texas and especially in California, as evidenced by the passage of two Propositions 187 (a law intended to bar undocumented people from receiving social services and public school education) and 209 (a law intended to end affirmative action programs throughout the state). These are only recent examples that threaten to spread to other parts of the country. The powerful blame the Latino community for its failure to be more aggressive when, in fact, it is the result of those who are practicing the story of capitalism, allied with racism, in the service of deformation that excludes the community from participation in the benefits of our nation. Either as victims or as victimizers, the four faces of our being are now profoundly wounded. Our personal face is erased, canceled out by those who hate us, but ironically, they also erase their own human faces in the process. With our political face, we experience the politics of anger, revenge, violence, and exclusion as victims. Our historical face is fundamentally more distorted as time goes on. Our sacred face is now linked to the lord of deformation who whispers that we are nothing and so cannot do anything or else inspires us toward revenge against the powerful, so that we can now take our turn at yielding absolute power over others. There is no way out from the logic of this rage and madness. We cannot possibly transform our lives, nor those of others, by having our personal face denied or by making the personal face of others invisible, because in that action the humanity of both the defeated and the perpetrator is crippled. Since we are all cut off from the deepest source of transformation, our personal faces cannot hear how to create the fundamentally new and better only to repeat the current story and way of life grounded in the lord of nothing. Thus our politics will be impoverished if we surrender ourselves to the same violence in response to violence. With our historical face we are incapable of creating a new story as things get worse. Our sacred face remains mired in the abyss of rage and hatred. This analysis of the four faces of our being in the service of deformation points out the inherent limits and destructiveness of deformation as a way of life. It is utterly bankrupt in its ability to change our lives for the better.[15]

This racist assault in the service of deformation, which threatens to exit our community from the core drama of life and into the abyss, makes us victims. But we do not have to respond as hopeless victims or fatalists or by rage and violence. We can choose to practice a politics of transformation. Our great guides and activists such as César Chávez knew that the answer was not more violence, but justice and compassion for everybody, including one's enemy because the enemy is also the victim of this deadly story.[16] Malcolm X came to realize at the end of his life that it wasn't white people who were the enemy, but white attitudes that led whites to believe that they were superior to dark-skinned people.[17] In other words, we have to deal with the deeper causes of racism, the underlying forming sources, the archetypal story of racism and the way of life of deformation that produces the white attitude. In her strikingly beautiful novel *Ceremony*, Leslie Marmon Silko tells us that it is not whites who are the enemy, but the stories of the witchery that took them over and victimized them as well as us.[18] But since neither whites nor people of color realize this, Latinos as a community too often say, "Now it is our time." For what? Our time for revenge, our time to take power and become just as arrogant and destructive as the Anglos, our time to restore a golden age that never existed, or our time to help build a fundamentally more loving and just society for all communities in this nation?

CREATING ALTERNATIVES IN THE SERVICE OF
TRANSFORMATION

We are the living carriers of the culture and of the traditions handed down to us by our forebears. We are free to analyze the stories and ways of life that hold us and to understand where we are arrested in the core drama of life. The cost to the four faces of our being of limited and partial ways of life has been too high. Analysis is not enough; the theory of transformation cannot be fulfilled unless we apply theory to action. It is up to us to break with those who hold us in the stories of capitalism; tribalism; patriarchy/matriarchy; possessive, romantic love; uncritical loyalty; and other such stories that are enacted within the ways of life of emanation, incoherence, and deformation. We need to break with these wounding stories and ways of life on the deeper level in Act II, Scene 2, and to empty them into the abyss. Once we have succeeded in liberating ourselves in this way, we can count on being filled anew by the deepest of all sacred sources, the god of transformation in Act III, Scene 1, and politically, with our neighbor, in the second scene of Act III bring about in practice a new and better turning point in our history.

Let us begin by using a strategy of subversion by reaching back and taking the best from our Latino heritage so that we can recreate and rediscover our culture in the service of transformation. Tayo, the American Indian protagonist in Silko's *Ceremony*, throughout the novel vomits out the poison of the lies that he has been told. As the novel comes to a conclusion, Tayo is taught how to create the alternative that affirms the life of the people and the endurance of the land by planting new seeds.[19] As we learned in The Popol Vuh, it is our heritage to know everything, to see everything, because it is within us to be *curanderas* and *curanderos*, healers. We can, like Betonie, the medicine man who serves as Tayo's guide, learn to understand the new outbreaks of deformation in our midst and create new rituals of transformation by which to defeat them before they become active. This means that we can be preventive by discerning the emergence of deformation and develop strategies of intervention before it becomes virulent in our society. We do not have to be the vessels of the destructive and jealous lords of emanation, incoherence, and deformation that blind us and cripple our capacity. We can choose to participate in practicing transformation, together with the deepest source of transformation.

Like Juanita in *La Carreta* (The Oxcart), we can say: "Porque no eh cosa de volver a la tierra pa vivir como muertoh. Ahora sabemos que el mundo no cambia por sí mihmo. Que somoh nosotroh loh que cambiamoh al mundo . . . ¡Asi volveromoh al barrio! Uhté y yo mamá, firmeh como ausuboh sobre la tierra nuehtra, y Luis dehcansando en ella!" "We cannot go home to live as dead people. Now we know that the world doesn't change by itself. That we are the ones who can change the world. . . . That's how we will return to our neighborhood! You and I, mama, strong like we used to be on our land, and Luis resting in it."[20] We also are returning to the promised land, not in some geographical sense, but home to the sacred terrain within our deepest self. This is the deeper meaning of Boricua and Aztlán (the land of origin of the Aztecs, one of the cultures, but by no means the only one, from which the Mejicano/Chicano nation derives its roots) and the strong longing of so many of us to go home again. Most of us are here to stay; we are part of the ongoing American experiment in democracy that is being re-created and redefined; home is wherever free Latinas and Latinos find themselves. But above all, home is the destination that we achieve when we have experienced the journey of transformation. In this way, we arrive for the first time in a place where we know who we are and wherein our story is being told and created ever anew.

La familia is a very important, if not the most significant, institution for la comunidad Latina. But we are coming to learn that there is no such thing as an ideal family. It is people like you and me who can and need to grow our own families in the service of transformation. This means that each member of the family is free to live his or her story and to travel through the core drama of life with parents as guides who are lovers and guides to each other. In this kind of family, each member has a personal face whose own dreams and desires are respected, a political face that is free to dissent and to help create both within the home and in the public realm a compassionate society in which everybody is included, a historical face of our being that enables us to judge the past and to bring about new and better stories that mark the turning point in the upward spiral of a new and more just history, and a sacred face that is no longer lamed in its connection to fragmented and jealous gods who possess us, but now to the deepest source of our being, the god of transformation, who needs us to finish the task of creating the world in justice and love.[21]

In a family in the service of transformation, *cariño*, affectionate love, is not used or withheld to instill fear, guilt, or possession, but to free the members of the family. To nurture people is to allow them and encourage them to find their *tonalli*, the Náhuatl word for the deeper self. In the service of emanation, *cariño* was used to keep people in the container by providing affection as a reward for docility and loyalty. In the service of incoherence, *cariño* is used to manipulate, to send up a smoke screen that hides the power of the authority figure; it is the use of the velvet fist. *Cariño* in the service of deformation is a lie that distracts the other while she is led into destructive death by the addict who says that if you love me, you will take the needle with me.

One of the most controversial aspects of the Latino culture is *machismo*. It is the energy of the male that has been misused in the story of patriarchy, the drama that justifies the systematic control of women by men and the practice of gay bashing that is endemic in the Latino community. Because the cultura belongs to us, we can practice subversion in regard to machismo. To subvert is to turn around from below (from the Latin *verso*), to redirect. In the context of the theory of transformation, when we turn around from below, it means to be radical, to go to the roots of the matter in its deepest sense and take something such as machismo and to end its misuse in the service of the underlying ways of life of emanation, incoherence, or deformation and to make it *use-full* in the service of transformation. We do not get rid of masculine energy; we redeem it by directing the energy of men away from maintaining the alleged superiority of men ordained by the lords of emanation, incoherence, and deformation that gave men permission to possess, dominate, and psychologically and physically assault women and children and to humiliate and hurt gays and lesbians. Machismo in the service of transformation means to reject these destructive uses of masculine strength in order to step forward aggressively to protect the humanity of the Latino community and that of all people. In this regard, one of the unfinished tasks of the Latino community as it confronts and rejects the destructive legacy of machismo is to move with determination to enter into a dialogue with our gay and lesbian brothers and sisters so that we can learn from one another how we can create a more loving and just community.

For example, when Latino veterans returned from World War II, they became the vanguard of the renewed efforts for ethnic and racial equality in our communities. They had traveled, had seen the world, were wounded and bloodied in battle, and realized the lies that they had been taught about their own lack of ability and courage. In the midst of battle, the story and myth of racism based on white supremacy was demolished. The Latino combat soldiers saw European Americans, Anglos, cry, become afraid, and at times refuse to go into battle. They found out that they as Latino soldiers were just as good as the white soldiers. When they returned home, they saw that nothing had changed. Their machismo had been used to make them into warriors to the point where as an ethnic group Chicanos had won more medals of honor than any other group. Their machismo was now aroused by signs saying NO MEXICANS ALLOWED. The dual-wage system was still in place, and there was little chance for a better life. The veterans did not riot or try to overthrow anything; they did something more dangerous: they helped to organize the people and convinced them that they could do for themselves what the government either could not do or would not do. The veterans, together with others in the community, redirected their machismo to demonstrate the strength and the courage to wage a nonviolent struggle for human rights. The miners in Arizona were a pioneering vanguard. As one of them said, ''Somebody been lying to me all these years. I went into the service as a private and came out a leader. If I could be a leader in the service, then why not in the mine?'' They helped to organize the first Mexican-American union in Arizona, the International Mine, Mill Smelter Workers Union, under the leadership of David Velásquez. The Phelps-Dodge Corporation refused to negotiate, and so the union went on strike on September 22, 1946, for fifteen weeks. The strike spread throughout the Southwest until 6,000 miners were on strike. Finally, the company gave in and met most of the demands of the workers, especially equal pay for equal work.[22]

The American GI Forum, a Mexican/Latino veterans' organization, under the guidance of Dr. Hector P. García, was founded to fight for the rights of returning veterans. The organization even found itself fighting for the right of the family of Sergeant Félix Longoria, whose body was being returned from the Philippines, where he had been killed in action, to have him buried in his home town in Texas. Others were being denied their GI Bill benefits. Returning veterans, as in Clifton and Morenci, Arizona, used their machismo to struggle not only for veterans, but for the whole gamut of issues being confronted by la comunidad Latina: education, employment, housing, unionization, voting rights, running candidates for office, and the general dismantling of the structures of exclusion. This kind of resistance, which had originally begun addressing local issues, soon spread throughout the nation and became the backbone of the Latino civil rights movement led by the Chicano and Boricua movements in the 1960s.

Since machismo is a masculine energy, it does not only belong to men; as full human beings, both men and women have masculine and feminine archetypal forces within them. Thus women as well as men are able to make use of machismo as a source of aggressive action to make personal, political, historical, and sacred changes for the sake of creating a fundamentally new and more loving society. This marriage of the masculine and feminine within each of us is beautifully expressed by Rosa Martha Villareal: ''I experience a masculine confidence in my feminine powers of healing.''[23]

In his award-winning film, *The Salt of the Earth*, for which he was blacklisted by the House Un-American Activities Committee and the movie industry (the latter viewed him as anti-American), Herbert Biberman tells the true story of Mexican miners in New Mexico.[24] They suffered from all the forms of racism shown in ''Los Mineros,'' about Arizona. But in their efforts to rid the mines of racism, they forgot that it was equally important to confront the story of the macho patriarch in their own culture. Esperanza, the leading female protagonist in the film, together with other Chicanas at a very crucial point in the strike, takes the initiative; this upsets her husband, Ramón. It is clear from her response to Ramón that neither she nor the other women see the strike as men's work any longer. As she says to him, ''The Anglos tell you to stay in your place. Is that what you want to tell me as a woman, to stay in my place? . . . I do not want to go down fighting; I want to win.'' The women organize and picket, asserting their own masculine, macho energy together with their feminine abilities. This redemption and subversion of machismo helps us to heal the split between the feminine and masculine wholeness of our personal face and so frees us politically to bring about a new and better connection between men and women who can work as equals to transform the history of neglect in our community to one of compassion. In this manner, we become the mercy, love, and justice of the deepest source of transformation.

As a community, we need to restore the story of healing, the drama of *curandería*, which has been a part of our heritage for thousands of years. This tradition of transformation keeps alive the understanding that to heal is to make whole, to heal the brokenness of the personal, political, historical, and sacred faces of our humanity and our mother earth. The great worry of the practitioners of healing is that nobody will practice the rituals and stories of restoration and transformation, and these will be lost, and we with them. Betonie the witch doctor warns Tayo: "It takes a lot of energy to be a human being."[25] The *curanderos* and *curanderas*, healers, at their best understand that their task is to guide us to achieve health by reacquiring, by rediscovering, by excavating our deepest self on the journey of the core drama of transformation. Illness and death come to a people when they forget their humanity and their specific expression of that humanity, their own stories and culture. They do not instruct us to blindly follow that culture, but to continue it by the healing power of transformative change. We are sick when we are split off from the deepest aspects of ourselves, thus fragmented. Our *curanderas* mixed herbs in the search for the medicines that would help us to become health-full, so that we could understand and see the deeper side of life as the world of the creative imagination. They knew that all of us have two selves, the concrete bodily presence and the *tonalli*, or deeper self, which comes from the deepest source of transformation. To break this connection was to become lost in the one-dimensional world of once-and-for-all answers, intoxicated by the search for power, envy, domination, violence, and death. These guides helped and continue to assist us to restore our memory, our remembrance of our best heritage, *gnosis* in the Greek, in Spanish, *conocimiento* and *conscientización*, consciousness, knowledge of the process of transformation. And our healers seek to restore the Indian understanding of time. They knew and know that the human psyche is not bound by space and time. Time is not in the world of our depths linear, the past aimed at the present to fulfill the future. No, time is a spiral that contains the potential of our humanity: past, present and future in the nowness of our life. Our memory of our past nourishes us, warns us, and sustains us now and prepares us for the work of transformation in the next moment of our ever-present future.

The concept of *mestizaje* has to do with our very identity. All Latinas and Latinos are the result of a *mestizaje*, the commingling of different cultures, races, ethnic groups, and religions. As a result of the story of tribalism, described above, many of us suffer from a loss of memory. Too many of us live in disguise, running away from our past. Racism turned the beauty of being multicultural, multireligious, and multiracial into a nightmare. We were born of the Arabic/Hispanic/Jewish/Muslim horsemen, of the African, and of the Indians. We are mestizas and mestizos who were disowned by our Spanish forefathers and by the Indians, both of whom sought to be pure blooded. As a result of this condition of being strung out among different cultures, some romanticized the Indian past and blotted out the Spanish side of our bones, calling the Spaniard the rapist who defiled the Indian woman and destroyed the manhood of the indigenous. The early Chicano movement was permeated by this kind of romanticism of our Indian culture, as many Puerto Ricans and other Caribbean Latinos are who look to the Arawaks and Taínos or to their African heritage as their gateway to a golden past. Mexicans especially consider themselves as sons of La Malinche, Malintzín Tenépal (called Doña Marina by the Spaniards), who allegedly betrayed the Indian cause by serving as an interpreter and concubine for Cortés. Latino males are so bound by this part of their past that they become insanely jealous, to the point of murder, when it comes to a matter of betrayal by women. As sons of La Malinche, we are doomed to seek revenge against the Spanish fathers who violated our mothers unless we can, through the process of subversion, conquer the Conquest, redefining and redeeming la Conquista, and free ourselves from the perpetual fear of castration. Again Rosa Martha Villareal is of great help to us in this regard. Doctor Magdalena, the protagonist in the novella, *Doctor Magdalena*, has a Spanish mother and a mestizo father who has tried to repress his mixed heritage. But in spite of himself, there is a deeper voice of authenticity in him that leads him to introduce his daughter, Magdalena, to her Indian past. It is he as a doctor who gives to Magdalena the mystery of the Indian *curanderas*. Her parents have lost their way and arrested the core drama in Act II, Scene 1, practicing the story of capitalism by exploiting their own *gente*, people, and refusing services to those who could not pay. It is Magdalena's task to redeem her parents outside of time by becoming a healer. She discovers the waters of life by combining the "masculine magic of my father's imagination and the secrets of ancient women."[26] So it is not only the Spaniards who conquered; they in turn were conquered by a new mestizo drama that has brought about a new transformation by melding Tonantzín, a mother goddess, with la Virgen de Guadalupe, the Mother of Jesus, with Gucumatz, or Quetzalcoátl, the plumed serpent, the god of culture for the Mayans, Toltecs, and Aztecs, and Jesus Christ, all of whom represent sacred sources of transformation.

I, too am a conqueror. I am their child. I have conquered the rivers of time with my desire. I can return to their conquered land and right the masculine wrongs: the rejection of the fathers of the children, and the sacrifice of the young woman, the virgin/whore, the mother of a new race. I have conquered my ancient fathers who denied to their bastard offspring their memory of the Indians. . . . What a forbidden secret! The fathers did not want us to know the secrets of the night for fear that we would undo their world, their conquests, their cities in the rivers of time, send them back, and thus, prevent our own birth.

They did not trust their mixed-blood children. . . . But their world lived on in the silence of the imagination.[27]

This is an extraordinary explanation of the ways in which we as Latinas and Latinos can take the past into our hands and create a new and better story. Villareal is clearly stating that we do not have to remain victims and that within the silence of our sacred and creative imaginations, we can see visions and, with the political and historical faces of our being, recreate history by conquering the conquest.

A ceremony from our past that we continue to celebrate can be of help to us in this regard. It is *el día de los muertos*, November 2, the day of the dead, when both Christian, Indian, and African rituals are practiced side by side. On this day, throughout the Latino world, people bring gifts of food and drink and prayer offerings to remember their loved ones who are not really dead but who have passed or are on the way and so require sustenance. Especially because they are still with us, we cannot deny them, our ancestors, who are European, Arabic, African, and Indian. We completely distort our past if we honor only the Indians or the Spaniards or the Africans. The blood of all these groups is in our blood. What was destroyed by the Conquest and racism was not forgotten; it remains hidden in us. We are indeed a mestizo people.

La Raza does not mean "the race," but the community. My grandfather always reminded us when we went out to eat in public that we should clean up after ourselves *"para que no digan mal de La Raza,"* so that nobody would be able to speak badly of us as members of the Latino community. He was concerned that the Anglos not be able to criticize us for displaying poor manners. He wanted us to have pride in ourselves as Mejicanos. "La Raza" was never meant to be a racial term that separated us from others but, rather, a concept that could help us to build a collective pride, for we were under attack in an alien culture. In fact, the term "La Raza" became a rallying cry for demonstrations against racism and bigotry, and it is once again a very significant term for the times in which we live. Because we want to know and celebrate who we are, we can work together with others to help one another to discover the resources of transformation within our cultures. We all need to transcend our own specific culture so that we can reach out to others to create a common humanity. To fulfill the story of democracy in our country we can create a new story, a *multicultural mestizaje*. We as a people have been multicultural for much of our history, although there have been times when we lost our way in this regard because of racism and ethnocentrism in our own community.

In the early 1960s the Chicano and Puerto Rican movements instilled pride in their communities by speaking about Brown Power and enhancing the status of La Raza. This was a necessary tactic in the development of community pride and unity. This history of struggle belongs to us; since we are the recipients of this tradition, we have the right and the duty to critique what it means for us now as a people. La Raza was used in an exclusionary way to highlight who was a member of the community and who was not. Now we can reinterpret the meaning of La Raza to include all people of goodwill, from all backgrounds, who care deeply about others.

The four faces of our being in the service of transformation can now come forth in their fullness. Our personal face emerges in all of its fullness and uniqueness, with new ideas, feelings, and intuitions. Our political face is one of compassion, inclusion, and justice that asks the question What is it that we can and need to do together to protect our humanity and that of all others? With our historical face we bring about a new story, a new Aztlán, a new Borinquén that has nothing to do with territory, but with a new people who create their own history since they are no longer victims of a past history. With our sacred faces we are colleagues of the god of transformation, who invites us to participate in the persistent creation of the cosmos and of our own humanity.

La Llorona, the woman who cries, is one of the saddest stories to come out of the collective experience of the conquest of Latino and Latina America. There are various renditions of the story. In all versions, a woman goes crying through the streets of the cities and towns at night, seeking her children, who have disappeared. One interpretation is that she drowned them to save them from the horrors of the Conquest; another, that the children represent the lost heritage of the Indians; still another, that the dead children represent the universal trauma that was felt when a whole age, world, and civilization ended. This story is so debilitating because there is no end to the depth of the sorrow and sense of loss; it is permanent night and death, with no resurrection. It is a story of continuous and totally discouraging victimization. But almost 500 years later, we have the response of another Latina woman who, together with Rosa Martha Villareal, says "Enough!" to victimization as the only meaning of la Conquista. In her short story "Woman Hollering Creek," Sandra Cisneros, as we have seen, tells the story of Cleófilas, who is caught in an abusive relationship with her husband, Juan Pedro. She had seen marriage only through the eyes of the characters in the telenovelas. She is terribly disillusioned when he begins to assault her. She finds herself living between Soledad and Dolores, loneliness and sorrow, the condition of many Latinas for generations. But, through the intervention of a woman friend, she is put in contact with Felice, which means happiness, fulfillment, joy, who will drive her to the bus stop so that she can leave her husband and go home to her father. As Felice drives across the arroyo, the creek, she gives a yell that startles Cleófilas. It is the shout of a woman who is free, who wears boots and drives a truck and is not about to let a man tell her what to do.[28] What a remarkable political statement this story is. Cisneros is telling us that there will be no more victims or crybabies; what we need now are women who yell out in protest and dissent against a society and culture that gave men permission to dominate them. But Cleófilas's journey is just beginning. She is leaving her husband to return to her father. Will she be a different Cleófilas, who will now also have the courage to resist her father, as she did Juan Pedro? Transformation is an ongoing story. This story is about the beginning of a new history and politics being told by women with their own personal faces, rooted in the deepest source of transformation.

THE UNITED STATES: PART OF OUR *MESTIZAJE*

It is clear to all who have seen the demographic projections for the twenty first century that by the middle of the century, the United States will be at least 25 percent Latino and Latina. This is a stunning realization. Because of this, we can no longer continue to use language that obscures the present and future reality of the ethnic and racial makeup of our society. Terms such as "minority," "subgroup," "marginal," "non-white" (which is the absence of color), "subculture," or "subclass," are political terms that disable people. They convey a sense of condescension, of permanent victimhood and powerlessness. To name one's self, to identify and name one's own people is a personal, political, historical, and sacred act of resistance and affirmation against those who define us by using their culture as the measuring rod. One of the most powerful tools in the arsenal of the dominant has been that of assimilation. To strip yourself of your own culture and to disavow your own community is an act of self- and collective hatred. The word "assimilation" derives from the Latin *simulo, simulare*, which means "to be like." To make yourself over in the likeness of others is to renounce your own identity.

La comunidad Latina continues to grow because of a high birth rate and the daily arrivals, who come from all over Latin America to seek a better life. Assimilation, as we have seen, means joining the powerful and accepting their story, which is that of capitalism, which arrests us in the first scene of Act II, wherein we are locked in perpetual struggles for power. But the American dream at its best is not about capitalism and power. Rather it is about democracy, participatory democracy in the service of transformation.[29] We also know that American democracy is still in process, a dream unfulfilled. The Declaration of Independence and the Constitution, together with the Bill of Rights, are the most important charters in the history of the United States. Above all, the Declaration of Independence is central because it is grounded on the primacy of the individual; each individual is sacred. This tradition of the individual as sacred needs to be seen in the context of community. "Individual" is not the so-called self-made man who pulls himself up by his bootstraps. That is the mean and petty kind of personality that results from the story of capitalism. By individual self, I mean the realization of one's deeper identity and the discovery of one's unique story as a result of having experienced transformation in at least one aspect of life. Having traveled through the core drama of life, these individuals are now prepared to guide others so that they can participate in the personal, political, historical, and sacred tasks of building a new and better community.

Each ethnic or racial group that came to this country, including those who were already present when the Europeans came and those who were brought against their will, have contributed something unique and valuable to our nation. As a nation, we have continued and need to continue to address the stories of tribalism, often in collusion with capitalism, in the service of the two truncated ways of life of incoherence and deformation. From the beginning of the Republic, we find racism and capitalism as two of the most powerful stories present. There were other stories, such as the story of community and stewardship based on biblical teaching, and the story of democracy, rooted in the small landowners who could daily ask the question, What is it that we can and need to do together to address the problems of our community? Again, as in the case of our *herencia Latina*, we can ask this question as citizens and residents of this country: What is it that we can and need to do together to rid the nation of racism and capitalism? In other words, because we are now citizens and residents of this country, we can participate in redefining the American tradition; we can assist in emptying our nation of those stories and ways of life that are destructive, nourish those which are conducive to justice, and create other, more loving and compassionate stories.

STRATEGIES OF TRANSFORMATION

To avoid the sin of assimilation and becoming arrested in the story of capitalism in the service of incoherence, we need to learn how to be simultaneously insiders and outsiders. This means living in the midst of the story of capitalism but not being seduced by it. To be in the world, but not of it, to live *in* the belly of the story of power, but not be *of* it, is a strategy of using the resources of the system not as intended, that is, to join the powerful by pursuing self-interest and power, but rather to gain leverage by which to bring about a new and better society. Such a strategy unequivocally rejects any talk or action intended to overthrow the system. This would be a form of rebellion that would lock us into a violent contest for power. As rebels, we would be caught by the story of capitalism, fighting for more power. No, we are after something much more radical than that. We are after the whole system itself: the underlying story of capitalism and the ways of life of incoherence and deformation that ultimately give to the concrete forms of capitalism their mysterious power over us. Our task is to create a parallel structure based on justice and love. In practical terms, this involves our young people getting good educations, so that they can become excellent doctors, lawyers, accountants, teachers, carpenters, police officers, and administrators. Once they have these skills, they are free to make a personal and political decision to use their competence to bring about a new and better history for people who are another face of the deepest sacred depths. We need a middle class not to pursue their own self-interest, but one that uses their competency to take risks, to experiment, and to search out new forms of justice for the community.

In the final analysis, any cultura Latina that we create in this country has an obligation to cross its own borders and to embrace others. If we discover who we are, as participants of transformation, we can share this gnosis, or knowledge, of the process of transformation with others who have gotten lost on the journey. As Latinas and Latinos, we need to struggle to become the creation that we desire for all others, what Villareal calls "a person who wants to heal the human flesh because it contains pieces of all our collective dreams, because the flesh and stories of all others is a piece of me."[30]

GUIDES OF TRANSFORMATION

As a community, we need to be vigilant about the tradition of *patrones, líderes,* and *caciques,* bosses, leaders, and chieftains. In la cultura Latina, we have been wounded by patriarchal and autocratic males who saw all criticism as a personal affront and therefore would allow no dissent. This aspect of our past still exists as a powerful fragment of emanation as a way of life. Many of us still have trouble resisting people in authority because we feel in our bones that we are being disrespectful to our fathers and to God the Father, who we now know is really the jealous lord of emanation that ties us in the knots of *pecado, vergüenza, y remordimiento*, sin, shame, and guilt. The stories of possessive love, patriarchy, and uncritical loyalty remain very powerful in our communities. What we need in the face of this is not leaders, role models, heroes, and authority figures to emulate, but guides. The true guide, like the healer, does not enhance her own power; she has a special gift to articulate the needs of the community. The guide's greatest concern is to draw people to their own creativity. The authentic guide is always in the process of putting herself or himself out of business, a sign of their success, since the other is now experiencing the meaning of his own life. Initially, the guide asks others to risk faith in her or him so that the others allow themselves to be guided out of stories and ways of life that have arrested them. One of the most difficult things that we are asking of our community is to give up stories that have given us meaning and security that now, however, are unable to respond to our needs. As Latinas and Latinos, we have a powerful attraction to strong men, father figures whom we ask to tell us what to do. We find ourselves lost and depressed when they are not present to lead us. I have witnessed community-based organizations that are run like personal fiefdoms wherein the director is a tyrant: "Yo mando en esta casa," I am the boss here. An authentic guide develops strategies by which to enable those with whom she works to realize their own potential by helping them bring forth their personal, political, historical, and sacred capacities. This does not deny the need for authority because real authority is guiding each person to be become an author of his or her own life and work.

Community-based organizations have the opportunity to become the basis for affinity groups made up of individuals who guide each other. In the barrios of this nation, small groups of people who care deeply about each other can build real community. We have in our history a strong tradition of such mutual aid, *mutualistas*, organizations like the ones organized after World War II among miners in New Mexico and Arizona which sprang up throughout the nation to protect the Latino community. My grandparents belonged to El Círculo Mutualista in Detroit. This group did everything from baby-sitting to helping people find housing and employment. There were also religious-based organizations like Los Caballeros de Colón, Knights of Columbus, Catholic laywomen's organizations such as Las Damas Católicas, Catholic Women, and Las Franciscanas, Franciscan Laywomen, and the Cursillistas, a Catholic layman's movement that reached out to the community to provide personal as well as social services. An affinity group is a group of from eight to twelve persons who are emotionally and intellectually connected to each other. They meet often to discuss what it is that needs to be done to help establish day-care centers, tutoring sessions, English classes, housing, employment strategies, and organizing other affinity groups. A network of such groups working on similar and different tasks can now form a political party, such as La Raza Unida in Crystal City, Texas; or a local or state organization, such as the United Neighborhood Organization, Council for Hispanic Advancement, or national organizations such as the National Council of La Raza, the National Puerto Rican Congress, the American GI Forum, or the United Farm Workers. The challenge to the administrators of these organizations, again, is to resist the temptation to become patriarchal leaders rather than guides. Another danger is that our organizations might join the powerful, becoming simply another interest group trying to get its piece of the action by competing with other interest groups. Once this happens, we lose our way and begin to see our organizations as other fortresses in a world of power. We have the opportunity to change the agenda by rejecting the way of life of incoherence, which limits us to seeing our relationship to other groups as contests for power. Indeed, as long as we remain in this partial way of life, the kind of change that we bring about will never be anything other than incremental change, that is, a reform of the story that holds us, capitalism, and an effort to make it a little less oppressive. As long as we remain caught in this story, we become just another interest group looking for legitimization from the system. If we remain co-opted and in competition with other groups, we cannot transform ourselves or our society. We remain partial selves, not fully connected to our own deepest source, and therefore wounded in our humanity. Manfred Halpern has explained it thus:

But what is not possible through any kind of incremental change is overcoming the intrinsically partial nature of our solution and the still partial nature and experience of our being and of all of our relationships—partial, that is, biased by our arrest and hence incomplete. With respect to any particular problem, the heart of the question is what will it take to overcome this archetypal drama and incoherence as a way of life which gives rise to this kind of problem.[31]

To free ourselves, we need to step out of the story of capitalism as the only game in town and release the creative imagination that will enable us to see new and better possibilities. A partial search for justice is profoundly wounding because it means that whereas we might achieve some gains for the Latino community, our hearts and minds are closed to the humanity of other groups, which, because we see them as competitors and threats to our gains, are rendered invisible and lesser human beings.

Transformation is impossible unless we open ourselves to be truly caring and concerned about the most basic and pervasive suffering of our time: We have turned ourselves into only partial human beings, and indeed we treat many others and ourselves as lesser or invisible. To face this deeply limiting reality as unbearable, untenable and however profitable for some, certainly at least as unfruitful to our being means also to seek to understand through a new, testable theoretical vision why we are where we are and how we can indeed discover and experience a fundamentally better way of life. Transformation will advance us towards ending ignorance and bigotry, eliminating poverty and oppression, nourishing peace and beauty, and also both nourishing and being nourished by nature. And thus also the core of our being is moved towards being understanding, loving, just and joyful with ourselves and with each other—hence towards becoming fully present and true beings.[32]

A strategy of coalition building will only be honest if we see the other communities of people of color not as competitors with whom it is better to join forces as a tactic, but as fellow human beings, with whom we share a common humanity that has been wounded. Together, we have a better chance of overcoming our partial justice, partial gains, partial and divided selves, and a partial humanity so that we can rediscover our own cultural uniqueness through the eyes of one another.

APPLYING THEORY TO PRACTICE

Community-based organizations on the local level and national organizations that represent the Latino community can do transformative work in our barrios by doing radical analysis and then taking action to address the problems. I would like to present here an example of how to apply the theory of transformation to a critical area in our society: education. This is an area of great importance to all of us because schools are readily available for us to begin the transformation of our communities. One of the greatest alternatives to violence in our society is access to a good education. Yet, ironically, our schools—and the future of the next generation of Latina and Latino students—are at risk precisely because of the violence in them. The outbreaks of ethnic and racial violence in our schools are symptomatic of the fissures in the wider society. We need to assist in transforming the relationships in the wider community in order to educate our children.

Given that it takes a community to educate children, we need to ask what kind of community is present. Many groups in our urban centers are radically disconnected from each other. We need to know why people who live and work and study in such proximity are really not close to each other. In fact, the growing number of disturbing violent confrontations in our schools is based on ethnic and racial differences, even between students from different Latino backgrounds; thus we have the fighting between Puerto Ricans and Dominicans in New Jersey and New York and the confrontations between Chicanos and Central Americans in Los Angeles. I believe that these outbreaks are symptomatic of the divisions in the wider community. Too often these violent clashes are merely papered over as soon as possible. But the problems remain on a deeper level. It is necessary to go beyond mere external appearances or behavior modification to understand how and why people are relating to each other in such a manner.

To discover the deeper meaning of the relationships that people have to each other, we can ask questions from the perspective of the theory of transformation.

As we have seen, the theory of transformation is a theory that allows us to ask fundamentally new kinds of questions. It is a theory that links together the empirical and the normative. Consequently, we can use this theory to help us to analyze the problem. After identifying several schools that represent the growing diversity in our city or town, we can use focus groups, personal interviews, personal written statements, participant observation, and dialogues in an attempt to determine the actual relationships and stories that people live within their family, school, workplace, and the wider community. It is possible to determine which relationships and stories are present, which are absent or forbidden, and which ones need to be broken (and new ones created) in order to transform a community. But these relationships and stories themselves, as we have seen, take place within a deeper and wider context, a way of life that tells us why, ultimately, we do what we are doing. There are four ways of life that organize the whole of our lives, often without our conscious participation: the ways of life of emanation, incoherence, deformation, and transformation. Only in the service of transformation can we participate with the fullness of our being in creating a fundamentally new and more compassionate society. The other three ways of life, since they are only fragments of the story of transformation, prevent us from dealing with the changes taking place around us. The way of life of emanation tells us that we already know everything necessary to live because it was revealed once and for all by a divine being. We dare not disagree, for this source is so powerful that all authority figures in our group accept it. In the way of life of incoherence, we live a story of power and the pursuit of self-interest as the most important value in life. Involvement with others that would compromise one's own power is to be avoided at all costs. In the service of deformation, this way of life tells us that we are the only valuable people and that others should accept their inferiority. If they do not accept their lower place, then we can use whatever means are necessary to assert our domination. As a result of fear and profound suspicion, this way of life makes it impossible to go beyond one's own racial, religious, or ethnic group.

As parents, students, and teachers, we practice the stories and relationships of our lives simultaneously, in more than one of these ways of life. As a result, we live fragmented lives because we are not free to be who we are anywhere. We are always adjusting ourselves to accommodate others and therefore always repressing very important aspects of who we are as people. We know that a constant stream of different ethnic and racial groups arrives almost daily in our communities. They are often representatives of the newest immigrants in the country. Persons from these communities bring with them stories and cultures that sustained them in their native land. When they arrive in this country, they are confronted with a different way of life, stories and relationships that they are required to learn in order to survive in this society. Their children, who are students in the schools, are under great pressure to assimilate and to learn how to belong as soon as possible, precisely by taking on the new relationships and stories necessary to get along in this country. This pull from their peers and the greater society pushes them away from their traditional cultures and homes. It is crucial to ascertain in the service of what way of life they enact the relationships and stories of their life. Let me give an example. In order to survive in U.S. society, one has to acquire relationships of autonomy and direct bargaining in order to step into the world of capitalism and competitiveness. These two relationships demand that we become competent in a particular skill that becomes our area of expertise. Together with the relationship of autonomy that allows us to carve out a zone of power, based on expertise, in a particular area such as law or computers, we learn to use our competence to bargain for a better standard of living, for more power. These two relationships in current U.S. society are usually practiced within the way of life of incoherence, that is, in the service of the pursuit of self-interest and power. The schools, of their very essence, prepare young people to succeed in this society by socializing them to become individualistic, competitive, and independent of others. But these relationships and this way of life contradict the traditional values taught in the way of life of emanation. In this way of life, the youth are raised to be respectful of authority, not to be critical, to repress their own interests and to avoid putting themselves forward. These are not just the views of their parents but, again, the will of an all-powerful sacred source.

Let us look a little more closely at the family and home situation from which many of our Latina and Latino students come everyday to school. Newly arrived fathers and mothers often do not know the language or the key relationships of the wider society. They often feel isolated and powerless. Their whole identity is at stake because all that they know is what they brought with them from their native land. The customs they confront are strange and dangerous; people from other ethnic groups at times intimidate them because they are too aggressive; jobs are hard to find and those that are available entail long, hard hours at minimum wage. All that the family has is itself and the unwavering support of its members. In the midst of this struggle for survival, the sons and daughters come home with strange requests: can they go to a dance, to a play, have some friends over, join a club, come to meet our teachers? Refusals lead to accusations that they are being held back: "We want to be Americans; other kids can do it, so why can't we? You are too old-fashioned." For families who were raised in the service of emanation, with relationships of respect and dependence, these are literally fighting words. Much violence in the family arises out of the incoherence that comes when the parents and the children live in different ways of life, and the young are practicing forbidden relationships. Why are they forbidden? Because the relationships of autonomy and direct bargaining in the service of incoherence legitimizes independence from parental authority and questions all authority, even that of the divine powers, in their world of emanation. The whole worldview of the parents is put in profound doubt.

The schools and the teachers are often insensitive to these conflicts, even though many teachers may have gone through a similar struggle with their own parents as they sought to enter the mainstream of American life. Many teachers have forgotten the history of struggle of their own ethnic group and so often cannot, or refuse to, identify with new immigrants, who are the newest Americans. Added to the mix of what is going on at home are the confused messages that they receive from teachers and their peers, who are not sure who they are in relationship to their journeys of transformation. When the students interact, whether they want to or not, they bring with them the world of their parents and the fears that their parents have instilled in them, especially regarding what group to avoid. Fear and suspicion tend to make students wary of each other and to hang with members of one's own ethnic group. In addition, the media and the wider society present a view of American society that is hostile to immigrants, documented and undocumented. This leads to a competition between different ethnic and even intraethnic struggles based on class and immigrant status. Feeling at odds with their parents and unaccepted at school, some students turn to gangs based on ethnic and racial identity, not because they are bad but because they are trying to create new families. This leads to competition between gangs for turf, prestige, and power. Violence occurs, and to repress the fear and tension, they will often turn to drugs and alcohol. Since they need resources that their families cannot provide, they turn to various kinds of crime to support their gang/family. This means that they are on the way to deformation, the creation of a fundamentally worse society.

In this situation, what is to be done? Good theory must be related to practice. There is a way by which to intervene, to bring the community to an awareness of the kinds of dynamics being described. People can come to learn and identify what relationships they have been limited to, the stories in which they are currently caught and the way of life in which they are living their daily lives. Traditional social science describes the horror that we are facing but has no clue as to how to transform the terror into new turning points for the better. The theory of transformation can identify the broken connections, stories, and ways of life that are not working and how to go beyond these to create strategies to bring about fundamentally new and more compassionate relationships in the service of transformation. Parents, teachers, and students organized together as affinity groups in the *mutualista* tradition discussed above can once again take responsibility for the community by helping to discover the underlying causes of their anger, pain, and disappointment. In applying theory to practice, we can in our neighborhood schools build focus groups of fifteen persons drawn from the community and led by two mentors, or guides. We can begin with five to ten schools. The guides will be parents, professionals who live in the community, and teachers in the schools. In this way, we can provide a valuable educational experience for people who are rooted in the community.

The guides are expected to live the core drama of transformation in their own lives. Members of the group come to know one another by participating in readings, discussions, dialogues, conversations, viewing of films, videotaping and interviewing one another (since nobody in this process is an observer), and writing that allows the stories, relationships, and ways of life of the participants to emerge. Guides will be responsible for leading their groups by means of a dialogue/research method as they meet with one another in preparation for their work in the community. This approach will allow them and the participants to do an analysis of the stories, relationships, and ways of life in which they are enacting their lives. This part of the process can take four to five months. Once the groups have learned to identify where they are in their personal and community lives, then the second part of the year, four to five months, can be devoted to strategies of transformation, that is, actually taking specific steps to transform their own personal, family, school and community relationships.

During the second year, the process of developing community guides of the first year can be repeated at several new schools. Now, however, some of the participants who have gone through the previous training can be involved as guides. The lessons learned during the first year can be incorporated into the program for the second year. By the end of the second year, a minimum of ten to twenty schools will have completed the program. At the end of the first year and the beginning of the second year, participants will be prepared, in groups of two or three, to lead groups of their own. In this way, we can concretely enact transformation. Mexican/Chicano, Salvadoran, Guatemalan, Chinese, Filipino, Egyptian, European American, Iranian, Dominican, Puerto Rican, African-American, or Chinese students, parents, and teachers can learn about their culture and that of others together and how this heritage has shaped their lives in a crucial and decisive way. Students, parents, and teachers can share their stories and their journeys so that they can come to see the differences in their various stories but still see that we are all on the same journey: to become whole persons who care deeply about their own lives and those of others.

But heritage is not destiny. Now it depends on what students, parents, and teachers do with this awareness. They are free to take the best of their tradition and to reject that which is destructive, such as patriarchy, which dominates all of our cultures. This critical analysis of their culture means that they are no longer blindly accepting all of their background. In addition, they can understand that the greatness of America is not to be found in the story of capitalism, but in the struggle to fulfill the story of democracy. In this way, the relationships of autonomy and direct bargaining, which were used in the pursuit of self-interest and power, can now be reacquired and used in the service of transformation because these relationships can also be used as leverage to create a more just society.

Many students, parents, and teachers are caught between ways of life. Some have rejected the old traditional ways because they are incapable of dealing with the new problems of a changing society; as a result they move quickly to assimilate, to become an American who is powerful and rich. A few will succeed in becoming successful in this way, but the majority obviously will not become wealthy. Many people from racial, ethnic, and religious backgrounds that are not valued will continue to be excluded by the nativistic, anti-immigrant, and often racist sentiments prevalent in the nation. Some who find themselves in this dilemma will be tempted to turn to violence against themselves and others by becoming involved in crime, drugs, gangs, early pregnancy, truancy, and other wounding behavior. Some will justify their actions by blaming white America, the rich, or the powerful. There is certainly some truth to this, but they are much more than victims. All of us have the transformative capacity to bring forth a personal face that empowers our political face to change our environment. This in turn leads to a new historical face, created by you and me, who, together as a community, draw our strength from the deepest source of transformation, capable of becoming guides of transformation for others. In this way, after just two years, there can be a critical core in the community who are prepared to introduce others to the story of transformation.

As to the kinds of issues that can be addressed in the focus groups, people from all ethnic or racial backgrounds can come to understand that, as they respond to the needs of the community, they can participate in transformation by breaking with destructive stories and ways of life and creating new and more just alternatives This understanding can only be achieved by archetypal analysis, getting to the roots of problems. Honest dialogue allows us to go beyond the smiles and other forms of ritualized avoidance that prevent us from seeing one another as real human beings. To get to this depth, those involved in the process need to be willing to risk the artifices carefully contrived to keep us hidden from one another's sight. To do anything less will only allow us endlessly to seek ways to manipulate ourselves and others, so that we end by being silenced by our dishonesty. There can be no peace, only a temporary pacification waiting for another outbreak of violence, unless we respond with a loving and understanding intervention. It takes a community to educate a child. The child's community has the main responsibility to see that this new individual is raised with the necessary love and guidance to tell her or his story, that is, to prepare the child to live his or her own journey of transformation. To do this, we need guides who themselves know where they are on this journey. Adults, teachers and parents, who are wrestling with their own transformation are the only ones we can ultimately trust with the education of our children. An authentic community can be defined as a group of people who are connected intrapersonally to their own selves, to one another, to common problems, and to the deepest source. This quality of connectedness is possible only in the way of life of transformation because it is only within this way of life that we are consciously and creatively fully present to ourselves, to one another, and to the deepest ground of our being.

CONCLUSION

Many of us years ago made a commitment to work with and for our people, La Raza. But we need once again to go through another conversion, another turning around of our being, and to ask ourselves why ultimately are we doing what we are doing? Are we members of organizations that are still asking radical questions? Do we ask what stories continue to block our way as individuals and as a community? Within what ways of life are we living the concrete stories and relationships of our lives? Do we approach others as loyal workers with no right to disagree? Do we see the members of our organizations as employees working for a paycheck, whom we can control? Are the very poor, for whom we exist to serve as an organization, group, political party, or affinity group, now become invisible to us as mere consumers of our economic or ideological plans? Or do we see ourselves and the community for whom we work as mutual guides who need one another's creativity in order to fulfill our task of creating fundamentally new and more just responses to all new problems? In regard to the four faces of our being, are we fully present, or do we have to repress, suppress, or violate crucial aspects of who we are as personal, political, historical, and sacred beings? As radicals, do we insist on dealing with the roots, with the causes of problems, rather than getting lost in symptoms? Do we, together with others, persist in exposing the underlying sacred sources and their concrete manifestations so that the real causes of poverty—exploitation, racism, patriarchy, possessive love, and violence—can truly be overcome? No lasting, authentic change is possible unless we descend into the depths, to struggle there with the dramas and ways of life so that we can empty ourselves of them and so create new and more loving relationships and stories. Transformation can only begin with persons, with Latinas and Latinos like you and me. The new Latina woman and the new Latino man, together with the new woman and new man from all ethnic and racial backgrounds, are those of us who have experienced a transformation that has so revolutionized the four faces of our being that our personal awakening leads to new insights, courage, and capacity that enable us to carry out the political agenda necessary to bring about a new and better turning point in the spiral of history that affirms our presence as sacred persons. The underlying structure of the journey through the core drama of life is always the same, and yet it is always unique. We live once again the transformative tradition of our guides such as Albizu Campos, Sor Juana Inés de la Cruz, Eugenio María de Hostos, César Chávez, Luís Valdez, David Velásquez, Frank Morales, Dr. José Rosario, Dr. Hector P. García, Rigoberta Menchú, Celia Dorantes, Archbishop Romero, Dolores Huerta, Sylvia Villa, Juanita Barbosa, Rosa Martha Villareal, Alberto Pulido, Demetria Martínez, and so many others when each of us, together with our communities, confronts our problems by practicing in our own unique way the journey of transformation for our own time.

NOTES

1. Octavio Paz, ''Reflections: Mexico and the United States,'' *The New Yorker*, September 17, 1979.

2. For an excellent book on our Spanish heritage see Américo Castro, *The Spaniards*, trans. Willard F. King and Selma Margaretten (Berkeley: University of California Press, 1971).

3. See in this regard Rodolfo Acuña, *Occupied America: The Chicano's Struggle for Liberation* (San Francisco: Canfield Press, 1972).

4. Frank Bonilla and Ricardo Campos, "Puerto Ricans in the New Economic Order," *Daedalus* 110, no. 2 (Spring 1981): 133–76.

5. David T. Abalos, "Some Reflections on the Creation of Latino Culture in the United States from the Perspective of a Theory of Transformation," in *Old Masks, New Faces: Religion and Latino Identities*, vol. 3, ed. Anthony S. Arroyo and Gilbert Cadena (New York: Bildner Center, City University of New York, 1995).

6. Octavio Paz, "The Sons of La Malinche," in *Introduction to Chicano Studies: A Reader*, ed. Livia Isaura Dúran and H. Russell Bernard. (New York: Macmillan, 1973), pp. 22–24.

7. David T. Abalos, *The Latino Family and the Politics of Transformation* (Westport, CT: Praeger, 1993), chapter 4.

8. Octavio Paz, *The Other Mexico: Critique of the Pyramid*, trans. Lysander Kemp (New York: Grove Press, 1972).

9. In this regard see Luciano Perena Vicente, *Derechos y Deberes Entre Indios y Españoles en el Nuevo Mundo Según Francisco de Vittoria* (Salamanca: Universidad Pontifica de Salamanca, 1991); and Bartolomé de las Casas, *In Defense of the Indians*, trans. Stafford Poole (DeKalb: Northern Illinois University Press, 1992).

10. Abalos, *The Latino Family*, chapter 4.

11. For the text of The Popol Vuh, see Miguel León Portilla, ed., *Native Mesoamerican Spirituality* (New York, Ramsey, Toronto: Paulist Press, 1980).

12. Abalos, *Strategies of Transformation Toward a Multicultural Society: Fulfilling the Story of Democracy* (Westport, CT, London: Praeger, 1996), pp. 98–106.

13. Manfred Halpern, "Underlying Forces Shaping the Fundamental Differences Between Incremental and Transforming Change" (paper presented at the annual meeting of the American Political Science Association, Washington, DC, August 28–31, 1997), p. 11.

14. Hector Galán, "Los Mineros," *The American Experience*, telescript by Paul Espinosa and Hector Galán, introduced by David McCullough, narrated by Luís Valdéz for PBS, 1990.

15. Abalos, *The Latino Family*, chapter 4.

16. Peter Matthiessen, *Sal Si Puedes, César Chávez and the New American Revolution* (New York: Random House, 1969).

17. Malcolm X, *The Autobiography of Malcolm X* (New York: Grove Press, 1966).

18. Leslie Marmon Silko, *Ceremony* (New York: Penguin Books, 1977). See especially pp. 132–39 and 191–204.

19. Ibid., pp. 224–27.

20. René Marqués, *La Carreta* (Rio Piedras, PR: Editorial Cultural, 1971), p. 172.

21. David T. Abalos, *The Latino Family*, chapter 5.

22. Galán, "Los Mineros," *The American Experience*.

23. Rosa Martha Villareal, *Doctor Magdalena* (Berkeley, CA: TQS Publications, 1995), p. 71.

24. Herbert J. Biberman, *The Salt of the Earth*, produced by Paul Jarrico and the Independent Productions Corporation and the International Union of Mine, Mill and Smelter Workers, 1953, San Marcos, New Mexico, renamed ZincTown, NM by the mine owners.

25. Silko, *Ceremony*, p. 230.

26. Villareal, *Doctor Magdalena*, pp. 74–75.

27. Ibid., pp. 71–72.

28. Sandra Cisneros, "Woman Hollering Creek," in *Woman Hollering Creek and Other Stories* (New York: Random House, 1991).

29. Abalos, *Strategies of Transformation Toward a Multicultural Society*, chapter 5.

30. Villareal, *Doctor Magdalena*, p. 48.

31. Manfred Halpern, "Transformation: Its Theory and Practice in Our Personal, Political, Historical and Sacred Being," chapter 6, p. 15.

32. Ibid., chapter 6, p. 30.

Bibliography

Abalos, David T. *Latinos in the United States: The Sacred and the Political.* Notre Dame, IN: University of Notre Dame Press, 1986.

———. *The Latino Family and the Politics of Transformation.* Westport, CT, London: Praeger, 1993.

———. *Strategies of Transformation Toward a Multicultural Society Fulfilling the Story of Democracy.* Westport, CT, London: Praeger, 1996.

———. "Strategies of Transformation in the Health Delivery System." *Nursing Forum* 17, no. 3 (1978).

———. "Rediscovering the Sacred Among Latinos." *Latino Studies Journal* 3, no. 3 (May 1992): 1–25.

———. "Latino Female/Male Relationships: Strategies for Creating New Archetypal Dramas." *Latino Studies Journal* 1, no. 1 (1990): 48–69.

———. "Some Reflections on the Creation of a Latino Culture in the United States from the Perspective of a Theory of Transformation," In *Old Masks, New Faces: Religion and Latino Identities.* Vol. 3. Ed. Anthony S. Arroyo and Gilbert Cadena. New York: Bildner Center, City University of New York, 1995.

Acosta, Oscar Zeta. *The Revolt of the Cockroach People.* San Francisco: Straight Arrow, 1973.

Acuña, Rodolfo. *Occupied America: The Chicano's Struggle Toward Liberation.* San Francisco: Canfield Press, 1972.

Alvarez, Julia. *How the García Girls Lost Their Accent*. New York: Algonquin Press, 1992.

Anaya, Rudolfo A. *Bless Me, Ultima*. Berkeley, CA: Tonatiuh-Quinto Sol International Publishers, 1988.

———, ed. *Making Face, Making Soul: Haciendo Caras, Creative and Critical Perspectives by Women of Color*. San Francisco, CA: Aunt Lute Books, 1990.

Anzaldúa, Gloria. *Borderlands, La Frontera: The New Mestiza*. San Francisco, CA: Aunt Lute Books, 1987.

———, and Cherrie Moraga, eds. *This Bridge Called My Back: Writings by Radical Women of Color*. Los Angeles: University of California at Los Angeles Press, 1980.

Appiah, Kwame Anthony. *In My Father's House: Africa in the Philosophy of Culture*. New York, Oxford: Oxford University Press, 1992.

Asturias, Miguel Angel. *Men of Maize*. Translated by Gerald Martin. Pittsburgh: University of Pittsburgh Press, 1993.

Attaway, William. *Blood on the Forge*. New York: Monthly Review Press, 1987.

Avineri, Shlomo. "Marx's Vision of Future Society." *Dissent*, Summer 1973, pp. 323–31.

Bellah, Robert, et al. *Habits of the Heart*. Berkeley and Los Angeles: University of California Press, 1985.

Berman, Marshall. *The Politics of Authenticity: Radical Individualism and the Rise of Modern Society*. New York: Atheneum Press, 1972.

Biberman, Herbert. *The Salt of the Earth*. Produced by Independent Productions Corporation and the International Union of Mine, Mill and Smelter Workers, 1953, San Marcos, (Zinc Town) New Mexico.

Blake, William. Ed. David V. Erdman, with commentary by Harold Bloom. *The Complete Poetry and Prose of William Blake*. New York, London, and Toronto: Doubleday, Anchor Books, 1988.

Bonilla, Frank, and Ricardo Campos. "Puerto Ricans in the New Economic Order." *Daedalus* 110, no. 2 (Spring 1981): 133–76.

Boswell, Thomas D. *The Cuban American Experience: Culture, Images, and Perspectives*. Totowa, NJ: Rowman and Allanhold, 1984.

Branch, Taylor. *Parting the Waters, America in the King Years, 1954–63*. New York, London, Toronto: Simon and Schuster, 1988.

Brown, Joseph Epes. *The Sacred Pipe*. Baltimore, MD: Penguin Books, 1972.

Burckhardt, Titus. *Alchemy*. Baltimore, MD: Penguin Books, 1971.

Campbell, Joseph. *The Hero with a Thousand Faces*. Princeton, NJ: Princeton University Press, 1973.

Castro, Américo. Trans. Willard King and Selma Margaretten. *The Spaniards* (Berkeley and Los Angeles: University of California Press, 1971.

Cisneros, Sandra. *The House on Mango Street*. Houston: Arte Público Press, 1988.

———. *Woman Hollering Creek And Other Stories*. New York: Random House, 1991.

Coles, Robert. "Education for a Moral Life." *Harvard Educational Review* 57, no. 2 (May 1987): 193–95.

Cooke, Michael. *Afro-American Literature in the Twentieth Century: The Achievement of Intimacy*. New Haven, CT: Yale University Press 1984.

Corbin, Henri. *Creative Imagination in the Sufism of Ibn Arabi*. Princeton, NJ: Princeton University Press, 1969.

Craven, Margaret. *I Heard the Owl Call My Name*. New York: Dell Paperback Books, 1962.

Cronon, William, et al., eds. *Under An Open Sky, Rethinking America's Western Past*. New York: W. W. Norton, 1992.

DeBeer, Gabriela. "Mexican Writers of Today." *Review: Latin American Literature and Arts* 48 (Spring 1994).

De las Casas, Bartolomé, Trans. Stafford Poole. *In Defense of the Indians*. Dekalb, IL: Northern Illinois University Press, 1992.

De Valdés, María Elena. "Verbal and Visual Representation of Women: *Como Agua Para Chocolate/Like Water for Chocolate*." *World Literature Today* 69 (Winter 1995).

Horno-Delgado, Asunción, et al. *Breaking Boundaries, Latina Writings and Critical Readings*. Amherst: University of Massachusetts Press, 1988.

Ellison, Ralph. *Invisible Man*. New York: Vintage Books, 1972.

Erdman, David V. *Blake: Prophet Against Empire*. New York: Dover Publications, 1991.

————, ed. With commentary by Harold Bloom. *The Complete Poetry and Prose of William Blake*. New York: Doubleday, Anchor Books, 1988.

Erikson, Erik. *Gandhi's Truth: On the Origins of Militant Non-Violence*. New York: W. W. Norton, 1968.

Esquivel, Laura. *Like Water for Chocolate*. Translated by Carol Christensen and Thomas Christensen. New York, London, Toronto: Doubleday, 1992.

Etulian, Richard W., ed. *Writing Western History*. Albuquerque: University of New Mexico Press, 1991.

Fernández, Rev. Avelino. "The Role of the Catholic Church in the Dominican Republic: Religion and Social Change." Lecture, Santo Domingo, Dominican Republic, January 10, 1997.

Fernández, President Leonel. "The Future of the Dominican Republic." Speech, Miami, FL, December 10, 1996.

Freire, Paulo. *Pedagogy of the Oppressed*. New York: Continuum Books, 1970.

Fuentes, Carlos. "Writing in Time." *Democracy*, 2, no. 1 (1982): 61–74.

Fuentes, Rev. Ferdinand. "An Overview of the Hispanic Context in the United States." Paper presented at United Church of Christ Latina and Latino Leadership Summit, Cleveland, OH. 1994.

Galán, Hector. "Los Mineros." Telescript by Paul Espinosa and Hector Galán. Narr. Luís Valdéz. *The American Experience*, PBS, 1990.

García, Cristina. *Dreaming in Cuban*. New York: Alfred A. Knopf, 1992.

Ghiselin, Brewster. *The Creative Process*. New York: A Mentor Book, published by the New American Library, 1963.

Gómez-Quiñones, Juan. *On Culture*. Los Angeles: University of California, Los Angeles, Chicano Studies Center Publications, 1986.

González, John Moran. The Politics of Ethnicity: Cultural Hegemony and Cultural Liberation in Contemporary Chicano Novels. Senior thesis, Department of English, Princeton University, 1988.

Griffin, Gail B. *Season of the Witch*. Pasadena, CA: Trilogy Books, 1995.

Griswold Del Castillo, Richard. *The Treaty of Guadalupe Hidalgo: A Legacy of Conflict* (Norman and London: University of Oklahoma Press, 1990).

Gutiérrez, Gustavo. *We Drink from Our Own Wells*. Maryknoll, NY: Orbis Press, 1984.

Gutiérrez, Ramón. *When Jesus Came, the Corn Mothers Went Away: Marriage, Sexuality and Power in New Mexico, 1500–1846*. Stanford, CA: Stanford University Press, 1991.

Hacker, Andrew. *Two Nations, Black and White, Separate, Hostile, Unequal*. New York: Charles Scribner's Sons, 1992.

Halpern, Manfred. "Transformation: Its Theory and Practice in Our Personal, Political, Historical and Sacred Being." Unpublished.

———. "Four Contrasting Repertories of Human Relations in Islam: Two Pre-Modern and Two Modern Ways of Dealing with Continuity and Change, Collaboration and Conflict and Achieving Justice." In *Psychological Dimensions of Near Eastern Studies*, ed. L. Carl Brown and Norman Itzkowitz. Princeton, NJ: Darwin Press, 1977.

———. "Choosing Between Ways of Life and Death and Between Forms of Democracy." *Alternatives*, January 1987.

———. "Why Are Most of Us Partial Selves? Why Do Partial Selves Enter the Road to Deformation?" Paper presented at the annual meeting of the American Political Science Association, Washington, DC. 1991.

———. "Beyond Present Theory and Practice: Transformation and the Nation State." Paper presented at a national symposium, Beyond the Nation-State: Transforming Visions of Human Society, College of William and Mary, Williamsburg, VA, September 24–27, 1993. To be published in *Transformational Politics: Theory, Study and Practice*, ed. by Ed Schwerin, Christa Slaton, and Stephen Woolpert (Buffalo, NY: State University of New York Press, 1998).

———. "The Archetype of Capitalism: A Critical Analysis in the Light of a Theory of Transformation." Paper presented at the annual meeting of the American Political Science Association, San Francisco, 1996.

———. "Underlying Forces Shaping the Fundamental Differences Between Incremental and Transforming Change." Paper presented at the Annual Meeting of the American Political Science Association, Washington, DC, 1997.

Hesse, Hermann. *Demian*. New York: Bantam Books, 1966.

Hijuelos, Oscar. *The Mambo Kings Play Songs of Love*. New York, Toronto, and London: Harper and Row, Perennial Library, 1990.

———. *Mr. Ives' Christmas: A Novel*. New York: HarperCollins, 1995.

Ibsen, Kristine. "On Recipes, Readings and Revolution: Postboom Parody, *Como Agua Para Chocolate*." *Hispanic Review* 63 (1995).

Idrogo, Curt. "Hispanic Americans." In *Guide to Multicultural Resources, 1997–1998*. Ed. Alex Boyd. Fort Atkinson, WI: High Smith Publications, 1997.

Isasi-Díaz, Ada María. "Ethnicity in Mujerista Theology" Paper presented at national conference on religion and Latinos in the United States, Princeton University, Princeton, NJ, April 16–19, 1993.

Islas, Arturo. *The Rain God*. Palo Alto, CA: Alexandrian Press, 1984.

Jaffe, Janice. "Hispanic American Women Writers' Novel Recipes and Laura Esquivel's *Como Agua Para Chocolate (Like Water for Chocolate)*." *Women's Studies* 22 (1993).

Jannuzi, Marisa. *Like Water for Chocolate*. Review of Contemporary Fiction 13 (Summer 1993).

King, Martin Luther, Jr. *Why We Can't Wait*. New York: Signet Books, 1964.

Kozol, Jonathan. *Savage Inequalities: Children in America's Schools*. New York: Crown Publishers, 1991.

Kuhn, Thomas. *The Structure of Scientific Revolutions*. Chicago: University of Chicago Press, 1969.

Lawless, Cecilia. "Experimental Cooking in *Like Water for Chocolate.*" *Monographic Review/Revista Monográfica* 8, (1992).

Lernoux, Penny. *Cry of the People*. Baltimore: Penguin, 1979.

Lerner, Gerda. *The Creation of Patriarchy*. New York: Oxford University Press, 1987.

Lewis, Oscar. *Five Families*. New York: New American Library, 1959.

Limerick, Patricia Nelson, et al., eds. *Trails Toward a New Western History*. Lawrence: University Press of Kansas, 1991.

MacCorkle, Lyn. *Cubans in the U.S.: A Bibliography for Research in the Social and Behavioral Sciences, 1960–1983*. Westport, CT: Greenwood Press, 1984.

Marqués, René. *La Carreta*. Rio Piedras, PR: Editorial Cultural, 1971.

Martínez, Demetria. *Mother Tongue*. New York: Ballantine Books, 1994.

Matthiessen, Peter. *Sal Si Puedes, César Chávez and the New American Revolution*. New York: Random House, 1969.

Morales, Alejandro. *The Brick People*. Houston: Arte Público Press, 1988.

Morris, Walter F. Photography by Jeffrey Jay Foxx. *Living Maya*. New York: Harry N. Abrams, 1988.

Neihardt, John G. *Black Elk Speaks*. Lincoln: University of Nebraska Press, 1961.

Neumann, Erich. *The Great Mother: An Analysis of the Archetype*. Princeton, NJ: Princeton University Press, 1974.

Orsi, Robert Anthony. *The Madonna of 115th Street: Faith and Community in Italian Harlem, 1880–1950*. New Haven, CT: Yale University Press, 1985.

Padilla, Elena. *Up From Puerto Rico*. New York: Columbia University Press, 1969.

Padilla, Félix. *The Struggle of Latino/Latina University Students, In Search of a Liberating Education* (New York, London: Routledge, 1997).

Paton, Alan. *Too Late the Phalarope*. New York: Scribner's, 1953.

Paz, Octavio. *The Other Mexico: Critique of the Pyramid*. Trans. Lysander Kemp. New York: Grove Press, 1972.

———. *Sor Juana*. Cambridge, MA: Harvard University Press, 1988.

———. "The Sons of La Malinche." In *Introduction to Chicano Studies: A Reader*. Ed. Livia Isaura Durán and H. Russell Bernard. New York: Macmillan, 1973.

———. "Reflections: Mexico and the United States." *The New Yorker*, September 7, 1979.

———. *The Labyrinth of Solitude*. Trans. Lysander Kemp. New York: Grove Press, 1961.

Perwin, Cynthia L. *The Ego, the Self and the Structure of Political Authority*. Ph.D. diss. Princeton University, 1973.

Pifer, Alan. *Bilingual Education and the Hispanic Challenge*. New York: President's Annual Report of the Carnegie Corporation of New York, 1979.

Poincaré, Henri. "Mathematical Creation." In *The Creative Process*, ed. Brewster Ghiselin. New York: Mentor Books, New American Library 1963.

Portilla, Miguel León, ed. *Native Mesoamerican Spirituality*. New York, Ramsey, Toronto: Paulist Press, 1980.

Preston, Larry M. "Theorizing Difference: Voices from the Margin." *American Political Science Review* 89, no. 4 (December 1995): 941–53.

Raines, Howell. *My Soul Is Rested: The Story of the Civil Rights Movement in the Deep South*. New York: Bantam Books, 1978.

Rich, Adrienne. *On Lies, Secrets, and Silence, Selected Prose, 1966–1978*. New York: W. W. Norton and Co., 1978.

Rilke, Rainer Maria. *Breife an einen jungen Dichter (Letters to a Young Poet)*. Leipzig: 1929.

Rivera, Edward. *Family Installments, Memories of Growing Up Hispanic*. New York: Penguin Books, 1983.

Rivera, Tomás. *. . . Y No Se Lo Tragó La Tierra, And The Earth Did Not Devour Him*. Houston: Arte Público Press, 1987.

Rodríguez de Laguna, Asela. *Notes on Puerto Rican Literature*. Newark, NJ: Rutgers University, 1987.

Said, Edward. *Culture and Imperialism*. New York: Alfred A. Knopf, 1993.

Schmidt, Heidi. "La Risa: Etapas en la Narrativa Femenina en México y Alemania, Una Aproximación." *Escritura* 6 (January–December 1991).

Sharabi, Hisham. *Neopatriarchy: A Theory of Distorted Change in Arab Society*. New York, Oxford: Oxford University Press, 1988.

Shockley, John Staples. *Chicano Revolt in a Texas Town*. Notre Dame, IN, London: University of Notre Dame Press, 1974.

Silko, Leslie Marmon. *Ceremony*. New York: Penguin Books, 1977.

———. *Almanac of the Dead*. New York: Simon and Schuster, 1991.

Solas, Humberto. *Lucía*. Produced in Havana, Cuba, 1968.

Stephan, Beatriz González. "Para Comerte Mejor: Cultura Calibanesca y Formas Literarias Alternativas." *Casa de las Américas*, October–December 1991.

Takaki, Ronald. *Strangers from a Different Shore*. Boston: Little, Brown and Co., 1989.

———. *A Different Mirror: A History of Multicultural America*. Boston, Toronto, London: Little, Brown and Co., 1993.

Tan, Amy. *The Joy Luck Club*. New York: Vintage, 1991.

Thomas, Piri. *Down These Mean Streets*. New York: Alfred A. Knopf, 1970.

Ulanov, Ann Belford. *The Feminine in Jungian Psychology and Christian Theology*. Evanston, IL: Northwestern University Press, 1971.

Vicente, Luciano Perena. *Derechos y Deberes Entre Indios y Españoles en el Nuevo Mundo Según Francisco de Vittoria*. Salamanca: Universidad Pontifica de Salamanca, 1991.

Villarreal, Roberto E., and Norma G. Hernández, ed., *Latinos and Political Coalitions*. New York, Westport, CT, London: Praeger, 1991.

Villareal, Rosa Martha. *Doctor Magdalena*. Berkeley, CA: TQS Publications, 1995.

Villaseñor, Victor. *Rain of Gold*. Houston: Arte Público Press, 1992.

Walker, Alice. *The Color Purple*. New York: Pocket Books, Washington Square Books 1982.

West, Cornel. *Race Matters*. Boston: Beacon Press, 1993.

Woolf, Virginia. *A Room of One's Own*. New York: Harcourt, Brace and Co., 1929.

X, Malcolm. *The Autobiography of Malcolm X*. New York: Grove Press, 1966.

Ybarra-Frausto, Tomás, and Joseph Sommers, eds., *Modern Chicano Writers*. Englewood Cliffs, NJ: Prentice-Hall, 1979.

Yezierska, Anzia. *Bread Givers*. New York: Persea Books, 1975.

Young, Iris M. *Justice and the Politics of Difference*. Princeton, NJ: Princeton University Press, 1990.

FILMS

The Ballad of Gregorio Cortez, directed by Robert Young, PBS American Playhouse, 1992

The Blood of the Condor, directed by Jorge Sanjines, Bolivia, 1969

Camila, directed by María Luisa Bemberg, Argentina, 1984

Like Water for Chocolate, directed by Alfonso Arau, México, 1992

Lucía, directed by Humberto Solas, Cuba, 1968

El Norte, directed by Gregory Nava, Independent Productions, 1983

La Operación, directed by Ana M. García, Cinema Guild, 1982

Operation Bootstrap, directed by Carl Dudley, Universal Education and Visual Arts, 1964

A Portrait of Teresa, directed by Pastor Vega, Cuba, 1979

The Salt of the Earth, directed by Herbert Biberman, Independent Productions Corporation and the International Union of Mine, Mill and Smelter Workers, 1953

Index

self of destructive stories and, 66; exiting from, 4–5, 12, 31–34, 48, 58, 63, 156; invitation to participate in, 154; journey through, 6, 11, 34, 45–49, 141, 181; lesser lords frustrating the, 157; our participation in, 155; stories and ways of life in, 157; as story and journey of transformation, 11–13, 154; three acts and scenes of, 4, 11–19, 72–73; transformation as the fulfillment of, 72–73, 155, 157; ways of life of emanation, incoherence, and deformation as fragments of, 44, 72

Cortés, Hernán, 152, 168

Council for Hispanic Advancement, 174

Counter tradition, 15, 78, 111

Craven, Margaret, 71

Create, nourish, and destroy: dialectics of change, 20–21; transformation and, 27, 36

Creative imagination, 123, 125–129; guiding students to, 58

Crusoe, Robinson, 86

Cultura Latina: creating a new, 89; critique of, 155–58, 164–65; dissent within by Latinas, 170, 172; patriarchal males in, 172–73

Culture: ahistorical, 72; carriers of, 163; creation of, 61, 71, 73, 151; creative and destructive faces, 153; critiquing both American and Latino, 3; definition and description of, 72, 152; dissent and, 170; emanation and, 47; four faces of, 72; grounded in deeper sources, 72; imperialism and, 152; losing one's memory of, 160; necessary to transcend specific, 4, 169; personal story and, 45, 47; in the service of transformation, 38, 61, 86, 162; transformation of, 153, 169

Curanderas/os: as guides, 167; as healers, 163; and story of healing, 167

Curandería, 166–68

Cursillistas, 173

Death squads. *See* El Salvador; Guatemale; Honduras

Declaration of Independence, 171

Deformation: arrested fragment of the core drama of life, 171; capitalism and, 160; colluding with emanation and incoherence as way of life, 45, 55, 62, 155; definition and description of, 4, 26–27, 68; education in the service of, 138–39; exiting the core drama of life, 12, 18, 48–49, 157; four faces of our being and, 48; Indians and, 156; Latinos and, 32, 63, 67, 157, 162; lord of, 12, 48 157; patriarchy, 66; personal story, 47; on the politics of and la comunidad Latina at risk, 85–86; preventive strategies against, 163; pseudoemanations as, 48; recognizing, 154; revenge and, 161, 162; on the road to, 5; sadistic/masochistic drama in the service of, 32–33; relationship of used to preserve partial ways of life, 32–34, 41; relationships of more serious than subjection, 27; tribalism and, 48, 61, 155–56, 160; underground capitalism and, 62; victim of, 47, 60, 158; and victimizer, 49, 60, 161; violence and, 44, 67; way of life of, 4–5, 17–18, 31–34, 49, 60, 63, 132, 159, 161, 164; white attitudes and, 162

de Hostos, Eugenio María, 181

de la Cruz, Sor Juana Inés, 181

Democracy: and American dream at its best, 171, 179; archetypal story of, 36; as experiment, 164; four faces of our being and, 36; multicultural *mestizaje* as a new face of, 164

Desaparecidos, los, 156. *See also* Argentina; Chile

Dialectical process. *See* Create, nourish, and destroy

Direct bargaining: definition and examples of, 24; Latinas and, 24; in the service of emanation, 41; in the service of incoherence, 53, 177; in the service of transformation, 68, 179

Doctor Magdalena (Villareal), 168

Dominican Republic, 144–45

Doña Marina. *See* La Malinche

Dorantes, Celia, 181

About the Author

DAVID T. ABALOS is Professor of Religious Studies and Sociology at Seton Hall University. He has lectured and written extensively on multicultural and gender scholarship and also on Latinas and Latinos in the United States from the perspective of the politics of transformation. He is the author of *Latinos in the United States: The Sacred and the Political* (1986), *The Latino Family and the Politics of Transformation*, a *Choice* Outstanding Academic Book for 1994 (Praeger, 1993), and *Strategies of Transformation Toward a Multicultural Society: Fulfilling the Story of Democracy* (Praeger, 1996).

ISBN 0-275-95892-2

EAN

9 780275 958923

90000>

HARDCOVER BAR CODE